Rangers: Triumphs, Troubles, Traditions

D0512878

Ronnie Esplin and Graham Walker (eds.)

Fort Publishing Ltd

First published in 2010 by Fort Publishing Ltd, Old Belmont House,
12 Robsland Avenue, Ayr, KA7 2RW

Printed by Bell and Bain Ltd, Glasgow

Front-cover photograph courtesy of Mirrorpix

Graphic design by Mark Blackadder

Typeset by 3btype.com

Contact from copyright owners welcome

ISBN: 978-1-905769-18-6

For my son, Alexander
Graham Walker

For my children, Kirsty, Alex and Mhairi
Ronnie Esplin

Contents

Introduction

Questions around the status, importance and relevance of Rangers Football Club in Scottish society, it seems, will always provoke heated discussion and debate.

The Ibrox institution – by the mid-twentieth century a natural sporting home for the majority of the indigenous population in Scotland – is now loved and loathed in almost equal measures. Like Manchester United in England, there appears to be no middle ground when it comes to views on the Govan club. Some of the antagonism stems from natural sporting rivalry and it is understandable that there is an element of resentment surrounding the success and power that the club has enjoyed for most of its existence.

In a rapidly changing Scotland, though, deeper disdain towards Rangers can be attributed to the ever-sensitive issue of sectarianism, the aspect of the 'Protestant' identity of the club that continues to bring controversies to the door of Ibrox.

Almost one hundred and forty years after the club's formation in 1872, the Rangers story is only just beginning to become clearer. The motivation of the founding fathers in forming the club – chronicled in Gary Ralston's book, *Rangers 1872: the Gallant Pioneers* – confirmed that the Light Blues were no different in conception to dozens of other clubs that emerged in the second half of nineteenth-century Britain as association football took a grip of the working classes. The McNeil brothers, Peter and Moses, and friends, Peter Campbell and William McBeath, all teenagers, had the idea to form a football team, which they called Rangers because, almost quaintly, they liked the name.

There was plenty of uncertainty about the club's future in the early years before it eventually grew into one of the strongest and most successful institutions in the country, notwithstanding the current financial problems, which promise another change in direction.

However, Rangers and its fans struggle to shake off the stereotype shaped by the middle years of the club's existence, when Ibrox became a bastion of anti-Catholicism. David Murray, the Scottish businessman who took over the club in 1988 when it was bossed by player-manager Graeme Souness, took the lead with the controversial signing of former Celtic striker Maurice Johnston. 'Mo Jo' was the first high-profile Catholic in decades to play for Rangers, and, aside from the fact that he was a fine footballer, his recruitment was an attempt to modernise the club while, ironically, taking it back to its roots, back to the days of the Gallant Pioneers when it was just about football.

In the intervening years the club has regularly made clear its desire to distance itself from what Murray called the FTP (Fuck the Pope) brigade. Some Rangers fans have found it hard to come to terms with the idea of adjusting the club's identity to reflect changing times. Tensions have developed between supporters and the club and between the fans themselves on this issue. If not quite a schism between fundamentalists and modernists, there remain two strands of thinking.

Of course, currently, the focus of most Rangers fans is on the club's financial problems and, amid broader concerns about the Light Blues' future, questions remain over how those problems will be addressed.

However, the question of identity remains central. What does Rangers Football Club stand for? Who are 'The People'? It was those queries, among others, that the editors' previous book on the club, *It's Rangers for Me? New Perspectives on a Scottish Institution* (*IRFM?*) sought, in all modesty, to address. Figures from all walks of British life, most of whom had a link of sorts to Ibrox, were invited to reveal their feelings.

And what a stir it caused.

Scotland on Sunday reported its publication as follows: 'A controversial new book . . . it has reignited the decades-old debate about the rights and wrongs of Old Firm rivalry.' According to the *Daily Record*: 'A new book on Rangers has sparked a fierce debate . . . and has left bosses at European governing body UEFA confused . . . Celtic fans were outraged . . . with websites flooded by complaints.' Television pricked up its ears and BBC's *Newsnight* programme, *Reporting Scotland* and *Scotland Today* all jostled to discuss the book's content and its significance.

While they say that all publicity is good publicity, there was an interesting sense of negativity in the reporting. Former Rangers player Gordon Smith was living life as a BBC pundit when he agreed to be interviewed for the book, but by the time of publication he had become the chief executive of the Scottish Football Association, which, of course, put a different perspective on his chapter. Smith remarked that religious segregation of schools in the west of Scotland drew the attention of pupils to differences between them from an early age. He asked for people to be more even-handed when apportioning blame for the sectarian problems, and offered his belief that there was an agenda against Rangers: 'Celtic have always thought that people were against them, but now Rangers are starting to feel the same.'

Smith's views provoked hysteria and many of the critics got into a further lather when reading the thoughts of lifelong Rangers fan Karen Gillon. The Labour MSP for Clydesdale made the national news, no less, with her 'revelation' that she had sung 'The Sash', a Protestant anthem, which has been for decades a regular part of the Ibrox song book. Gillon had said: 'Yes I have sung "The Sash". I would be a liar to deny it and I am not a liar,' and those apparently anodyne words could not have been analysed more closely had a parliamentary inquiry been commissioned.

What was interesting to many Rangers fans, and not just the funda-mentalist wing of the Light Blues support, was how the topic was framed by some in the media. Keith McLeod writes in the *Daily Record*: 'In it [the book], one MSP owns up to singing sectarian songs,' while Marc Horne's piece in *Scotland on Sunday* sat under the headline, 'The cry was no offender as MSP comes clean on singing "The Sash"'. Horne writes about a passage in the book that 'includes an admission by Labour MSP Karen Gillon that she once belted out choruses of "The Sash"'. To Ibrox diehards, terms such as 'owns up' and 'admission' revealed mainstream attitudes in contemporary Scotland towards Rangers supporters and provided more evidence for that growing rump who believe the club has become fair game for its detractors.

Smith and Gillon were not only branded as bigots. There were also plenty of people who wanted to hound them out of their jobs. A *Sunday Mirror* columnist was one who called for sackings.

> Gordon's arguments belong in the bar room and not in the halls of the SFA. As for Karen Gillon. What makes her think she can represent all the

people in her constituency when she says she defends the singing of 'The Sash'? The get-out-of-jail card that she is married to a Catholic doesn't wash. She would deny she is a bigot, but if nothing else it displays a mind too small to represent me. Both should be shown the door.

That type of negativity, however, did not translate into unconditional support from the book's target audience. A section of Rangers fans – unhappy at the inclusion of journalist Graham Spiers and former Celtic winger (but boyhood Rangers supporter) Davie Provan as contributors – refused to embrace the project. Indeed, there was an active bid on a fan website to instigate a boycott. Moreover, on the Amazon website, one fan going under the pseudonym 'hyram' was clear and concise in his condemnation: 'I would urge ALL Rangers fans to avoid this book.' A. D. Brunton was no less virulent: 'What an opportunity lost. The book puts the boot into every generation of Rangers supporter from all walks of life. Certain contributors cannot seem to conceal their hatred for the club and everything it stands for.'

There were some prepared to accept the book's concept and A. C. Gavaghan offered his support.

> This is a book for thinking people interested in reading a range of perspectives on Rangers and its support. Some of those perspectives I agree with, some I find interesting but unconvincing, others I find very weak. But that's just the point – it displays a range of views. To boycott the book because of one, or maybe two, chapters by non-Rangers people is, I have to say, a bit childish, especially given that some of the 'reviewers' on here appear not even to have read the thing!

More encouragement came from Stuart Campbell.

> I'm somewhat surprised by a few of the negative reviews on here for this book. To my mind it's long overdue and should be pretty much curriculum reading for all Rangers fans out there. . . . This book does a superb job in framing where Rangers grew from as a Scottish institution and looks at the many complex factors that have shaped the club. It allows the reader to celebrate where Rangers have come from and be proud of the club's heritage whilst behaving in a modern manner.

Newspaper reviews were in the main, positive, with *The Belfast Telegraph* saying: 'Esplin and Walker step into the world of the blue side of Glasgow and the result is a refreshing tale unlike those of a stereotypical "boy done well" variety. A fine insight into what is a Scottish institution.'

Who would have thought that as *IRFM?* was making its way to the bookshops, Rangers would be making their way to a European final for the first time in thirty-six years? And who would have thought that a song sung by some Rangers fans – the 'Famine Song' – would usurp 'The Sash' in the controversy stakes?

It is the discussion of those two topics which makes up the bulk of *Rangers: Triumphs, Troubles and Traditions*, a follow-up of sorts to *IRFM?* Between 150,000 and 200,000 fans of the Light Blues descended on Manchester and its surrounding areas for Rangers' first European final since they captured the European Cup Winners Cup with a 3–2 win over Moscow Dynamo in Barcelona in 1972. However, the 2–0 defeat by Zenit St Petersburg, managed by former Rangers boss Dick Advocaat, was not the only disappointment for the Ibrox club. Trouble ensued in one of the Manchester-city-centre fan zones after a big screen that was to show the game for the thousands of supporters who could not get tickets went blank before kick-off. The crowd disorder escalated from bottle throwing to battles with the police, with television coverage of the mayhem shown all over the world. Not for the first time, questions were asked of the Ibrox club and its support.

Some of those questions, we hope, are addressed in the book's opening section: Manchester Revisited.

Graham Walker draws on the subsequent report of Manchester City Council, as well as his own recollections of the day, to frame a discussion on the relationships between the club, its fans and wider Scottish society. Peter Millward, a Wigan supporter, provides an outsider's take on how matters unfolded during the course of the day in Manchester city centre and explains how the situation was in his view mishandled by the authorities.

Ronnie Esplin uses a variety of voices, mostly from the media, in an attempt to give a rounded version of the run to the final and the day itself. Television commentator Peter Drury, almost unwittingly, became part of the UEFA Cup narrative with his description of the dramatic penalty-shoot-out win against Fiorentina in Italy. Englishman Drury recalls the journey through the latter stages of the tournament to an 'extraordinary' day in Manchester, which left him with some abiding images: 'I can't believe I will ever see anything like that again.' Journalists from Manchester and Moscow recount the build-up to the game and the day of the final itself while Zenit supporter Alexey Morozov reveals the enthusiasm among the travelling Russian fans and those back home in St Petersburg.

'To see ourselves as others see us' is the theme of Scott Dougal's Manchester experience. Dougal – a Rangers fan born in Berwick, but Scottish through his parents – lives and works in Yorkshire and so was well placed to see how England reacted to the 2008 UEFA Cup final in general and the invasion of Manchester in particular. He sums it up as the 'view of Scottish culture through English eyes'. Like many Rangers fans, Dougal cites Manchester as a career highlight but the pride he felt even in defeat was 'rendered ridiculous the moment I felt the crunch of broken glass under my feet'.

Andy Kerr was vice-president of the Rangers Supporters Assembly during the 2007/08 European campaign (he is now president). A son of Biggar, but now a member of the Harrogate True Blues in Yorkshire, Kerr has come to the fore in recent years as a calm and articulate voice of the Rangers support. He recalls how the UEFA Cup final crept up on the club and its fans and explains his semi-formal role in the build-up, while admitting the final was not a totally positive experience for him either. As part of the Rangers sponsors' party, he was caught up in the city-centre melee following the match and admits that Manchester was 'a scary place'. While accepting that some fans let the club and their fellow fans down Kerr offers a strong defence of the majority and argues that the Manchester authorities were not only reluctant hosts but also ill-prepared for such an occasion.

The trouble in Manchester rekindled dim and distant memories of disturbances at places like Newcastle, Barcelona and Aston Villa but the furore surrounding the 'Famine Song' brought a new problem to the marbled halls of Ibrox.

Both Old Firm clubs piled in to an argument over the issue, which came to the fore following a 4–2 win for Rangers at Parkhead in 2008 and the bitterness spilled out of the sporting arena with the topic becoming the subject of a nationwide debate. Rangers asked fans not to sing the song ('Why don't you go home?, Why don't you go home?, the famine's over, why don't you go home?') but for a while those pleas fell on deaf ears and the controversy escalated when the song became integral to a case in the criminal courts.

On 19 June 2009, appeal-court judges ruled that the song was racist. The Justiciary Appeal Court upheld a conviction against William Walls over his conduct at a Rangers away match against Kilmarnock in the previous year. Walls's defence counsel, Donald Findlay QC, a former Rangers director, had put up the free-speech argument. However, Lord Carloway said the lyrics called on people to leave Scotland because of their racial origins and it is from these two separate viewpoints – free speech versus alleged racism – that the issue continued to be debated.

Section two of the book is entitled 'Controversies' and includes specific discussions about the 'Famine Song', which widen out at times to include general controversies surrounding the club and its supporters.

David Edgar, spokesman for the Rangers Supporters Trust, is a knowledgeable, humorous and enthusiastic voice of the Gers support. He asks for the chant – for it is more of a chant than a song – to be put in to the context of traditional fan rivalries. He points to double standards in regards to the treatment of the issue by the media and the authorities, and reveals the growing feeling among the Ibrox support that, in terms of trying to appease their numerous critics, they have 'gone as far as they are likely to go'. Expanding the argument in the sphere of a more general disgruntlement among the Light Blues support, Edgar asks for Rangers to battle harder to protect the image of the fans and the club. He also explains the chasm between many at Ibrox and the modern-day Tartan Army, which he believes is all but unbridgeable.

Roddy Forsyth is one of Scottish football's most experienced and respected journalists, working for, among others, *The Daily Telegraph* and radio station BBC Five Live. In one of his other guises, though, Forsyth occasionally has to explain the madness of the Old Firm to newspaper readers in Ireland, many of whom are less au fait with the nuances of the Glasgow giants than might be imagined. The 'Famine Song' controversy was one such issue that elicited 'general bemusement' in Ireland which, as Forsyth explains, 'engaged two governments and the police . . . and at one stage had the chairmen of both Celtic and Rangers snarling at each other'. In an entertaining way, and with oblique references to comedians Woody Allen, Ricky Gervais and Steve Coogan, Forsyth sets the controversy surrounding the song against the vast changes that have taken place at Ibrox and in wider Scottish society in recent years. In assessing the agitation some Rangers fans continue to have with all things Irish-Catholic, Forsyth wonders about those Ibrox supporters who, he says, resemble 'those Confederate rebels who fought on, raggedly and forlornly, for years after the Civil War'.

Daniel Taylor adds to the 'Famine Song' debate amid a wider examination of sectarianism in Scotland. He points at media obsession with an issue that lacks clarity in definition and throws up the possibility that the song, like many others in football, is simply part of the mutual antagonism which is part and parcel of supporter culture. This tit-for-tat attitude among football fans also permeates Steve Bruce's chapter 'No Pope of Rome: Football Fans Wearing False Noses'. Bruce, professor of sociology at the University of Aberdeen, highlights the dilution of cultural identities that were once strong amid fans of Celtic and Rangers. He argues that 'there is now little – apart from football – which divides the fans of the Old Firm'. Boiling down the current angst surrounding football chants to the traditional abuse of opposition supporters, he concludes that: 'The fans of both teams wear false noses. Each lot pretends to find the noses of the other ugly and grotesque while claiming to be deeply hurt by the cruel remarks that those scumbags have made about our noses'.

Rangers fan, Alan Truman, however, believes that the fuss surrounding the 'Famine Song' is just part of a 'propaganda onslaught from powerful and influential antagonists'. In a passionate essay, which dismisses long-held beliefs that Rangers are Scotland's establishment club, he claims the Govan club and its fans are now fair game for, among others, politicians, academics and the media.

The 'Home and Away Fans' section of the book is more diverse and allows a range of supporters to recall their own particular stories and experiences of Rangers.

Most budding footballers grow up dreaming of playing at the ground of their boyhood heroes and, in January 1987, Bobby Barr found himself fulfilling that dream at Ibrox, albeit as a Hamilton Accies player. Ironically, the home of Rangers was the only stadium in Scottish senior football in which Barr had yet to perform before he pitched up for the SPL match as one of John Lambie's men. However, the former Alloa midfielder's dream turned in to a nightmare when he sustained a broken leg in a tackle by Light Blues defender Terry Butcher, a tackle that effectively ended his Premier League career. It did not stop Barr – still in plaster – from travelling up to Pittodrie with the Kirkintilloch RSC at the end of that dramatic season to witness Rangers win the SPL title for the first time in nine years, with Butcher, ironically, scoring the vital goal in a 1–1 draw. Barr's injury saw him miss out on Accies' finest hour, the 1–0 Scottish Cup win against Rangers, although his rehabilitation brought him in to close contact with Ibrox legend Jock Wallace. For those who wonder how lower-league players reconcile their affiliations with the Old Firm while retaining a professional approach, Barr's story make fascinating reading.

Elaine Sommerville's Rangers credentials are unimpeachable. She has been a season-ticket holder at Ibrox since the mid-1970s, long before it became commonplace for women to be seen at 'the fitba'. Sommerville retraces her journey from Willie Waddell to Walter Smith, recalls her friendship with the late Davie Cooper and includes nuances that only female football fans will recognise. Much of her story belongs to a different era. She remembers a young Derek Johnstone agreeing to open her school fete – and driving to the former Rangers striker's house with her teacher to pick Johnstone up. Tales of the Nou Camp, Easter Road and Manchester bring Sommerville's diary up to date and reveal a supporter as passionate as any who continue to follow, follow.

There are, of course, Rangers fans further afield than the United Kingdom and Ireland and one of the oldest supporters clubs is Toronto Number One. The old Ibrox song 'If We Only Had the Rangers Over Here' was written with the Scottish diaspora in mind and the city of Toronto was renowned for the number of Scots and Irish who moved there in the 1960s and 1970s. Bobby Smith was just one of thousands of Scots who travelled to Canada in search of a better life and he has been a member of the club since the mid-seventies. In a poignant chapter he discloses the problems that the club – based in Scarborough in the west of the city – faces and acknowledges that, due to the changing nature of Toronto's demographics, there is an ongoing struggle to keep it alive.

Steve Clark is a founder member of one of the newer Rangers supporters clubs, the Dublin Loyal, whose emergence provides an obvious talking point for those who are cognisant of the Old Firm's relationship with the island of Ireland. 'Were we being mischievous starting up a Rangers supporters club in Dublin? Too right we were,' says Clark. Originally from the north of Scotland but now living on the outskirts of Dublin, he traces the club's foundations and the difficulties it faces as an organisation 'behind enemy lines'. Somewhat ironically, though, Clark takes the view that its biggest battle is with those who call the shots at Ibrox.

The Irish theme continues with Gregory Campbell, Democratic Unionist Party (DUP) MP at Westminster and government minister at Stormont, who has been an avid Rangers fan since his boyhood in Londonderry. Campbell is always quick to produce his Rangers credentials and, among other memories, he reveals how, in 2008, he was behind a House of Commons motion to celebrate the centenary of the birth of fellow Ulsterman Sam English (whose life is covered in greater depth later in the book). The Irishman scored a record-breaking forty-four goals in a single season for Rangers but his career was overshadowed by an accidental collision with John Thomson during an Old Firm game, which resulted in the death of the Celtic keeper. Campbell also recalls travelling across the Irish border to see the team play against Dundalk in the Fairs Cities Cup in season 1968/69.

In *IRFM?*, space was given to Hearts fan Ian Wilson to provide an alternative view of Rangers and Hibernian supporter Ian Wood offers a similar service in these pages. While examining the relationship between the Easter Road club and Rangers since the days of the 'Famous Five' at Hibs, he makes clear that the Leithers and Celtic, despite being from the same Irish-Catholic stock, are not simply two sides of the same coin, as many at Ibrox still believe to this day.

The righting of historical wrongs, or at least re-examining important episodes in the club's past, forms the backbone of the 'Legends and Forgotten History' section of the book.

There is no better example of that than the story of Sam English, recently inducted to the Rangers hall of fame. In a poignant and well-researched article, Terence Murray discovers how English found what it was like to live 'less as a person than one half of an accident' until his death in 1967. Murray traces English's path from a farm cottage in the hamlet of Crevolea, County Londonderry to the shipyards of Govan where Bill Struth tempted him to Ibrox, fending off the advances of Arsenal's equally famous manager, Herbert Chapman. However, English's world turned upside down on 5 September 1931 when he collided with Thomson. While the keeper's family, Catholic newspapers, Celtic players and a fatal-accident enquiry exonerated him of all blame, Parkhead boss manager Willie Maley 'did more than anyone to keep the bitterness going'. English recovered to score a record-breaking forty-four goals that season. Struth controversially sold him to Liverpool but the player was never to escape the 'whispered asides and furtive glances that followed him wherever he went'.

Sam English came before Campbell Ogilvie's time at Ibrox but there are few people more steeped in Rangers than the man generally accepted as being one of Scottish football's finest administrators. Now working as managing director of Hearts, Ogilvie's Ibrox lineage goes back to the sixties, growing up around the club where his father was the reserve-team doctor. Ogilvie's professional bond with Rangers dates back to 1978, to the time of irascible club legend Willie Waddell who recruited him from his administrative post with the Scottish League.

Waddell was not the only strong personality Ogilvie worked with at Ibrox. He shared his Rangers years with huge characters such as Jock Wallace, John Greig, Graeme Souness, Walter Smith and David Murray, and other men of influence such as David Holmes and Martin Bain. Ogilvie, who has known nine Rangers managers, reveals the trials and tribulations of working with Waddell et al and discusses the vast changes he oversaw both on and off the park as Rangers moved from a family club to a commercial behemoth.

As Ogilvie is well aware, there are fewer heroes bigger among the Rangers support than the late Jock Wallace. His first period as manager, from 1973 to 1978, saw him win two domestic trebles but his second spell in charge, following the departure of John Greig in 1983, was less successful and preceded seismic changes at the club. Alex Totten, primarily a Falkirk man, and indeed a living Bairns legend after spells as player and manager at the club, was assistant to Wallace during that turbulent second period. Totten reveals the sense of pride he felt at being asked by Wallace to take the walk up the famous marble staircase. However, while some fans yearn for the return to the club of Wallace's passion for Rangers, in truth, those frugal pre-Souness years were fraught. Totten, now business-development manager at Falkirk, accepts he may have been in the right place at the wrong time. However, he fondly remembers the bond between the fans and Wallace which, as so often happens in football, grows stronger with the passing of time. Totten also recalls the pressure he and Wallace were under at a difficult time in the club's history, when money was tight and the four-way competition in Scottish football that involved old rivals Celtic and the New Firm of Dundee United and Aberdeen, was unprecedented and fierce. Nevertheless, missing out on becoming Wallace's successor, as was mooted at one point, remains a regret.

Craig Paterson was a Hibs and Scotland under-21 defender in 1982 when he was bought by John Greig and he also played under Wallace. Paterson reveals that Ibrox was probably not a happy place in his time there and recalls the difficulties he suffered in his Rangers career due to a misdiagnosed injury, which saw him succumb to the twin evils of machismo and cortisone. When the injury was eventually cleared up to his satisfaction, Souness had taken over from Wallace and Paterson was soon to be replaced by big-money buys from England. The boyhood Hibs fan, while harbouring a lingering frustration about his time in light blue, also reveals a touching pride in playing under Greig and Wallace and in captaining Rangers to League Cup glory, a memory that still warms the cockles of his heart when cold winds whip round the television gantries.

While Wallace's time at Ibrox has been well-chronicled in these pages through Totten and Paterson, David White is, by comparison, almost a forgotten Gers manager. His short managerial stint at Ibrox from 1967 until 1969 is reviewed by Rangers historian David Mason. Based on a recent interview for Rangers TV, conducted by Mason, the chapter provides an important reassessment of the man who moved in to the hot seat when Scot Symon stepped down. This look at the late 1960s period reminds us how close Rangers came to ending the dominance of Jock Stein's all-conquering Celtic. It also points to a time when attitudes towards the club were changing in certain parts of Scottish society, which, in many ways, is where this book comes in as it seeks to address, as previously noted, 'questions around the status, importance and relevance of Rangers Football Club'.

Despite an increase in Rangers publications and productions in recent years, it remains the case that many aspects of the club's history are less well known and understood than they should be.

However, once again we, as editors, hope that we have contributed to a more informed, historically aware and lively appreciation of this remarkable football club.

MANCHESTER REVISITED

'So Much to Answer for': Rangers Fans in Manchester, 2008

Graham Walker

The 2008 UEFA Cup final witnessed 'the largest known migration of supporters for a single match'. So stated the introduction to the report on the event and the accompanying crowd chaos by Manchester City Council (MCC). This report estimated that the city hosted between 150,000 and 160,000 supporters; others put the figure at over 200,000 and point out that thousands of Rangers fans also travelled to surrounding Lancashire towns simply to be, in the words of UEFA president Michel Platini, 'close to their club in one of the most crucial moments of its history'.[1]

It was an occasion that reminded the world of the magnetism of Rangers FC and the prodigious weight of communal aspiration which the club continues to bear. The investment in Manchester 2008 went far beyond the financial outlay for fans whether they came from Scotland, Ireland, the USA, Canada, Australia, New Zealand and a myriad of other places around the globe which delineate the Rangers diaspora. This was a journey which thousands had longed to make from the moment in their younger lives when an ineradicable passion was forged. As the representatives of the fans later put it 'many years of hope came to the surface'.[2] For many it was a case of regarding the final as something that would most likely never come again in their lifetimes.

Arriving, then, in Manchester on the sun-drenched morning of 14 May was, for this lifelong fan, akin to approaching the rainbow's end. The pride in surveying such a mass of people revelling in the club's achievement and anticipating the ultimate glory was immense; that it was later accompanied by other less exalted feelings cannot dim it in my memory. It may have been as good as it got, but, along with the build-up in the stadium to the match itself, it was sublime.

The story, however, proved not to be about the joy of the day, or even about the team's capitulation to a capable Zenit St. Petersburg outfit; rather it inevitably focused on the crowd disorder in Manchester city centre. Out of this flowed another inquest concerning the alleged sectarianism associated with Rangers and their fans, and a national examination of the club's place in Scottish society and culture. For many of the wrong reasons, in the end, Manchester 2008 was indeed a crucial point in the club's history.

*

It might be best to deal first with the actual trouble. Much media attention has been paid to this and many fans' personal accounts have found their way on to websites along with footage of incidents.[3] Other chapters in this volume will provide more detailed reports of it. However, some comment is necessary, and the MCC report is the most authoritative single published source upon which to draw for the purpose.

The report is reasonably balanced, much more so than the representation of it in the popular press subsequent to publication. For many Rangers fans it appears to have been the press reports of the MCC report, rather than the document itself, which led them to denounce it as a 'stitch up' and a device for deflecting blame from what they regarded as the Manchester authorities' failure to cope with the massive influx of fans, mistreatment of supporters and general incompetence.

The report refers to the briefings that Manchester City Council received in the weeks running up to the match from Strathclyde Police and Rangers. Estimates of the number travelling were regularly revised upwards to a figure of 100,000 by 9 May. As it transpired even this was hopelessly below the mark. If there is a suggestion of 'buck-passing' in the report it is that the advice coming from north of the border could have been more accurate, and that Rangers might have made it known sooner that they would show the match on a big screen at Ibrox. In the event 30,000 attended this screening with many more unable to gain access. However, none of this can excuse the council and the Manchester police for the confusion that was caused in first stating that ticketless fans would not be welcome and then reversing that position to give the impression that the city was ready for them and, indeed, the ideal location for a party.

In the report the 'right to party' question is addressed and the view firmly placed on record that it was a 'right' that could not be conceded.

Nevertheless, many thousands of fans interpreted the volte-face on the part of the Manchester authorities as an invitation to a football Glastonbury. As the sun blazed down the mass influx into Manchester for a time bore the hallmarks of a Club 18–30 trip to Ibiza. Indeed, it should be borne in mind that there were at least some who travelled, probably having only decided on it at the last minute, in the spirit of partygoers or holidaymakers.

For many more, however, the party theme was strongly linked to the Old Firm football rivalry. For Rangers fans, this was their chance to party en masse in the manner of Celtic fans in the Seville sunshine in 2003.[4] Around this theme a strong competitive drive emerged to ensure that this would be an even bigger and better party. Rangers fans recalled the saturation media coverage of Seville and looked forward to the same. The Celtic fans' taunt of 2003 – 'You'll be watching *The Bill* when we're in Seville' – was met with 'We'll be having such fun in the Rover's Return.'

It needs to be emphasised that the party feeling was genuine and good-humoured if extravagant and inevitably alcohol-fuelled. It was maintained among the great majority of fans in the city in the face of the disappointment of the result. The MCC report notes that the majority remained 'good-natured' in defeat, and acknowledges that the trouble which erupted involved 'hundreds' with 99 per cent of Rangers fans having no involvement. In its submission to the MCC report, Manchester City Football Club's representative states: 'The Rangers fans that were in the stadium, and we believe this to be approximately 37,000 of the 44,000, were extremely well behaved and good humoured – a credit to their football club.'

The MCC report also makes clear how good the event was for the city's economy: an estimated £20 million worth of business was brought to the city. Even in venues such as Irish bars, from which the police expected Rangers fans to stay away for religio-political reasons, there was a 'party atmosphere' with the many fans who patronised them being described as 'well behaved'. This was an eloquent rejoinder to assumptions about the supposed sectarian blinkeredness of Rangers fans and their attitudes. Even incursions into Manchester's gay village occasioned only camp hilarity best likened to an inebriated Stanley Baxter routine. Moreover, the Rangers security officer Kenny Scott's submission to the report makes the telling point that in the nineteen previous European games over the season in which the team reached the UEFA final, nine European countries were visited by Rangers supporters and not a single arrest had been made.

The serious trouble which began in the early evening was centred on the Piccadilly fanzone, one of three designed to accommodate the bulk of those who congregated in the city centre. In this respect the sheer volume of fans who arrived in Manchester on 14 May upset all the calculations about crowd safety and the capacity of the city's infrastructure, facilities and services to cope with people's needs. The Piccadilly and Albert Square fanzones had a notional capacity of 12,000 each with the third zone at Cathedral Gardens capable of holding around 5,000. With well over 100,000 fans in the city centre, the potential for trouble and even disaster was apparent. As it turned out Albert Square and Cathedral Gardens, although both overcrowded, saw no large-scale violence. The report makes a point of noting in relation to Albert Square that 'the festival atmosphere' persisted throughout the day. The most serious overcrowding was at Piccadilly, which, given its proximity to rail and bus stations and services, was always likely to be the most popular zone. Fans had gathered in this area in particular since 12 May. The MCC report candidly admits the unsuitability of the Piccadilly location for a large-scale event, and it seems clear that not enough thought had been given to the dangers of a build-up of people in this area. Even at 10 a.m. on the day of the match this fanzone was thickly populated, and the MCC report refers to the first reports of anti-social behaviour taking place here at 11.30 a.m. It was also clear from an early stage that there were problems with the big screen that was to show the match: its position was not advantageous to communications with technicians.

The Piccadilly zone was also meant to accommodate the travelling Zenit fans. Some duly congregated and friction developed between them and those Rangers fans whose alcohol intake was in evidence from very early in the day. Walking through the Piccadilly zone in the morning I sensed an undertow of menace not apparent anywhere else in the city. Many Rangers fans in this area gave free voice to the songs that had landed their club in trouble with the UEFA and Scottish football authorities not long before. For these fans, at least on this day, that ordeal for the club may as well not have happened. Some would probably have been fans who either did not possess a season ticket for Ibrox or had been banned from attending or who had not been regular attendees at Rangers matches for some time. It was one of a number of indications of a 'retro' feel to the whole occasion. It was as if these fans interpreted Manchester as a chance to support the club in what they believed was a 'traditional' manner; that the occasion gave them license to turn back the clock and dust off the old standards in their repertoire.

In the Piccadilly zone the official entertainment acts soon had to abandon their performances as fans pelted the stage with missiles. Before long the 'party songs' (in the peculiar Scottish and Irish usage of the term) were accompanied by a flute band. As the alcohol continued to flow and the match itself grew nearer the heady cocktail of exhilaration, anticipation, drunkenness and aggression turned Piccadilly into a cauldron. Walking around the perimeter of the fanzone around six in the evening the mayhem was obvious. There was a distinct lack of litter and toilet facilities, anti-social behaviour was rife and the police were clearly readying for confrontation. I witnessed one fan literally go berserk and smash his fist through a restaurant window. Drugs rather than drink may have been responsible for such incidents but it was the prodigious quantities of booze consumed that accounted for most of the disorder. The MCC report justifies the decision to allow a 'relaxed' stance on alcohol on the grounds that it would have been counter-productive to have imposed a ban. Again, with hindsight, forbidding fans from taking drink into the fanzones while permitting its sale within them, may have been a wiser option.

The violent clashes between groups of fans and the police followed the breakdown of the screen at Piccadilly shortly before the start of the match. The MCC report claims that the violence of the fans forced staff to flee and that had the fans behaved, they could have fixed the problem. However, the report's admission that the company responsible for the signal for the screen, Vodafone, was unaware until the day of the match of the decision to utilise the screen, tends to suggest that there had been a significant failure of communication and preparation around the issue of the functioning of the one screen which would be watched by the greatest number of people. As it was, Vodafone could not account for the failure of the signal. On the Rangers fans' websites conspiracy theories about the failure of the screen abounded.

Following the screen's blackout it was claimed that thousands had been transported to the alternative indoor venue of the Velodrome, close to the City of Manchester stadium. While many fans did end up at the Velodrome it appears that very few were taken there on buses laid on for the purpose. The fans' frustration over the failure of the screen was compounded in the vast majority of cases by the inconvenience of the alternative or indeed the belief that there had been no alternative plan put into place. After the match there was sheer pandemonium at Piccadilly station, which I personally experienced; as a poster on the 'Follow Follow' website later put it, the station was like 'a refugee camp'. It appeared to most people by then that the city's services had totally collapsed, and that the police were simply left to prevent a chaotic situation becoming something tragically worse. That they managed to do so through the ensuing night hours while thousands milled around was a testimony in this case to the restraint exercised by most fans and to the fact that many had expected to sleep rough after the match in any case. The question of how to get home had not been uppermost in the minds of those who had fondly imagined a long night of celebration.

*

The critical backlash against the behaviour of those Rangers fans in the Piccadilly area began almost immediately. Politicians and media commentators lined up to condemn and demand that the culprits be identified and held to account. This was only to be expected, as was the recourse on the part of some pundits to the equation of the Manchester problems with the dominant narrative of Protestant sectarianism to which Rangers and their fans have been habitually related. From this perspective the story wrote itself: there was a ready template to which the Manchester events could conform. Thus, in a sense, Rangers were victims of their past: the practice of not signing Catholic players for many years, the crudely sectarian chants and songs once sung on the terraces and stands and the episodes of hooliganism in eras such as the 1960s and 1970s when Rangers visited England for matches, including Manchester.

Rangers fans in the wake of the UEFA final were resentful that the incidents involving a small minority were allowed to disrupt the 'good news' story of the biggest invasion of football fans for an away match. They were inclined to reflect on how trouble involving Celtic fans on the way to and surrounding the 2003 final was not so pejoratively contextualised and was not allowed to upset the positive spin put upon the whole adventure. Some believed that escapades involving the Tartan Army were similarly indulged and finessed out of the coverage of that phenomenon. Giulianotti's research has demonstrated that Rangers fans surveyed in the 2003–5 period felt that they had not been credited, as Celtic fans and the Scotland team's support had, for good behaviour abroad, while they were keen moreover to point out that Rangers fans did not feel it necessary ostentatiously to advertise that they could get on with the locals.[5]

One contributor to the 'Follow Follow' website confronted the critical assault on Rangers fans around the sectarian theme in the following trenchant terms: 'Any suggestion that a more ecumenical outlook from Rangers fans would have led to events unfolding differently in Manchester . . . is, at best, misguided . . . or more probably and more sinisterly, further evidence of an ongoing demonization of Rangers and their supporters.' Such sentiments were typical of those fans who had long perceived an anti-Rangers cultural and political bandwagon operating in Scottish society, resulting in the denigration of what many considered defensible traditions and displays of identity. Such attitudes had in fact led them to castigate the Rangers chairman David Murray, chief executive Martin Bain, former player Sandy Jardine and security officer Kenny Scott, all of whom had been central to efforts to rid the club of the songs, chants, banners and so on which constituted precisely the baggage from the past which commentators could seize on to depict the club in a critical light.

Manchester signalled both how far those in charge of the club had succeeded in their quest to change the supporters' culture, and how far they still had to go. The Herald sportswriter, Hugh Macdonald, made the valid observation that Rangers had achieved significant advances in curbing the singing of certain songs inside grounds when the team played, including the UEFA final, but that many fans in Manchester were only too ready to sing them outside.[6] However, others were less willing to acknowledge that the club and at least a substantial section of supporters had changed – in this they were arguably as stuck in the past as those Rangers fans who saw it as a matter of honour to withstand the pressure to stop singing their old favourites. A recurring theme in the Scottish press, post UEFA final, was the despairing voice of exiled Scots who had typically emigrated in the 1970s or earlier, assuming that sectarian problems were just the same now as when they had left, and evincing a lack of knowledge of developments in the recent past. Rangers now have a considerable record of sponsoring anti-sectarian and community-development initiatives, and it is seldom appreciated that their efforts in this regard have to address both the demands (often facile and ill-informed) from wider society about sectarianism, and the perceptions among their own fans about being unfairly scapegoated and singled out for the persistence of the same phenomenon in Scotland.

However, the theme of religious sectarianism did not monopolise the post-match debate quite as much as on previous occasions when the Rangers support had been involved in well-publicised disturbances. This time it was accompanied by a striking degree of comment on the subject of national identity and allegiance. Among journalists, letter-writers and bloggers there was much chat about Scottishness and Britishness and the extent to which the overt Unionism of so many Rangers fans was now so peculiar in twenty-first century Scotland as to deserve comment and, very often, vilification.

In a reflective piece before the match, the journalist Melanie Reid struck the note of nostalgia which was to be something of a motif around the coming events. She evoked the stereotype of the Rangers fan as the pro-Union working man whose heyday was probably the period from the Second World War through to the late 1960s, identified by one eminent Scottish historian as 'The Moment of British Nationalism'.[7] This was a time when skilled manual workers still occupied a pivotal political and cultural position, at one and the same time a repository of hopes for a more egalitarian order and a force for upward social mobility and the rewards of a more affluent age.

On the day of the match *The Herald* featured a cartoon depicting Alex Salmond – the Scottish National party (SNP) leader and Scottish First Minister – observing Union-Jack bedecked Rangers fans departing for Manchester and musing to himself that this might be an opportune moment to hold an independence referendum. During the post-mortem into the trouble in Manchester there were jibes about Rangers supporters representing 'the sinister underbelly of Unionism' and 'sectarian/Unionist imperialism'; the fans were described as 'wrapping themselves in the butcher's apron' and displaying 'a nasty and aggressive form of British Unionism'. One commentator contended that the incidents would be likely to have a baleful impact on Anglo-Scottish relations at a time when tensions in the Union were self-evident.[8]

The Union flag was certainly the predominant emblem favoured by the Rangers support in Manchester. There was nothing at all new or surprising about this. Indeed, it may have been more noteworthy that there was also a great deal of Scottish national symbolism on display which was ignored by those with an anti-Unionist political agenda. Saltires and Lion Rampants were much in evidence, and many fans wore kilts and glengarries. Some even wore T-shirts with the message 'Manchester 2008 – We're coming down the road', the latter slogan borrowed from the Tartan Army. The occasion, moreover, bore more than a few similarities to Wembley trips on the part of Scotland fans in days gone by, including a fair dose of anti-English antagonism. In recent years as many Rangers fans have drifted away from active support of the national team there has nevertheless been a notable tendency to reflect nostalgically upon the time when, before the 1980s, they supplied the bulk of the Scotland support. Manchester was in this sense as well as others an occasion to reclaim a cherished part of the past.

The Rangers fans' profile in this regard was distinctly double-sided, again not a new phenomenon. It can be suggested, indeed, that there is a unique edginess here on the part of many fans, which derives from the tension between different national allegiances and the difficulties they have in expressing both simultaneously. Many fans may be resentful about being considered not properly Scottish on account of all the pro-British sentiment which surrounds the Rangers fan base and this, coupled with the continuing solidarity with Ulster Loyalists, arguably produces a profound defensiveness. The overall mindset becomes simply too complex for some fans to articulate. Celtic fans may experience tensions around Irish and Scottish allegiances but they appear to resolve them more easily, and overwhelmingly, in favour of the celebration of one kind of Irishness.

The time when the articulation of the sentiment 'Scottish, British and Proud' – which adorned a massive banner hung from a bridge near

Piccadilly station – was straightforward and 'normal' has long passed in Scotland. The Rangers fans' loyalties are now widely viewed as problematic, peculiar, schizophrenic and outmoded. One *uber*-Nationalist blogger in *The Scotsman* actually claimed that the Rangers supporters in Manchester were not Scots: 'They weren't flying the Saltire. It was Gordon Brown's underpants they were flying.'[9] Thus, according to this perspective, you cannot be a true Scot if you wave the Union Jack, and Rangers fans, like Gordon Brown, were either traitors to Scotland or not deserving of the appellation 'Scottish' any more.

The events of Manchester may have exposed the behaviour of some Rangers supporters as chauvinistic, bigoted and intolerant; yet the same adjectives can be applied to the response of many of their detractors of a Scottish Nationalist bent. Such critics also undoubtedly deduce too readily that the display of the Union Jack and the bellowing of Loyalist songs in a football context will translate into particular political beliefs and voting behaviour away from football. They underestimate the degree to which fans' conduct has become ritualised; if there was real political substance to it then the current Scottish political landscape would look very different indeed. A correspondent to *The Scotsman* following the UEFA final made the interesting point that he observed much support for Alex Salmond's SNP among Rangers fans and that 'the Union of most interest to the average Rangers fan is that of Northern Ireland with Great Britain'.[10] Clearly, the only safe conclusion is that identities of a national and cultural kind can be complex and labile and difficult to reduce to the one simple 'truth' beloved of capital 'N' Nationalists everywhere, in this case both Scottish and British. Manchester 2008 simply shows how far we have to go in creating an environment which accommodates different identities and combinations of them.

On the other hand there is another angle from which to look at the issue. What renders the Rangers fans' behaviour relatively anomalous in the context of contemporary Scotland is not perhaps the willingness to subscribe to a British allegiance; rather, it is the manner – some would say jingoistic manner – in which it is expressed. There is a suggestion that an affinity with Britishness still remains in Scotland, but that this tends to dwindle as the more British symbolism is foregrounded and celebrated. It is as if most Scots are happy to retain a British identity but – crucially

– in a low-key manner and decidedly as a supplement to a strong primary Scottish one. Britishness might be said to work best and gain greater popular acceptance in the modern era when it sits lightly on top of other identities. The forms of Britishness that celebrate an imperial past have little purchase today however much they may well be pointing to some vital aspects of Scotland's historical role in the Empire.

It is in this connection that some of the Rangers fans' cultural talismans might be seen as problematic. Few Scots these days are given to passionate renderings of 'God Save the Queen', far less 'Rule Britannia'. The latter may have been written by a Scot but it was written for the age of an empire that is long since gone. Moreover, it is a song that was adopted by the neo-Nazis among the English national team's support in the 1980s, and in adding it to their repertoire a few years later Rangers fans only ensured that they would take on the same associations. The practice of singing it by much of the Rangers support may then have been shaped by the changing political situation in Scotland and thus underpinned by a desire to appear defiant in defence of the Union. Or, more prosaically, it may have been sung in the spirit of terracing tribalism to 'wind up' opposing fans. Even if this is all so, the choice of such a song only tarnishes the cause of the Union and British identity as it has now come to be reformulated. Equally, proclaiming such a brand of ultra Loyalism has in general attracted the worst kind of allies from England in terms of the club's wider international reputation. By most accounts some of the troublemakers in Manchester were English extreme-right-wing hangers-on attracted to Rangers on account of the Loyalist image and the singing of songs like 'Rule Britannia', although it might be added that to such people the religious ditties which have landed the club in trouble with the football authorities mean little or nothing.

The Rangers fans' defence of the Union and Britishness has lost sight of the most constructive aspects of these two phenomena: their subtlety, their expansiveness and their flexibility. They have simply answered certain kinds of narrow and chauvinistic Nationalism with the British version. Then again, when have such characteristics as subtlety been a feature of football fans' behaviour anywhere? Rather, football has tended to be an arena where old 'certainties' are reaffirmed.

*

At the heart of the celebration of Unionism and Loyalism by Rangers supporters over the years lies the Irish question. One of many jaundiced comments about this in the wake of the UEFA final referred to Rangers supporters making common cause with 'the Ulster Unionist basket case'.[11] Even on the 'Follow Follow' site there were, albeit untypical, views expressed about Loyalism no longer being 'relevant'. Manchester 2008 served to hold up to scrutiny even what most observers would have regarded as axiomatic and immutable: the Rangers fans' vociferous support for Northern Ireland's place in the Union.

While the debate over this, if such it can be considered, was hardly more than superficial skirmishing and the floating of notions which would previously have been viewed as heretical, it nonetheless deserves acknowledgement. In a way Rangers fans have now started to mirror the tensions in the Celtic support regarding the apparent predominance of Irish symbolism and cultural promotions over Scottish. In the Manchester aftermath, there were Rangers fans who materialised to ask whether the Orange and Loyalist 'heritage' and 'culture' was holding the club back. Their suggestions were met with fundamentalist responses about it being imperative not to 'placate our enemies', but it might be wondered if a section of the Rangers support now wishes to distance the club from the Ulster Loyalist cause or at least make radical changes to how that cause and the Ulster link is maintained and expressed. Arguably, the concerns of these fans might have been felt to be less pressing had solidarity with Ulster not segued so often into an apparent British National Party (BNP) brand of Loyalism. As is the case with some Unionists in Northern Ireland, there seems to be a tendency on the part of some diehards in the Rangers support to welcome allies regardless of who they are and what they stand for, simply because allies are hard to find in a chilly political and cultural environment for the cause of the Union.

As it was, the Ulster connections were much in evidence in Manchester including the waving at the match of a flag bearing the logo of the Vanguard political movement of the 1970s. There was something quite symbolic about this beyond the Vanguard associations; it was as if nothing had changed since the peak of the conflict at that time and that there had been no peace process and no new governmental institutions set up in the Province. Indeed, the way the Rangers fans still sing and chant in support of Ulster betrays a mindset which refuses to contemplate the changes that have taken place and the way the problem itself has evolved and has been reshaped. Of course, such fans are not out of step with the persistent 'No Surrenderism' in Ulster Loyalist political culture; yet this is now only one strand in the Unionist tapestry, and many more Unionists have chosen engagement over self-exclusion in the quest to build a secure future while retaining the Union. It may well be the case that for the thousands of Ulster men and women who travel to see Rangers, a sense of recreational fundamentalism is enjoyed at football matches which compensates for its contemporary irrelevance and outdatedness within the political realities back home. Once again there are interesting parallels to be drawn with Celtic fans and displays of support for Irish Nationalism and Republicanism.

Yet it needs to be noted that in a world in which 'identities' are exhaustively analysed and discussed and obsessed over, there has been a modern (or post-modern) twist to the Scottish-Ulster solidarity. This has largely come through the revival of the movement to promote Ulster-Scots language and culture which emerged purposefully in the 1990s and has now a substantial history of cross-channel initiatives behind it. Rangers' relationship to this movement is tangential, and may be problematic for some activists, but it is undoubtedly part of the package.[12] Moreover, Ulster-Scots, while open to criticisms about cultural misrepresentation and the dangers of ethnic exclusivism, may help direct the Rangers dimension to the enterprise away from the fans' hitherto dominant concern with Orangeism and the politics of sheer defiance. If the movement helps people to feel that their identity and culture is being recognised then perhaps an Ulster more at ease with itself and its differences around cultures and traditions might translate to the fans at Ibrox in a positive way.

However, this kind of speculation runs the risk of neglecting the continuing tribalistic and 'us and them' essence of the football crowd and indeed football fandom. As a contributor to the website 'Spiked' put it in relation to the events at Manchester, football is 'no place for democracy'; 'moralistic politicians and commentators', he suggested, should stop 'policing' the behaviour of fans in respect of uncouth songs and chants.[13]

Political correctness, it seemed to be suggested, was again intervening where it was not wanted or, at the end of the day, required. Certainly it can be claimed that Rangers fans in particular have reason to feel victimised by PC lobbies who know they are an easy target. In this respect, as Giulianotti shows, it is plausible to regard Rangers fans as cultural underdogs notwithstanding the fact that their emblems, songs, chants and so on appear to celebrate historically powerful forces in society.[14] For many Rangers fans their self-understanding is of a group targeted for being unfashionable and honest about it, while the bigotry and intolerance of other clubs' fans is overlooked on account of their more 'acceptable' political and/or cultural profile. Such perceptions and resentments were a feature of the fans' reaction to the spotlight shone on them by Manchester 2008.

The price of breaking all records for a travelling support was the steep one of national, and even international, critical comment about Rangers as a club and the image it projects. Much of this comment drew lazily on well-established narratives fashioned around selective aspects of Rangers' history and episodes of supporter misconduct from over thirty years before. It should not be allowed to obscure either the positive features of the whole Manchester occasion or the relatively trouble-free record of Rangers fans at games abroad over recent years. Nor should it prevent acknowledgement of the efforts of some fans in the aftermath to take initiatives such as fundraising for policemen injured in the Manchester violence, and of the commendable self-examination conducted by fans who recognised that it was not enough simply to complain about 'agendas' in the media against the club.

Rangers are an extraordinary institution. The club's awesome support base is worldwide and as passionate as can be found in football. Along with this goes a glorious yet deeply controversial history. For many fans contentious issues around identity, politics and culture complicate straightforward football fanaticism. The debates around such issues will continue. Manchester was another demonstration that being a Rangers fan often means, fairly or unfairly, that there is much to answer for.

Notes

1 MCC Report

2 MCC Report

3 For an examination of the way the event was reported see R. Boyle and R. Haynes, *Sport, the Media and Popular Culture* (Edinburgh University Press, 2009), ch. 8.

4 For discussion of the Seville events see R. Giulianotti, 'Celtic, Cultural Identities and the Globalization of Football: Notes from 2003 UEFA Cup Final in Seville', *Scottish Affairs* No. 48, 2004, pp. 1–23.

5 See R. Giulianotti, 'Popular Culture, Social Identities, and Internal/ External Cultural Politics: The Case of Rangers Supporters in Scottish Football', *Identities* Vol. 14, 2007, pp. 257–84.

6 *The Herald* 16 May 2008.

7 C. Harvie, 'The Moment of British Nationalism', *Political Quarterly* Vol. 71, 2000, pp. 328–40; Melanie Reid article in *The Times* (Scotland) 12 May 2008.

8 *Scotland on Sunday* 18 May 2008. The assortment of readers' comments is drawn from the coverage in *The Herald* and *The Scotsman* in the days following the UEFA Cup final.

9 Comment posted on 19 May 2008.

10 *The Scotsman* 19 May 2008

11 *The Herald* 19 May 2008

12 See Chris Williamson, 'Rangers and the Ulster Scots', in R. Esplin and G. Walker (eds.), *It's Rangers for Me?* (Fort Publishing, 2007).

13 Viewed on 20 May 2008.

14 Giulianotti, 'Popular Culture'. See also article 'Rebel Rebel' in *Follow, Follow* ('The People's Fanzine') No. 199.

Manchester Brace Yourself

Ronnie Esplin

'Manchester brace yourself . . . Rangers are coming! Scotland will have its big night. . . . The Scots are heading for Manchester and you know what? Manchester may not be big enough! They won't need passports, they won't need visas but the battle for tickets starts now!'

Rarely has a commentator been as prescient as Peter Drury was on 1 May 2008, when, at the end of the shoot-out, Nacho Novo slammed in the winning penalty against Fiorentina in Florence to take Rangers to their first European final in thirty-six years.

The impressive City of Manchester stadium would be the venue for the UEFA Cup final and Russian club Zenit St Petersburg, managed by former Ibrox boss Dick Advocaat, would be the Gers' opponents. Englishman Drury – who was providing the television commentary for ITV Sport – vividly remembers the climax in the Stadio Artemio Franchi and recalls the thinking behind the words that became the soundtrack to what is now an iconic moment for Rangers supporters.

> If I successfully summed it up then that's fantastic. In truth, we commentators sometimes get lucky and I was, in a sense, wrapped up in the Rangers experience and it all came spewing out. I went with my gut instinct and set myself up for the moment. I blurted out 'Manchester brace yourself' but if Novo hadn't scored then I had nowhere to go. It would have gone to sudden death and I couldn't have used that phrase again. And it was obvious to me that, with Manchester being so close to Scotland, there would be thousands down for the final.

While the little Spaniard was still on his way over to celebrate with the small band of Rangers fans penned in at the corner of ACF Fiorentina's inhospitable ground, chased by the rest of the Ibrox squad, an explosion of 'ticket texts' shook Scotland and beyond.

While as a journalist I was, I hoped, assured of my media pass for the final I knew I would be under pressure to source tickets for friends and family and in the subsequent minutes, hours and days, people I hadn't heard from in years got in touch, as I myself made contact with long-lost friends, spurious acquaintances and, in some cases, complete strangers.

The search for tickets became the dominant issue in the fortnight before the final but the restrictive capacity of a stadium originally built for the 2002 Commonwealth Games in Manchester, around 44,000, promised disappointment to the majority of Rangers fans hoping to see their club win its second European trophy. As the days passed it became clear that for tens of thousands of punters, simply being in and around Manchester would have to suffice.

During the stormy and uneasy early years the threat of extinction hung over the club on a few occasions, none more so than for one game in the late 1880s when only five hundred turned up to see the Light Blues take on Partick Thistle.* That well over two hundred thousand Gers fans mobilised for a match well over a century hence – and who knows how many were cheering on from their armchairs – was without precedent in the history of the global game. For all the disdain aimed at the Ibrox club in modern-day Scotland, its size, strength and status as a Scottish institution was reaffirmed.

In his first spell as Ibrox manager in the 1990s, Walter Smith had enjoyed years of big spending on stars such as Brian Laudrup and Paul Gascoigne to achieve domestic domination but to the great frustration of the Light Blues support, apart from one exciting campaign, real success in the Champions League had remained elusive. On his return to Govan in 2007 to mop up the mess left by failed Frenchman Paul Le Guen, working within vastly reduced financial parameters, and with a squad full of journeymen, Smith had guided the club to a European final.

The journey, though, was far from smooth.

Rangers had dropped out of the Champions League with the jibes of arguably the world's greatest footballer ringing in their ears. Barcelona superstar Lionel Messi had accused Smith's side of playing 'anti-football' in their drab, goalless Group E encounter at Ibrox. While the mesmeric Argentine was clearly peeved at the way a disciplined Rangers side had shackled him and his superstar teammates – without resorting to the dubious tactics traditionally associated with his fellow countrymen – most Gers fans while cheering the result probably agreed with the assessment in the cold light of day. The Ibrox side, in some ways pioneers of European club competition, had set out from the first whistle to hang on for a point.

Nick Harris of *The Independent* described it as the 'the sweetest of stalemates' in the context of keeping Champions League hopes alive but, ultimately, it was a performance that would be replicated and honed in the less rarefied environs of the UEFA Cup. The home point against Barca helped secure third place in a group that also contained Lyon and Stuttgart. What faced Rangers thereafter was a second-rate European tournament, a competition that the giants of the game all but ignored and which has seen unfashionable clubs such as Espanyol, Alaves and Middlesbrough competing in recent finals.

The lingering disappointment surrounding another Champions League failure took some time to dissipate and in consequence the initial knockout rounds of the UEFA Cup were low-key. After a dreary goalless encounter against Panathinaikos at Ibrox, a 1–1 draw in Greece, courtesy of a Novo goal nine minutes from time, saw Rangers through to the next round. A 2–0 home win over Werder Bremen – thanks mostly to uncharacteristic mistakes by visiting goalkeeper Tim Wiese – meant that Rangers could afford to lose 1–0 in Germany in the return leg, although that match against the Bundesliga's second-placed side was not without some nervy moments and a wonder save from Allan McGregor.

As the European run unfolded, there was the feeling in some quarters that Rangers were bound to go out sooner rather than later so why let the tournament detract from wresting the SPL title back from Celtic. It was thought likely that Sporting Lisbon would put Rangers out at the quarter-final stage although by kick-off the Light Blues had opened up a six-point lead over Celtic at the top of the SPL with a game in hand. But only a late miss by Sporting striker Tonel let Smith's side off the hook in the first leg at Ibrox. Against the odds in Portugal, after surviving an early onslaught, classic breakaway goals from Jean Claude Darcheville and Steven Whittaker had the Govan men facing the hitherto unlikely prospect of a European semi-final and at last people sat up straight and took notice. The first leg was at Ibrox and there was almost an expectation that Rangers would concentrate on keeping a clean sheet and so it proved as yet another goalless draw was played out. Former Chelsea star Adrian Mutu became the latest superstar to leave Ibrox frustrated and he branded the match 'one ugly game of football'.

Like most neutrals Peter Drury, who had begun commentating on Rangers games at the quarter-final stage, was not enthralled.

> The football was not sparkling, it was functional. Walter Smith had a game plan with the lone striker and he made it work. The first game against Sporting Lisbon was a classic example of the style of football Rangers were playing. It ended up 0–0 but it was almost minus goals. I thought then that it was over but then you had Whittaker going through like Lionel Messi to score the second goal in Lisbon. It made no sense. When I thanked Walter for his help afterwards, he said 'are we still in this?' with a twinkle in his eye. That summed it up. He knew he was getting lucky.

The semi-final first leg against Fiorentina at Ibrox was almost a carbon copy of the game against Sporting. But, upon checking my notes, I see that Barry Ferguson and Kevin Thomson were suspended, and that Burke, McCulloch, McGregor, Beasley, Adam and Naismith were injured. You had names like Jordan MacMillan in the squad, names that with all due respect should not have been near a European semi-final. I also noted that Rangers had a game against Celtic in between the two legs. So you have to take that into consideration.

In Florence, although Rangers were battered for most of the game, I remember thinking, 'this is going to happen'. There was a sense of destiny about it. When Cousin was sent off – after picking up his second booking of the night for clashing with Liverani in injury time – I was almost angry. I remember feeling he had been inexplicably stupid and that he had blown it for Rangers, a feeling that stayed with me when Ferguson missed the first penalty in the shoot-out. But then Alexander saved from Liverani and when Christian Vieira missed his penalty I thought it was back on, and then, of course, Novo scored the winner.

Novo's penalty was a genuine 'where were you when it happened?' moment and it completed the rehabilitation of the tournament in Ibrox eyes. Rangers fans realised the final was probably going to be a once-in-a-lifetime occasion. The UEFA Cup turned from an inconvenience into a cause.

Celtic's visit to Seville for the 2003 UEFA Cup final against Porto had elicited great enthusiasm and after lionising their Spanish experience – even in defeat – Parkhead fans could hardly criticise the fervour surrounding Manchester. In consequence, the build-up to the 2008 final was mostly free from the sniping that usually accompanies any semblance of success by either Old Firm side. Rangers fans were determined to eclipse the fuss made over Seville and the novelty of a cup final against a team managed by a former Ibrox boss added a little spice, if it was needed.

Advocaat's profligacy in his time at Ibrox, from 1998 to 2001, had all but bankrupted the club but with no better Champions League record to show for the spending, although there had been more solid performances against Europe's elite. European success for him had subsequently come with the nouveau riche St Petersburg club, who were to contest their first European final. A phone call to the Dutchman minutes after Rangers had clinched a place in the final found him in fine fettle. Earlier in the day, Zenit had crushed Bayern Munich 4–0 in Russia to book their trip to Lancashire with a remarkable 5–1 aggregate. Never one to get too excited, Advocaat reiterated his fondness for the Ibrox club – which is undoubtedly genuine – but stressed that he was looking to take the trophy back to Russia.

> After this game the circle is closed. I've said for months that I would love to play Rangers in the final and it's great that it will happen. It is a major achievement for Rangers and for us, and I look forward to seeing David [Sir David Murray] and Walter in Manchester. I watched the Rangers game on television after our match had finished. I think Walter aged a bit during that game – and so did I. But it just shows you that if you work hard then you can get your rewards.

Advocaat also knew from experience the support Rangers would bring to Manchester.

> It could be like a home game for Rangers. I'm not sure how many of our fans will be at the game but it is not easy for them to get to Manchester. There might only be four or five thousand and if that is the case, then Rangers will have around 40,000. One thing is sure: there will be many more Rangers fans than Zenit fans.

The nationwide interest in the game was part-reflected and part-fuelled by the media, which went into overdrive. Football coverage on television, radio and on the internet in recent years has complemented, if not supplanted newspapers, which for years had the pitch to themselves.

Newspapers, though, had traditionally exercised restraint when covering even the biggest matches. When Rangers first reached a European final in 1961 – losing the European Cup Winners Cup final to Fiorentina over two legs – the *Daily Record* gave just two pages to the 2–0 first-leg defeat at Ibrox. In 1967, when Rangers faced Bayern Munich in the final of the same competition in Nuremburg – a week after Celtic had won the European Cup in Lisbon – there were just two pages devoted to the preview. The day after Rangers had lost 1–0 in extra time, within a two-page match report, Ibrox boss Scott Symon was afforded just three paragraphs of quotes.

Five years later, when Rangers fought their way through to the Cup Winners Cup final against Moscow Dynamo, they had to compete with the Scotland national team for space. As Willie Waddell's side trotted out in the Nou Camp, Scotland were playing Wales in a home-international match at Hampden. Although the *Daily Record* printed a souvenir pull-out, there was barely a page devoted to the final, which was not televised live, but was instead broadcast on Radio Four with delayed television highlights.

By complete contrast, and as evidence of the increased importance of sport to modern-day media, there was wall-to-wall coverage of the 2008 UEFA Cup final. Space and time appeared unlimited. Novo's winning penalty made the *Daily Record*'s front page, two news pages inside and formed the basis of a sport special that ran to nine pages. From then until the day of the final, the game did not leave the front page and on the eve of the match a sixteen-page pull-out was produced. On the day of the game the *Record* published messages of support from famous Scots such as Gordon Brown, Alex Salmond and Colin Montgomerie, with the game being discussed on the front page, the back fourteen pages, plus another five pages inside. On the morning after the final, events of the previous evening were splashed over eight news pages plus fifteen sports pages. The game, as we now know, also made the front pages.

The saturation coverage of the event was not unique to the *Daily Record*. The reportage was similar in all other mainstream Scottish newspapers and on radio, television and the internet. By the eve of the final, though, there was almost nothing left to say. At the pre-match media conference – held in a makeshift tented area just outside the stadium – Advocaat looked relaxed and confident, and was philosophical about losing the services of the tournament's top scorer Pavel Pogrebnyak. The Muscovite's two-goal display against Bayern – which took his total to ten for the campaign – was soured by the yellow card that kept him out of the final. 'We will be missing the striker who scored ten goals for us so that is a blow,' the Zenit boss said. 'But as a coach, you can only worry about the players that you can choose and we have others that can come in.'

Smith was more pensive. There were no rallying cries, certainly none that screamed conviction. Victory, if it came, would come courtesy of another well-practised defensive display. It wasn't the style of football that most Rangers fans wanted to watch – as opinion polls, phone-ins and message boards testified – but, on the whole, criticism would be saved for another day. This was a time to keep believing that the last hurdle could be overcome.

However, Pavel Astafiev, a journalist for *Sport Daily*, a Moscow-based newspaper, could see only one outcome.

> Scottish football is not so popular in Russia so a lot of Rangers players weren't even known over here. And it was almost obvious that Zenit were favourites to win, as they had beaten Bayern, Bayer, and Marseille, who were all stronger than Rangers. In Russia, there is also the view that Scottish football is rather simple in style so it was thought that there should be no problems beating Rangers.

Zenit fan Alex Morozov was also confident as he prepared for the trip to Manchester: 'After thrashing Bayern 4–0, the Zenit fans had wings. To be honest I didn't know much about Rangers except the fact that our coach was their coach several years previously.'

Most Rangers fans conceded that Zenit looked to have a better team but there were no hang-ups about the tag of underdogs. The game would look after itself. The whole occasion was to be enjoyed but there were signs beforehand that Manchester might be ill-prepared.

Manchester City Council had hesitated before publicly welcoming the Rangers supporters. The fact that the three fan zones set aside in an already-cramped city centre were unlikely to cope with the sheer volume of visitors was glossed over. As it transpired, the number of Rangers fans who headed to Manchester exceeded all forecasts. For that reason it was soon obvious most fans had to find somewhere other than the stadium to watch the match.

Luckily, after numerous phone calls, I had procured tickets for my son, Alex, and nephew Derek, who were to travel with my brother, Stuart, and Derek's friend Ryan early on the day of the game. Another couple of tickets were promised, although I was to pick them up at the stadium before kick-off. I drove south on the Monday afternoon for the game on Wednesday night with a friend, John Allardyce, and we enjoyed the calm before the storm. Manchester city centre was relatively quiet that night with a few Zenit supporters mingling with those Rangers fans who had also arrived early.

The next day, though, our hotel at Salford Quayside, close to Manchester United's Old Trafford stadium, buzzed with excitement as Gers supporters began arriving from all over the world, most of them without tickets. Three generations of one family – gran, daughter and grandson – set up base camp in the hotel, the adults content to be within a few miles of the stadium and a few yards of the bar. The chaos in the hotel restaurant at breakfast the following morning confirmed my earlier suspicions that many of the rooms were over-populated by enterprising Rangers fans keen to keep costs to a minimum. It was another early sign, though, of the mayhem that was to unfold.

Drury, a veteran of major football events at club and international level, was taken aback by the extent of the invasion.

> Commentators get accused, and often rightly, of hyping things up too much. But I don't think I will ever see anything like that day again. At 8 a.m. I came out of my hotel in the middle of Manchester and you couldn't walk on the pavement it was so busy. We were only three miles from the stadium but I made sure I got over there at noon; I couldn't take the chance of getting caught up in the crowds. It was simply extraordinary. I can't believe I will see anything like it again.

The eight to nine thousand Zenit fans, most of whom had flown direct from St Petersburg, were swamped as rail, roads and airports acted as tributaries flowing towards an ocean of red, white and blue. Morozov was one of the few Russians who flew to London before getting a train north and although he had anticipated that Zenit fans would be outnumbered, the extent of the disparity surprised him.

> Scotland is much closer to England than Russia and Rangers fans did not need to take a plane to get to Manchester so I expected to see crowds. However I was stunned to see the sheer amount of Rangers fans in the city centre. Most of them were peaceful and I even was offered a Rangers scarf – however, I politely refused to accept.

Long before noon, amid the growing excitement in the city centre, there was a slight but noticeable malevolence in the air. Earlier I had nipped in to a packed cafe in the Piccadilly Gardens fan zone to use the toilet and witnessed two shaven-headed Rangers fans belligerently and brazenly sniffing cocaine off the Formica table, their glazed eyes almost begging for confrontation. The police, at that point, were hands-off but some officers' grins were fixed as they struggled to comprehend what stood before them. Or what was struggling to stand before them. The slabs of lager that were being carted around by some already-tipsy supporters made the problems that were to arrive seven or eight hours later predictable, if not inevitable.

I met some colleagues at the edge of one of the fan zones and, as we swapped stories of what we had witnessed, I half-jokingly said to one of them, 'They'll be throwing bottles at that screen before the night is out,' only to be dismissed out of hand. Still, supporters continued to flood in to the already-claustrophobic city centre by the minute.

Local surrealists would have appreciated the sight of a flute band from Harthill snaking its way around the streets at lunchtime, as workers and shoppers looked on in bemusement. As tram services slowly ground to a halt, and taxis and buses struggled to move, we decided to get over to the ground early where I was to pick up my other two tickets. The City of Manchester stadium, basking in heat like the rest of the country, was relatively tranquil and in the car park I bumped into radio broadcaster Mark Donaldson, who asked for an impromptu interview that was to go out live in Scotland. I mentioned the prodigious amount of alcohol that was being demolished and hoped it would not lead to anything unsavoury. Donaldson expressed fears that it might already be too late.

Broadcast journalist Nina Warhurst – then working for Manchester television station ChannelM – also witnessed some stereotypical behaviour.

We placed a massive emphasis on the event and leading up to the game there was great excitement and a fantastic atmosphere. Most Mancunians are very proud of the city and international sporting events are a great opportunity to show it off and dispel some misconceptions. But it was certainly apparent, even the day before the game, that there were far more fans than ticket-holders in the city. I was working a breakfast shift on the morning of the game, and en route to the studio there were men literally sleeping on the roads, using their Rangers flags to cover them. The fact that there were so many fans became the top line of the story.

There was a real buzz to the city that day though. It was beautifully sunny and there was no hint of anything sinister – I remember feeling like I was at a festival. Although there was obviously lots of binge-drinking going on, I didn't encounter any aggression at all, and was really charmed by most of the fans I met – both Scottish and Russian. I remember laughing with a colleague at what was happening in the supermarket opposite our offices. Some Rangers fans were drinking cans of lager then placing the empty tins back on the shelves. The security guards had completely given up and were even laughing about it.

Far from the madding crowds the Ibrox squad contemplated the prospect of making more history. Rangers were fighting to win four trophies, the Co-operative Insurance Cup having been already captured in March following a dramatic penalty shoot-out win over Dundee United. A Scottish Cup final against first-division side Queen of the South would close the season and the traditional battle with Celtic for the championship was heading for a last-day conclusion. Arguments about fixture congestion would dominate the Ibrox agenda in the closing weeks of the season but the only debate in the hours leading up to the final was which starting eleven Smith would choose.

The only certainty was that Kris Boyd, the club's top scorer, would be on the bench and in the event it was Darcheville who was used as the lone striker, in place of the suspended Cousin. Midfielder Kevin Thomson passed a late fitness test to partner Barry Ferguson with Steven Davis and Brahim Hemdani both also drafted in as Novo once again had to settle for a place on the bench. Rangers lined up: Alexander, Broadfoot, Weir, Cuellar, Papac, Hemdani, Whittaker, Ferguson, Thomson, Davis, Darcheville.

Aside from the loss of Pogrebnyak, Advocaat's side was at full strength, the names of Malafeev, Aniukov, Krizanac, Shirokov, Sirl, Tymoschuk,

Zyryanov, Denisov, Faitzulin, Fatih and Arshavin cheered by the vociferous Russians, keen to help the St Petersburg side, playing in all-white, make their own history.

Rangers fans had descended from near and far, evidenced by the banners displayed around the sun-bathed stadium. Name checks were given to supporters clubs from Stranraer to Orkney, Largs to the Isle of Harris, as well as others from places such as London, Derby, Ipswich, Larne and further afield to Lanzarote and Melbourne.

Former Rangers players and players with an affinity for the club were spotted making their way into the ground. Northern Ireland star David Healy was greeted by fans with an enthusiasm that would not be enjoyed by some of the Ibrox players out on the pitch. Sandy Jardine, John MacDonald, Gus MacPherson, Arthur Numan and Jorg Albertz were just some of the former players who were spotted in and around the stadium, as were Frank Lampard junior – who would score for Chelsea in the following week's Champions League final – and his father, the West Ham legend.

Sir Alex Ferguson beamed when on arrival he was given a rousing cheer by Rangers fans. The former Light Blues striker has enjoyed a fractious relationship with the club's supporters since leaving Ibrox in acrimonious circumstances in 1969 but there remains a sense of pride among many Gers fans that one of the best managers ever and a living legend is, at heart, still a bluenose.

My two other tickets eventually materialised. One came from an English colleague and was for my brother. The other ticket – which was sourced from a Zenit fan – was for another friend who had travelled up from London that afternoon, coincidentally on the same train as said Zenit fan. We needed one more ticket and it came – as is often the case with big games – in fortuitous circumstances, when a man with a UEFA blazer wandered out to the perimeter fence with a spare.

From my seat in the press box, through the banners, balloons and oversized footballs, I could see a Rangers flag draped over the top tier. It urged: 'THIS IS YOUR CHANCE. THIS IS YOUR TIME. BECOME LEGENDS.' Melodramatic, certainly, but true nonetheless. The Champions League final between Chelsea and Manchester United in Moscow a week later was irrelevant. In the eyes of Rangers fans, wherever they were, the biggest event in the club's recent history was taking place in the City of Manchester stadium.

Weeks of preparation, speculation and fevered hype were coming to an end. Drury took his place in the gantry alongside regular co-commentator Jim Beglin, and surveyed the scene below him.

> As the two teams came out on a beautiful sunny evening, past the UEFA Cup and on to the park, for selfish purposes I took a breath and allowed myself a moment. I said nothing and let the pictures tell the story. I just looked around at the magnificent scenes and it gave me the chance to remind myself how lucky I was to be at such a wonderful occasion. In many ways, I was a gatecrasher. I knew how desperate Rangers fans were to get tickets and I was neither a Rangers fan nor a Scotsman. If there was an Olympics for getting tickets then Scottish football fans would win a gold medal. There will be thousands of individual stories about how fans got their tickets and we knew there would be more than the official allocation inside the stadium, some of whom would have got there by hook or by crook. If the final had been in the Maracana stadium, the Rangers fans would have sold it out.

However, the Light Blue legions did not see, nor did they expect to see, Brazilian-style football. Former Spurs captain Danny Blanchflower once said: 'The great fallacy is that the game is first and last about winning. It is nothing of the kind. The game is about glory, it is about doing things in style and with a flourish, about going out and beating the other lot, not waiting for them to die of boredom.' He could have been speaking after watching Rangers continue with their cautious approach.

A competent but not great Zenit side were sharper, slicker and more purposeful while Rangers defended resolutely during an unremarkable first period, which, to no one's surprise, ended goalless.

As the second half unfolded, with the game still waiting for its first goal, the Scottish media, at least, were making mental preparations for extra time and penalties. How much extra copy was required? Would there be time to make first-edition deadlines? There was another requirement from duty editors. Word had started to filter through that some Rangers fans had turned violent when a big screen in the Piccadilly Gardens fan zone packed in just before kick-off.

The extent of the problem, or who was to blame, was unknown but I knew, like in Barcelona thirty-six years previously, that even if Rangers won the cup the feat would share the headlines with any outbreak of hooliganism. Sports desks primed journalists to seek official reaction from the Ibrox club after the game.

Most of those inside the stadium were oblivious to the trouble taking place just a few miles away, as they enjoyed the growing tension. Around the sixty-eighth minute the television cameras pan round to the Zenit fans, who are enacting their own version of the 'bouncy' before the Rangers fans respond in kind momentarily to shake the ground to its foundations. For many Gers fans it remains the highlight of the occasion. As the game takes a breather, Drury gives his impressions.

> It would be inaccurate to report that only Rangers fans have brought passion to this final . . . here comes the response and there is only one winner. How dare you take us on? It seemed to crystallise the night. For a few seconds, you could hear and see the Zenit fans and then the Rangers supporters said, 'okay, you've had your ten seconds of fun' and then swamped them again.

However, the Ibrox show of strength was confined to the stands. Zenit midfielder Igor Denisov eventually got the breakthrough in the seventy-second minute following a one-two with the wonderfully talented Andrei Arshavin. Rangers fans looked for their side to throw off the shackles in search of an equaliser but it was not in the team's European DNA and there was no do-or-die cavalry charge at the end either. The one genuine chance fell to Novo, on for Sasa Papac after the loss of the first goal, but he blazed over the bar. Lee McCulloch replaced Hemdani, and Boyd, who would finish the season with twenty-seven goals, came on for Whittaker with four minutes remaining. It was too little too late.

In stoppage time, with Rangers running on empty, Konstatin Zyryanov doubled Zenit's lead with a tap-in after being teed-up by a Fatih Tekke cutback. The dream was over. The majority of Rangers fans stayed behind to cheer their favourites after the final whistle and witnessed the exuberant Zenit players and fans celebrating the capture of the club's first European trophy. Morozov fondly recalls the scene.

> The atmosphere inside the stadium was great. My friends and I almost lost our voices trying to out-sing the Rangers fans. It wasn't the most interesting game in the history of football; there were too many nerves for

that. I had the impression that Rangers were trying to play for penalties and so what a relief it was to see the first goal from Denisov. I started to receive celebratory text messages right after the second goal went in. There was unbelievable happiness, it was the moment when a dream came true and St Petersburg did not sleep that night.

My friends told me that even in the remote districts of the city, people were in the streets waving flags and singing. My father sent me a message that night, which said, 'It is five a.m. and people still in the streets celebrating!' It was one of few moments in the city's history when the whole St Petersburg was happy as one.

However, just as not all of Scotland had wanted Rangers to triumph, Russia was not four-square behind the side from St Petersburg. Russian journalist Pavel Astafiev watched the match at home in Moscow with his father and brother and made the following observations.

Can I say that all of Russia was glad that Zenit won? No. We also have antagonism between rival fans in Russia and supporters of teams such as CSKA and Spartak weren't very happy. My father and brother were behind Rangers because they are CSKA fans. Of course, all of St Petersburg was joyful as everyone there is a Zenit fan. But it should be accepted that the best team won. The troubles in Manchester after the game could have been predicted. Scottish fans – British fans in general – have a long history and tradition of alcohol ingestion and fan disorder. Of course, in Russia, there is the same problem.

Many Rangers supporters trudged back to the city centre to catch trains or find hotels, while others boarded cars and buses to begin the journey home. Former Rangers striker John MacDonald found himself, like many Gers fans, struggling to get back to the friend's house where he was staying. 'I walked back in to the city centre with my wife Margaret but there were no trains or buses. There was a taxi dropping off at a nightclub and we jumped in that and wouldn't get out until he took us to our hotel.'

After celebrating with his fellow Zenit fans, Morozov also headed for the city centre.

I had a safe journey to the train station after the match. Next morning I heard about the fights in the city but I hadn't seen anything. Rangers fans were in sorrow but they were not aggressive at all. Some of them were too drunk but when any of them tried to clash with us, they were immediately taken away by their friends. The train station was a mess; it looked like an evacuation point in times of a natural disaster. People were sleeping on the floor and in places it was hard to get past them but I expected that so it was no surprise.

While colleagues headed for the post-match press conference, where Smith and Advocaat relayed contrasting emotions, I made my way down to the mixed zone looking not only for player reaction but also a statement from Rangers about the alleged misbehaviour of some fans. Ibrox security chief Kenny Scott obliged, insisting that the club would 'take the appropriate action' against troublemakers.

Scott's utterances were appropriately cautious but it soon became clear that the matter would not blow over. Sickening television pictures of Rangers fans – or people purporting to be Rangers fans – battling with police, smashing windows and overturning cars were beamed all around the world. Due to their repeated screenings, they came to define the occasion, at least for some. It was a throwback to darker days at places like St James' Park, Villa Park and Old Trafford, when Rangers fans were involved in acts of hooliganism, only this time the evidence was more compelling.

Mancunian journalist Warhurst became aware of a sudden change in the local mood.

I remember getting angry with a colleague who said she thought things were going to take a bad turn. I hate it when people expect the worst in others and I saw no reason why it would turn ugly. That's why it was such a shock to come in to work the next morning and see the front pages of the newspapers. I think the *Manchester Evening News*'s splash read, 'The battle of Piccadilly'.

It was terrifying to think that an atmosphere could change so quickly. The footage captured by closed-circuit television was truly shocking, as were some of the eyewitness accounts. There was disbelief among my colleagues; we were all really quite shocked and even frightened that the police had appeared to lose control.

There has also been a great deal of subsequent anger. Manchester City Council is quite liberal and it encourages the use of the city centre for events. The fan zones they had established were, in retrospect, insufficient, but many people believe that night of violence has discouraged them from allowing and even encouraging big sporting events in the city. I would be lying if I said that it hasn't left a lasting impact, which is a shame, because as with all of these things, the vast majority of the visitors were great fun and brought a real vibrancy to the city. But I know that it won't be forgotten.

The next fixture Rangers faced was the blame game, which began in earnest on the Thursday morning. While the Ibrox club warned offenders that they would be dealt with harshly, there was enough evidence to suggest that Manchester had failed in its duty to provide the proper resources and facilities to accommodate such a gathering. In what looked like an attempt to deflect blame, the Manchester police and council in my view hyped up the trouble caused by some Rangers fans, leaving Ibrox chief executive Martin Bain, and everyone else connected to the club, on the back foot.

> Unfortunately a screen went down in the centre of Manchester without maybe a separate feed coming in as back-up, and it has obviously been the catalyst for some incidents. Those scenes obviously are dreadful and I've seen them myself and we have been informed . . . that those scenes were caused by supporters who don't normally attach themselves to our support. Therefore we are extremely disappointed and we will do every-thing we possibly can to help Manchester police find out who those perpetrators are.

Stephen Smith, of the Rangers Supporters Trust, backed the club's bid to find those renegades who had spoiled what had been a great occasion, even in defeat. 'It was a very small minority who were responsible and the vast majority were a credit to the club. We would want any of those individuals who are identified to be receiving punitive sanctions from the club, and I am sure they will.'

A clearer picture was to emerge over the following months. Suggestions that Manchester's riot police – who had come on duty later in the day – had been seeking confrontation were given some credence. On 6 April 2009, almost a year after the final, the *Daily Record* reported that Rangers fan James Clark had been cleared of rioting by a Manchester jury, which rejected the evidence of not one, but five, officers. Clark told the jury how he had been battered by police batons and savaged by police dogs, a story told by many Rangers fans with no axe to grind. However, by that time the reputation of the club and its supporters had been irreparably damaged. And there was another reminder when eleven people were arrested and charged with violent disorder at the beginning of October 2009.

Mention of the 2008 UEFA Cup final in Manchester will probably always elicit two responses. In myriad ways, tens of thousands of Rangers fans enjoyed the excitement of looking forward to and witnessing a long-awaited European final, played on a beautiful May night in a fantastic stadium. Those memories will remain precious and untarnished by defeat.

For others, the occasion was hijacked and ruined by a hooligan element that continues to frustrate the Ibrox hierarchy and the club's decent supporters. On 4 May 2009 – when discussing the UEFA Cup competition on the English-based radio station, TalkSport – *Daily Express* journalist Mick Dennis retorted: 'We know that Rangers got to the final last year because their fans smashed up Manchester.'

Perhaps we should leave the last word to Drury, who, unwittingly, became a star of Rangers' UEFA Cup-final story.

> The Rangers fans were brilliant and the Zenit fans were also terrific. You had to work hard to find the Russian supporters but outside the stadium before the game the Rangers fans were interacting with them and it was great fun. I know there were some bad headlines afterwards but the majority of Rangers fans were well behaved. Some of them had too much to drink but let's forget about them.
>
> Don't let them spoil the memories.

Note

* The club's birth and development is examined at greater length in *Rangers 1872: the Gallant Pioneers* by Gary Ralston (Breedon Books, 2009).

To See Ourselves as Others See Us

Scott Dougal

The border between England and Scotland follows the river Tweed east until it gets a scent of the sea. Then it turns north at close to ninety degrees before skirting the outer reaches of Berwick-upon-Tweed. I was born in Berwick, on the north bank of the Tweed. By an accident of history – and there is a fair bit of that in the old place – that means, like Trevor Steven, I am technically English. What is more, I have lived in England for almost my entire life. I make my living in England; my wife is English, as are my two boys. But for all that and as proud as I am to be British, there is only Scottish blood in my veins. I love Shakespeare but Robert Burns is mine and, while I love English football, I don't support an English team. I follow the Rangers.

However, and maybe because of my cross-border heritage, I believe I am sensitive to what separates the Scots and the English and what unites us. Rangers are part of that. Or rather the Old Firm are. In English eyes you do not get one without the other. Let us leave aside the sizeable, hostile, 'Mickey Mouse-football' constituency. In my experience English attitudes to the Old Firm fall into two distinct camps: the enthusiasts and the indifferent. Among the enthusiasts, there are those who have inherited a preference from fathers or grandfathers. Then there are those whose political or religious sympathies point them in one direction or another. More than once, an Englishman with no Scottish or Irish antecedents has told me he supports Celtic because he is a Catholic. Oddly enough, I have never heard a similar sentiment for Rangers from a member of the Church of England but I have heard our 'Britishness' cited as reason enough for some English backing. Beyond that, there are remnants of the support we picked up in the Souness era on the back of the number of England internationals in the team.

In truth, the indifferent are in the majority and for them – even the football fans among them – the run to the 2008 UEFA Cup final was only of mild interest. Certainly, there was nothing to compare to the news churn created by Celtic's progress in the same competition in 2003. That was partly fuelled by the defeat of two English teams along the way but also because there was a definite tendency south of the border to overestimate the achievements of Martin O'Neill because he was that rare creature – a manager in Scotland who had enjoyed some success in England. If three league titles and a UEFA Cup final with Celtic was enough to get O'Neill linked to the England job then someone ought to tell Walter Smith to brush up his CV and get on LinkedIn because he is clearly missing a trick.

Our 2008 defeat of Sporting in Lisbon, for example, might have been as impressive an away win by a Scottish team in the last twenty years or so. But, in England, it was nothing compared to a win over Blackburn for O'Neill's lavishly funded team. So, even when we won in Florence, there was not enough of the media chatter that might have prompted urgent action by the authorities in Manchester. Little of the hilarity that greeted chief superintendent Gerry Donnellan's request for fans without tickets to stay away was heard south of the border. For the Rangers support, Nacho Novo's penalty hitting the back of the net at the Stadio Artemio Franchi was a starting pistol. And, in common with thousands of others, I began pulling as many strings, calling in as many favours and nagging as many contacts as was necessary to get hold of a ticket.

It was not until the week of the game that I was sure I had got tickets for me and my friend Macca. In actual fact, I pulled some strings a little too hard, triggering a complicated process that meant relaying tickets to friends of friends outside such-and-such a place before heading to another rendezvous to meet someone else who I couldn't miss because he was wearing a Rangers top. I ended up driving into Manchester – I lived in Leeds at the time, only a short hop down the M62 – on the afternoon before the game to collect tickets from the stadium, which I had to pass on to someone else the following day.

I must have driven to the Eastlands area of Manchester dozens of times but, inevitably, on this occasion I got lost so found myself navigating through the centre of the city. That took me past the big Wetherspoons by Piccadilly station about teatime, where I got a taste of what Manchester had coming. Rangers fans were spilling out into the street and there were more arriving from every direction. Eventually, I found the City of Manchester stadium – big place, looks a bit like the San Siro if you squint – and managed to appear respectable enough to collect someone else's tickets before heading back up the motorway.

On the day of the game, most of my supporters club were meeting in Leeds station at 9 a.m. for some early refreshment before getting on the train. But for me, Wednesdays mean Daddy Daycare so, in between nappies, I watched the build-up on television. The breakfast reports were a view of Scottish culture through English eyes. Maybe with the 2006 World Cup in mind, when the Germans set up campsites on the outskirts of host cities, camera crews were dispatched to find some jolly fans enjoying their cornflakes.

Of course this wasn't Berlin, this was Manchester. So the film crews had to head for the city centre. I'm not sure what they were expecting at half-seven in the morning in Piccadilly Gardens – maybe some hungover but basically fresh-faced young men with the odd furtive can of lager – but what they got was bottles of Buckfast and the party in full swing. Nothing wrong with that, as such, I'm casting no stones and it was no surprise to me. But on reflection, it seems just another pointer that the English didn't wholly understand what was about to happen.

The flood of Rangers fans into Manchester should have caught no-one on the hop. If Celtic took eighty thousand to Seville, it was simple mathematics that Rangers would take more to a city within a day's drive of most of the United Kingdom. But it amazed me at the time – and I still find it hard to believe – that large numbers were allowed to drink on the street, not just immediately before the game, but all day. I can't pretend that I knew there would be trouble but it didn't feel right. Having said that, I mostly had that cup-final feeling times ten as the clock ticked on. My wife came home about four and, although I had intended to get the train and have a few beers, at the last minute I decided to ignore the official advice and drive into Manchester. I hadn't been able to get out of work on the Thursday and besides, I thought, it would be nice to have a totally clear head for what might be a once-in-a-lifetime experience. As things turned out, it was an unusually brilliant decision on my part. Had I gone on the train, I might still have been standing on the platform in Manchester when my shift started the following morning.

I left the car in a city-centre multi-storey – plenty of spaces – and joined the blue tide washing up the road to Eastlands. That was a great part of the day – loads of smiles, loads of songs, hello friendly Russians, hello Manchester – although I didn't have a lot of time to enjoy it. There were three tickets in my pocket but none of them were mine. In chronological order I had to: meet the punters they belonged to – although I'd never clapped eyes on any of them before – meet my contact to get my tickets, find Macca, find our seats, then watch Barry do a John Greig.

Not all of it went to plan.

Even with Magellan's sense of direction, finding anyone that day would have been murder. So I had to orbit the stadium twice before I was able to pass on the tickets I had picked up the day before. And Macca and my contact found each other long before I found either of them. I'd arrived in Manchester about half-five but all that left about forty-five minutes before kick-off. Then there was the next great bit of the day – you know when you get tickets for an unfamiliar ground and you think to yourself: 'I wonder where they are?' We were directed through a gate then along a concourse before hitting what we thought was a dead end. Not so, said the nice steward, go through this door, down the corridor, then up the first set of steps on the right. There was the usual rush when you get the first view of the pitch then we took in our immediate surroundings.

'Eh, isn't that Michel Platini?'

'Aye, and there's Sandy Jardine.'

Good seats, right enough, even if we did feel a little self-conscious.

Then I saw our fans. Three-quarters of the ground in red, white and blue. Flags everywhere. Singing. I'd never felt prouder to be a Rangers fan. Most Scots – most people from small countries for that matter – secretly want the approval of their bigger neighbours. So, as much as I enjoyed the moment, there was a part of me that hoped England was watching. This is what we were about.

The match went the way it did. Suffice to say, I'm still not sure what our plan B was for when the Russians scored. Like most of the Rangers fans in the stadium, I stayed behind to applaud our team and the Zenit players as they collected their well-deserved medals. Thinking of the Celtic fans' response to Porto five years earlier, I turned to Macca and said something about the moral high ground.

That sentiment was rendered ridiculous the moment I felt the crunch of broken glass under my feet.

We had walked back into the city centre as part of a subdued but philosophical mass, oblivious to what had been happening while the match was on. It took me three hours to drive what is normally a forty-five-minute journey home. The first hour or so of crawling through Manchester was enlivened by a series of Rangers supporters knocking on my window and asking to be taken to – among other destinations – Salford, Stockport and, bizarrely, Eastlands. But most of the time was spent listening to depressing reports on the radio. Outraged citizens of Manchester, clearly out of patience after surrendering the city centre for two days, rang in to lambast our fans.

The English papers the next day concentrated on the match and some – Henry Winter in the *Daily Telegraph* springs to mind – praised the Rangers support. Clearly, the fighting had broken out too late to be worth the bother for most night editors. But, on television and radio, there was no doubt what the story was: Rangers fans had rioted. And, despite whatever any of us might feel about either the policing or the preparations of the Manchester authorities, there remains little English interest in scrutinising the small print.

It seems to me now that there were two English misapprehensions at work that day. The first was the size of the Rangers support. The Old-Firm-in-the-Premiership debate is pretty much worn out – especially in England – but while south of the border the talk is of Celtic and Rangers as big clubs, I think in the popular imagination this means something like Everton or Tottenham, not clubs that can mobilise multitudes that most national teams would struggle to match.

The second is: just how much fun it is to have large numbers of people drinking heavily in your city centres? Possibly, the media stereotype of the Tartan Army was at play here; the notion that hard-partying but good-natured football fans are a colourful and jolly background to a football match. No doubt, it looks that way when the match is in Oslo or Paris and you're sitting in Manchester or Glasgow. The reality of thousands of drunkards – some of them vomiting and/or urinating in the street – blocking your way as you try to get into work is a lot less attractive. The mass migration of supporters without tickets – celebrated by the media and now tacitly sanctioned by the football authorities – is a relatively new phenomenon, and one to which we in the United Kingdom have not yet had to adapt. It certainly post-dates Euro 96. Can you imagine an alternative reality in which Scotland got to host a Euro 2008 for which England qualified? The 2006 World Cup saw unprecedented numbers of England fans travel without hope or even ambition of getting into the stadium, something reported with close to glee here. Of course, there was no trouble – at least of the water-cannon and café-chair-chucking type – but there wasn't much English consideration for the extraordinary efforts the Germans made to accommodate them.

The citizens of Manchester probably see it differently now.

From 'Party' to 'Riot': Rethinking Manchester '08 – A Neutral's Perspective

Peter Millward

There was a lot of litter and a lot of chanting. And some of it wasn't very pleasant. There were empty cans, bottles and food wrappers and the streets carried a strong scent of urine. There were too few toilets and even fewer bins. But this was the least of the 'social disorder' problems. A group of young, seemingly drunk, male Rangers fans chanted 'bullied at school, you must have been bullied at school' at a large number of police officers who had lined the backstreets of Piccadilly Gardens in Manchester city centre. Less than one hundred metres away, Tactical Support Group officers and football supporters were clashing: the scenes were not easy viewing.

The date was Wednesday, 14 May 2008 and Rangers were contesting the UEFA Cup final with the Russian club Zenit St Petersburg at the City of Manchester stadium on the southern fringes of the city centre. Rangers eventually lost the match 2–0 but sport was not at the forefront in the minds of those in the vicinity: ordinary people were hurt; some quite badly.

In the days which passed after the event, news coverage reported that forty-two Rangers fans had been arrested in Manchester on 14 May and unfairly paralleled this with the fact that one Zenit St Petersburg fan was stabbed (at the stadium). CCTV footage was released of a police officer being tripped to the floor and being surrounded by a 'mob of twenty [Rangers] fans' (*The Guardian*, 16 May 2008). The television channels that screened the clip universally told us that all of the supporters were attacking the man. Newspaper reports informed readers how 'Glasgow Rangers fans went on the rampage in the city after their UEFA Cup final defeat' (*The Guardian* 22 May 2008), when the trouble actually began fifteen minutes into the game (with the score incidentally tied at nil-nil at that point).

An image found its way into the media of a Rangers supporter being attacked by a police dog, yet the *Daily Mail* discredited this possible story by reporting the photographed man as a 'convicted murder'.[1] The article quoted an 'unnamed' prison officer arguing that the man involved 'shows the calibre of people who were involved' (*Daily Mail*, 17 May 2008). *The Times*'s views were equally strong, as it ran a news headline describing Rangers as '[a] club with a poison at it its core' and ending the same article with the damming verdict that 'the once-proud name of Rangers FC will always trigger thoughts of yobbishness and bigotry' (16 May 2008).

The day after the match, the prime minister, Gordon Brown, himself a Scot, referred to the events as 'a disgrace to see people misbehaving . . . and it was completely unacceptable' (*The Guardian*, 15 May 2008). Unsurprisingly, the incidents were viewed in an unfavourable light and football supporters were universally blamed for the disorder. My experience during the day – as an academic and an English football fan, with no ties to Rangers – meant that I formed a slightly different view of the huge numbers of Rangers fans and their conduct. This chapter will tell that story.

Rangers: the 2007/8 season

The 2007/8 season promised much glory for Rangers. While the club did capture both the Scottish Cup and League Cup – beating Queen of the South and Dundee United in each final – a heavily congested fixture list contributed to the club narrowly losing out to local rivals Celtic in the quest to win the SPL title. However, an early-season priority was to progress to the highly lucrative Champions League group stages, which was secured with victories over FK Zeta and Red Star Belgrade, who were the reigning champions of the Montenegrin and Serbian leagues.[2]

In Group E of the Champions League Rangers beat German champions VfB Stuttgart and French league winners Olympique Lyonnais but failed to qualify for the next round of the tournament, finishing third in the four-team mini-league. This meant that Rangers' participation in European competition continued, albeit in the far less profitable UEFA Cup. The club progressed to the final of this competition, knocking out Panathinaikos (Greece), Werder Bremen (Germany), Sporting Lisbon (Portugal) and Fiorentina (Italy) along the way. This sketches out the point at which the chapter's fieldwork begins, namely in Manchester, where the 2007/8 UEFA Cup final was held.

Rangers fans have often voiced anger at what they believe to be mistreatment by some police constabularies, which results in behaviour that becomes criminalised as 'hooliganism'. These views may be substantiated as O'Neill, in her study of football police in Scotland, notes:

> [Police Constables] often hold predetermined ideas of what each visiting team's fans will be like. Supporters of Glasgow Rangers Football Club are generally held to be the worst behaved.

> (O'Neill 2005: 73)

Here, O'Neill is clearly suggesting that the police treat Rangers fans differently to other clubs in Scotland. She also points out that, from her experience, heavy-handed policing methods tend to produce fan unrest. This is especially noteworthy given that Rangers have recently been fined £13,000 and £8,280 for disturbances during their European away games at Spanish clubs Osasuna (2007) and Villareal (2006). On both occasions, there were claims made by Rangers supporters that the police had used heavy-handed and brutal tactics. The next section of the chapter will discuss the ways in which the UEFA Cup final and the arrangements for fans were organised.

Down in Manchester

On Thursday, 1 May – thirteen days before the 2008 UEFA Cup final – Rangers beat Fiorentina in a penalty shootout to secure their trip to Manchester. Two days later, *The Times* (3 May 2008) reported that two fan zones would be set up in the city but, as a deterrent to those supporters who planned to travel without legitimate match access, would be open only to those fans with tickets to the final. The same day, *Manchester Evening News* stated that around 43,000 Rangers supporters without tickets – alongside 11,000 with tickets – were likely to descend upon the city (3 May 2008). The actual number of Rangers supporters who did travel to

Manchester on 14 May was impossible accurately to calculate. However, estimates on the day of the match varied between one hundred thousand and two hundred thousand, but the number of fans was significantly greater than it appears that Manchester City Council and Greater Manchester Police (GMP) first accounted for.

Despite the initial conservative estimates, there were clear indications that fans would travel in their droves to Manchester. For instance, the *Manchester Evening News* (3 May 2008) pointed out that in 2006 a friendly match with Bolton was cancelled on the advice of GMP after it was discovered that twelve thousand supporters would travel to the game, outstripping the ticket allocation of five thousand. The grounds upon which Manchester City Council and GMP believed that fewer fans – even without tickets – would turn up for a major European cup final than a pre-season friendly are unclear. There was also a similar warning voiced by the Rangers' head of security, Kenny Scott.

> Clearly, it will be inconvenient because of an influx of 50,000–60,000 people coming into the daily lives of those who live in the city and that is going to cause an amount of disruption. But this is our ninth away tie in Europe this year and we have taken thousands of people across the Continent. We took 20,000 to Barcelona alone and we have had no arrests[3] . . . Let's not tell any lies. Our supporters like to enjoy themselves and like to drink. . . . They like to party and enjoy themselves and, hopefully, Manchester can look forward to a friendly invasion from Scottish supporters.
>
> (Kenny Scott in the *Manchester Evening News*, 3 May 2008: 2)

Although Scott also misjudged the number of Rangers fans who travelled to Manchester, his estimate was more accurate than those emanating from Manchester. Second, he points out that during the UEFA Cup run, Rangers fans had been well-behaved, although they had shown that they 'like to drink . . . party and enjoy themselves', and, third, perhaps most crucially, Scott hints that an already busy city centre may not be able to cope which such a influx of extra people – football supporters – who were likely to roam the streets. His final point is very important, given that there is no shortage of open space and parkland on the fringes of Manchester city centre where fan zones could have been erected. This would have taken them away from the shopping and business districts of the city.

On 7 May, just one week before the match, the *Manchester Evening News* ran an 'exclusive' story which reported that 'Manchester will set up "fan zones" – serving food and drink – when up to sixty thousand Glasgow Rangers fans arrive for the UEFA Cup final'. This story illustrates two points associated with the event's organisation: first, the number of Rangers supporters had spiralled beyond the original estimates, but was still much lower than the number who would eventually travel and, second, seven days to organise public events for ticketless (as well as ticketed) Rangers fans is a very short period of time.

Further, a day later, the same newspaper 'exclusively' reported that 'big screens for up to one hundred thousand Rangers fans' were to show the game in the fan zones (*Manchester Evening News*, 8 May 2008). Indeed, the article quotes Pat Karney, spokesperson for Manchester City Council, as saying: 'In the light of Rangers qualifying for the final and the massive reported demand from fans for bigger and better provision, we've arranged for big outdoor screens for fans to watch the match.' (*Manchester Evening News*, 8 May 2008: 4)

This evidence suggests there was a chronic underestimate by Manchester City Council (and quite possibly GMP) about the enormous number of Rangers fans travelling to the city on the day of the final, and related to this a lack of preparation in key facilities dedicated to the event, particularly in the fan zones. The chapter will now present the fieldwork findings collected in Manchester on the day of the final to show that Rangers fans were looking to party before this descended into confrontation with the police.

The Big Day – and a Big Party to Match

The striking factor throughout the pre-match period in Manchester was that Rangers fans were intent on having a party. A great number of supporters – who were almost all shirted in official and unofficial club attire – wore the words 'Manchester 08 Party' on the reverse of their replica club shirts. I shared a train with supporters, on a journey that ran for forty-five minutes, spanning 10.40–11.25 a.m. On the train, Rangers supporters were very friendly, as they sought local knowledge about the city centre.[4] Fans were only too aware that occasions like this did not occur regularly – the club were last in a European final in 1972 – and that the proximity of Manchester to Glasgow meant that a (possibly unprecedented) large number of supporters (many of whom would not travel to non-British European away fixtures) were due in the city.

To the supporters on the train – much like those found in the city centre – a party invariably meant getting drunk together before the match. Indeed, large quantities of alcohol were consumed as fans notably drank spirits and Tennents lager communally, with bottles and cans being freely passed around; the fans on the carriage appeared to embrace everyone in a friendly manner. Perhaps significantly, I did not meet any fans on the train who were actually going to attend the match at the City of Manchester stadium; indeed, all planned to watch the game in the fan zones, with many anticipating spending the day in Piccadilly Gardens.

Away from the train, Exchange Square, which forms part of the Millennium Quarter, was packed with fans. The square has been rebuilt in recent years with significant investment since the IRA bombings in 1996. Although at around 11.30 a.m. there was not a great deal of collective singing, the noise from the crowd was very loud with the sound of people talking and laughing. The public houses in the square were very busy as the theme of alcohol consumption continued. A street peddler was selling air horns and the noise of fans sounding them was also very audible.

At one in the afternoon in the Piccadilly Gardens fan zone, the atmosphere was exactly the same. The area was very busy as police and stewards randomly checked the bags of supporters for weapons. Again, the behaviour was party-like, with much alcohol drunk and plentiful singing but no hint of violence. There were very few Zenit St Petersburg fans in the vicinity but those present were warmly met by the often drunk Rangers supporters. The atmosphere was jovial and, at this point, anti-Celtic songs were not evident. Despite this, there were large numbers of Union Jacks and Loyalist Northern Ireland flags inscribed with 'We are the People'.

Outside the Piccadilly Gardens fan zone, a Manchester man in his late sixties told me:

> Last night, I was just stood hanging around and some scary-looking fella walks up to me and asked if I'd like to have three cans of bitter [he shows me one can of John Smiths bitter]? He says 'ey are' [here you are], I don't like 'em. They just wanna have a good time.

This interaction is a further illustration that Rangers fans appeared to have caused no disorder at that point and that they simply wanted to enjoy the festival atmosphere, fuelled by alcohol. The inclusive atmosphere would begin to change slightly within the next hour in Albert Square, where a second fan zone had been erected.

At 2 p.m. inside Albert Square, many anti-Celtic songs were being chanted, including some with sectarian undertones. These were the first anti-Irish Republican chants I heard that day, despite the common pro-British attitudes amongst the Rangers fans and the club's great rivalry with Celtic. However, from that point, such discriminatory overtones became the norm. Indeed, at about 2.45 p.m., a group of Rangers fans tried to display a flag that declared 'Fuck the Pope' but stewards removed it: a response that did not appear to be inflammatory to those supporters in close proximity (most of whom appeared to be drunk).

It is also noteworthy that – presumably as a response to the combination of heavy drinking and too few public lavatories – fans had set up their own 'pissing areas' on the fringes of the fan zone, away from most other supporters. That men would queue in their dozens for several minutes in order to relieve themselves against a wall hinted that they did not want to wreak havoc and, amidst the chaos, had established their own (unconventional) rules. It would have been easier to urinate anywhere in the fan zone, but fans chose to impose their own order, presumably as a way of respecting fellow supporters.

The drunken 'party' did become more exclusionary as the day wore on: as well as anti-Celtic chanting, the drunken, predominantly male supporters became more laddish. Outside the Seven Oak public house, on the edge of the Chinatown district of the city centre, two local women – blonde, slim and in their mid-twenties – walked down the road to the sound of wolf whistles from a large group of Rangers fans. As they escaped this attention two other young Scottish men, who were not part of the larger group, tried to stop the women for a chat. Additionally, at the It's a Scream public house on Oxford Road, a group of seven supporters – who ranged in age between thirty and fifty – leered at female students on their way to the nearby universities. Yet, however uncouth this laddish behaviour appeared, it did not compare to the events that unfolded during and after the match in the Piccadilly Gardens area of the city.

Then the Trouble . . .

At seven o' clock I returned to Piccadilly Gardens, where the queue to access the fan zone was sizeable but orderly. The waiting supporters were told that the temporary arena had reached its capacity and that there would be no more entrants. However, shortly before half-past seven I was granted access. Inside, I stood by the entrance as music was played to the fans, most of whom appeared very drunk and in high spirits. There was much anticipation and excitement as pro-Rangers and anti-Celtic songs were belted out.

At 7.40 p.m. – five minutes before kick-off – the huge television screen was still not switched on and the crowd became restless. At 7.45 a sign was displayed on the screen pointing out that there was a problem with the transmission even though – according to fans – the television had showed clips from past matches throughout the day. A loud collective groan was given by the fans, some of whom began to chant 'you're not fit to have the game' and a relatively small number of bottles were thrown at the screen. Then, at around eight o' clock – fifteen minutes into the game without the fans having seen any of the action – the sign on the television was removed. There were large cheers from the supporters, who clearly anticipated this meant that the technical problems had been resolved. But the screen stayed blank.

Very shortly thereafter, rumours spread that the match would not be shown but still there was no official confirmation. At this point, droves of restless fans began to stream toward the exits to watch the match elsewhere. However, at the exit closest to me, the police officers and stewards blocked off the route and pushed the supporters back. The numerical density – and alcohol-induced physical instability – of people in the zone meant that many fans moved away from the exit in a domino effect. This caused a collective panic and people begin to push each other as they tried to create space. Inevitably, this panic – alongside the heavy alcohol consumption – gave rise to a number of minor scuffles between supporters. As a limited amount of empty space appeared, gossip spread about a temporary gate panel that had been removed by fans, allowing them to leave the fan zone.

The consequence was that many fans moved toward the self-made exit, while others charged at the official exits and broke free, moving toward the public houses and betting shops in the area. As this happened, there were some minor altercations with police officers and security staff as fans hurriedly tried to flee the area. Had a large number of public houses in the vicinity been open at this point (they were closed because GMP had asked publicans to ensure that their businesses had extra safety provisions, such as stewards, which meant that some would have to spend an extra £3,000 before the day of match), it is likely that the disorder would not have escalated beyond a minor level.

Within minutes of these incidents, GMP's Tactical Support Group arrived on the scene, with the aim of moving people away from the area. Despite subsequent reports that a new fan zone was hastily arranged at the Manchester Velodrome – by day a national cycling centre – close to the City of Manchester stadium, there was no audible announcement. Indeed, it is uncertain where the Tactical Support Group officers were planning forcibly to relocate fans to as they chased them. Further, as Tactical Support Group officers rounded up some supporters, they knocked others to the ground. Not all of these supporters were young men; they were of both genders and of varying ages.

From my vantage point on a wall at the edge of Piccadilly Gardens, it appeared that some police officers were hitting fans with batons if they questioned their approach and many of those who were hit had approached officers with open-body postures, which body-language experts agree is not symptomatic of hostility. The police approach appeared to be adversarial as greater numbers of intoxicated Rangers fans moved into the scene and threw bottles at Tactical Support Group officers. The growing number of fans meant that the Rangers supporters ceased to run away from Piccadilly Gardens and some returned to seek vengeance. As a result, more Tactical Support Group officers appeared at the scene as the police officers and football supporters took turns at 'charging' each other.

This deepened the level of violence: an increasing number of bottles were thrown by Rangers fans and police batons were used more frequently. At about 8.30 p.m. – half-time at the match – many supporters, some of whom appeared to be completely innocent, were being randomly hit with batons. The number of Rangers fans charging against the police diminished quite rapidly around this point as a result of injury. One young man walked over to me at my vantage point with a large quantity of blood pouring from his left ear. I told him that he must seek medical attention, but we could not find any official first-aid attendants. Other solitary Rangers fans approached me and said that they had not instigated trouble but that the Tactical Support Group officers had attacked them. At the same time, conflict between supporters and the police continued, with the former chased back toward Exchange Square.

At just after nine, I decided to go home and headed for Piccadilly station to catch a train. However, police officers had blocked off the main routes, so I had to walk to the station via the side streets, which most visitors to the city would not have known about. On the way, I noticed that book-makers were packed with fans trying to catch a glimpse of the last half-an-hour of the final. As I arrived at Piccadilly at quarter past nine, more pandemonium ensued as platforms 13 and 14 – used for trains to Blackpool, Bolton, Liverpool, Southport, Warrington, Widnes and Wigan (among other places) – were closed to the public because, as a station attendant told me, there were 'too many people' waiting to board. It was clear that the sub-sequent trains, after the match had finished, would see greater, not fewer, numbers of people waiting around the platforms. At that point, one woman – in her fifties and not intoxicated – told me how the police just charged at her and her family in Piccadilly Gardens. Another man, also apparently sober and of a similar age, told me how he had to pull his innocent son from under a police baton. Neither had seen any match action.

At the station, a local man, who had witnessed the turn of events, offered his opinion that Manchester City Council 'couldn't organise a piss-up in a brewery'. Like the media he was sure where blame lay, although he blamed another group entirely. The ways in which responsibility was passed between the various groups connected to the disorder will now be discussed.

Deciphering the Blame Game

In the aftermath of the disorder, the blame game started in earnest. The fans who were at Piccadilly Gardens blamed the event organisation, while Manchester City Council's official response concluded that Rangers supporters were the perpetrators of the violence. Rangers Football Club was keen to stress that the failure of the television in Piccadilly Gardens was at the root of the problem, while the police took the view that responsibility lay with a 'minority' of fans.

First to give an opinion was Sir Richard Leese, leader of Manchester City Council, who released the following official statement on 15 May 2008.

> We are having a full inquiry into the failure of the screen in Piccadilly. The vast majority of fans spent a peaceful evening in our city centre in a spirit of friendship and respect. But this has been spoiled by the bad behaviour of a minority. We cannot tolerate missiles and bottles being thrown.

Leese points out here that the council is having a full inquiry into the failure of the screen in Piccadilly Gardens, which most people would interpret as a reasonable course of action. On the other hand – and in an attempt in my view to take the moral high ground – he argues that the 'other' group involved, the Rangers supporters, engaged in 'bad behaviour' by throwing missiles and bottles, an action that he 'cannot tolerate'. Rangers fans might with some justification respond that they cannot tolerate elementary organisational mistakes, such as technological failure. Leese framed responsibility for the disorder on a minority of (nameless and faceless) football supporters. GMP used similar techniques to shift blame onto fans.

Eleven days prior to the final, GMP superintendent Gerry Donnellan was keen to show his force in a positive light, with the following statement: 'We have been planning for almost twelve months and we have liaised with our colleagues at Strathclyde Police. It is a world-class event and we want to make sure it's policed in a world-class fashion.' (*Manchester Evening News*, 3 May 2008: 2)

Donnellan refers to GMP as both well prepared ('planning for almost twelve months') and 'world class'. This undoubtedly created a positive image of his organisation. Evidence outlined earlier in this chapter suggests that it is unlikely that a great deal of detailed planning had taken place before Rangers qualified for the final, which was just two weeks before the City of Manchester-stadium fixture. After the trouble, Justine Curran, a GMP assistant chief constable, made the following statement: 'I am sure the majority of Rangers fans will be as disappointed as we are that this event was marred by this unnecessary and unacceptable behaviour by a small number of fans.' (*The Guardian*, 15 May 2008a)

In my view Curran was trying to gain support for her force's actions by isolating a minority of 'unacceptable' fans from the 'majority' of supporters, who, she inferred, had acted in an 'acceptable' way. There was no reference in the statement to the fan-zone-television-screen failings, which might have caused some reflection on the general organisation of the event (of which GMP were part).

For his part, Martin Bain, chief executive of Rangers, took a different position: 'The police and council have identified the failure of a big screen in the city as a key point in the evening.' (*Manchester City Council* 15 May 2008)). Here, Bain avoids putting any element of blame onto his fans, instead placing responsibility for what transpired on the failure of the television screen to work. This is important as attacking an element of the club's support may have called into question his commitment to the Rangers supporters, while criticism of either the police or Manchester City Council could have had serious repercussions for the club.

The fans were less diplomatic. While some who were not in Piccadilly Gardens blamed a minority of their own support, others ascribed responsibility to the police and the council. Two views which placed fault with the police are given on the virtual fan exchange:[5]

> Fan [1]: One minute GMP are saying that we are 'Some Great Group of Fans', and the next we are not. It seems the only thing that changed things was when they started bashing in heads. NB The vids, etc I've seen of the other stuff shows some scum pieces of work on the GMP side.

> Fan [2]: I was talking to a policeman today, who was down in his capacity as a loyal Bear.[6] He reckons every copper in Manchester city centre was changed at 6 p.m. as part of the policing plan. The new lot couldn't understand the blocking of paths, road junctions etc and went about keeping order in a totally different manner from the first shift.

> (Comments articulated on http://forum.followfollow.com/
> on 19 May 2008)

Both supporters blame the Manchester police. Fan 1implies that the police had heavy-handed officers ('scum pieces of work on the GMP side') who changed their perceptions of Rangers fans when they started attacking them, whereas Fan 2's grievance is with the (unconfirmed) GMP policy of collectively changing the officers on duty at 6 p.m. Both supporters held the police accountable for the disorder but for different reasons. Fan 3 also blamed the police and did so in quite unequivocal terms.

> There is no way I am going to apologise for the small minority of mindless thugs who helped to ruin an amazing party atmosphere, as in my view if they are big enough to start it then they should be big enough to take responsibility. However, I believe that most of the blame has to lie with the GMP and Manchester City Council. For the last two weeks in the run up to Wednesday there were countless posts on this forum about how many people were going to descend on Manchester. As the day got closer the numbers estimated got bigger. I think this was probably the main factor as to what went wrong, GMP didn't expect this many fans but they were well warned in advance.
>
> The police did entice trouble and the reaction from the 'fans' was unacceptable. Now after seeing certain footage, although the reaction from a section of 'supporters' was totally stupid, I can totally understand it.
>
> Look on Youtube, you will see for yourselves. Numerous fans just innocently walking past the riot police and getting pushed about; fans putting their hands out in gesture to the police to calm down; and *numerous* unprovoked attacks on innocent bystanders.
>
> And we still get the blame?
>
> (Fan 3, 19 May 2008 from http://forum.followfollow.com/)

Fan 3 suggests that responsibility for the disorder lay with both the police and a 'small minority of mindless thugs'. However s/he then points out that the 'majority of blame has to lie with GMP and the local council'. Fan 3's point is that the event organisers chronically underestimated the number of Rangers fans who travelled to Manchester and that on the evening of the game, the police 'entice[d]' trouble, as evidenced by Youtube footage. S/he also acknowledges that the Rangers fan base includes a hooligan element by placing the words 'fans' and 'supporters' in quotation marks (paragraph 3), implying that their loyalties do not lie wholly with the team. Still, the message largely frames GMP (and to a lesser extent Manchester City Council) for the violence.

Conclusion: From Party to Riot – Rethinking Manchester 2008

My main conclusion is that no party was completely innocent in the unsavoury events of 14 May 2008. The 'fan party' degenerated into a 'hooligan riot' for five reasons.

First, Manchester City Council and GMP chronically underestimated the number of Rangers fans who were likely to travel. For unknown reasons, neither organisation appeared to realise that a UEFA Cup final, just a few hours' drive from Glasgow, would attract a huge number of ticketless supporters who wanted to take part in a 'fan party'. When this reality became clear, arrangements were made to accommodate supporters in three city-centre fan zones, which served food, alcoholic and non-alcoholic drink and intended to screen the football on giant television screens. However, such plans were only announced on 8 May, six days before the final. This timescale was far too short to plan an event that was to attract more than one hundred thousand people.

Second, and connected to this point, the geographical location of the fan zones was unsuitable. Manchester city centre thrives with shoppers and service-sector workers seven days a week. Adding hundreds of thousands of extra people to the same area was far from ideal, yet Manchester City Council and GMP encouraged this by locating the fan zones in some of the city's busiest areas. Instead, larger fan zones could have been located in either Heaton Park or Platt Fields, which are on the fringes of the city centre and retain easy access to the city's major train stations (most notably Oxford Road station) while reducing the burden on the city centre.

Third, it is widely recognised that had the television screen in Piccadilly Gardens functioned to show the match, it is highly unlikely that the disturbances would have broken out. Manchester City Council and its television-screen supplier, Lightmedia, must in my view take responsibility for this most elementary organisational error. Further, the fan zones were sufficiently large to merit more than one screen each, which would also have acted as an insurance mechanism against possible technological failings.

Fourth, although the media in general were unnecessarily critical of Rangers supporters, many of the fans were heavily intoxicated when the screens failed to function. Although it is clear that the link between alcohol consumption and football hooliganism is not mono-causal, intoxication played some part in the trouble. There is an argument that Manchester City Council and GMP could have been less relaxed in their rules around public drinking during the day but had such an approach been adopted, it is highly likely that heavy drinking would still have taken place. Therefore, supporters must take some of the blame for what happened.

Fifth, there was a marked difference in the number of police officers deployed at different times on 14 May, and in the tactics they used. During the day, there were fewer officers in and around the fan zones. Those officers that were present allowed the light-hearted fun to prosper, with some even joining in by having the tips of their noses painted blue. During the evening, more draconian measures were adopted, especially by the Tactical Support Group officers who appeared to use unnecessarily 'heavy handed' methods. Indeed, the *Manchester Evening News* (2008: 1) reported that by 3 June, there had been sixty-three separate complaints against GMP, with thirty-eight on the grounds of 'excessive force' (almost as many as the forty-two fan arrests). The approach adopted by the police appeared to inflame, rather than quell, disorder.

The excessive drinking of supporters did not help the situation, but it was noticeable that Support Group officers knocked innocent Rangers fans to the ground during the disturbances and were hitting those who questioned their tactics. In short, and consistent with O'Neill (2005), the strategies adopted around Piccadilly Gardens after seven that evening showed scant respect for Rangers fans, especially when they are compared to the police approach earlier in the day .

Despite this complex behavioural and organisational picture, the media continued to produce headlines that held Rangers supporters solely accountable for the disorder. Establishment figures, such as the British prime minister, accepted this version of events. This is not a new phenomenon: 'ordinary' football supporters have frequently been held liable for unrest at matches. For instance the Heysel disaster, in which thirty-nine Juventus fans were tragically killed during the 1985 European Cup final (which was contested with Liverpool) saw prime minister Margaret Thatcher castigate all Liverpool fans and call for all English clubs to be banned from European club competition for five years.[7] This was despite the subsequent Belgium parliamentary commission of inquiry pointing out that

Heysel stadium was 'dilapidated' with both structurally weak 'columns, crush barriers and steps' and poorly maintained terracing that was sixty years old (Scraton 1999: 25).[8]

In addition, four years later, ninety-six Liverpool FC fans were killed during the Hillsborough disaster before an FA Cup semi-final with Nottingham Forest. Whilst it is still unclear why the incident occurred, within days Thatcher's press secretary, Bernard Ingham, publicly spoke about how a 'tanked-up mob' of Liverpool fans caused it (Scraton 1999). Future inquiries showed this was not the case but sections of the media uncritically reported the story as an accepted 'truth'.[9] Despite media sensationalism, which feeds into public interest for stories that denigrate football fans, the truth is that supporters are often not unambiguously to blame for disorder at football events.

On the strength of the evidence offered in this chapter, it is clear that responsibility for the trouble must be apportioned to GMP, Manchester City Council *and* a small number of Rangers supporters. Without critical reflection into the organisational errors, disorders will recur. The causes for the degeneration of a 'fan party' into a 'hooligan riot' were multiple but the conclusion must be that, contrary to widespread media reports, there were organisational factors which played a negative role in the disturbances: Rangers supporters were not solely responsible.

References

Banks, S. (2002) *Going Down: Football In Crisis, How the Game Went from Boom to Bust*, (London: Mainstream)

Manchester City Council 'Latest News – 15 May 2008' http://www.manchester.gov.uk/site/scripts/news_article.php?newsID =3654 [accessed 5/2008]

Manchester Evening News (2008) 'City set for tartan invasion' 3 May.

Manchester Evening News (2008) 'Fan zones for Rangers faithful' 7 May.

Manchester Evening News (2008) 'Rangers fans get big screens' 8 May.

Manchester Evening News (2008) 'Rangers fans blame police' 3 June.

O'Neill, M. (2005) *Policing Football: Social Interaction and Negotiated Disorder*. (Palgrave MacMillan: Basingstoke)

Parkes, R. (2005) 'UEFA Champions League – the Icing or the Cake?' *The Football Money League: The Climbers and Sliders*, (Manchester: Deloitte)

Scraton, P. (1999) *Hillsborough: The Truth*, (London: Mainstream)

Daily Mail (2008) 'Rangers fan mauled by police dog at UEFA Cup final is convicted murderer' 17 May.

The Guardian (2008) 'Manchester football violence a disgrace, says Brown' 15 May.

The Guardian (2008a) 'Carnival mood sours as police confront Rangers fans' 15 May.

The Guardian (2008) 'Moscow's plan to avert Manchester-style chaos' 16 May.

The Guardian (2008) 'Safety fears rule out United parade' 22 May.

The Times (2008) 'Ticketless fans urged not to travel' 3 May.

The Times (2008) 'A club with a poison at its core' 16 May.

Notes

[1] Further reading of the article shows that he committed his crime twenty-one years before this event, when he was just eighteen years old and it is assumed that he had not been in trouble with the police since.

[2] To give some idea of the Champions League's riches, Banks (2002: 128) points out that in the 1997/98 season the Champions League generated £185 million, with £100 million awarded to participating clubs. The size of the potential revenues underline the revenue-driven importance of qualification, with many big clubs framing group stage qualification as the 'minimum acceptable level of on pitch success.' (Parkes 2005: 22)

[3] Rangers achieved a highly creditable goalless draw at Ibrox and then lost 2–0 in Barcelona's Nou Camp stadium whilst both clubs were in Group E of the Champions League.

[4] Indeed on the train, a Scottish man who was leading much of the singing offered his seat to an older local woman. He repeatedly asked her if she was 'okay' with the singing and helped her off the crowded train at her chosen stop.

[5] Virtual fan exchanges/comments given in this article were found on the Rangers e-zine – that is a virtual fanzine, which is independent from the club

and owned by fans – *Follow Follow online*. This is the online component of *Follow Follow*, which is one of Rangers' most popular paper fanzines.

[6] A 'bear' is what Rangers fans call their fellow supporters.

[7] In Liverpool's case the ban was elongated to seven years.

[8] Therefore the inquiry did not explicitly blame Liverpool or Juventus fans – although there was undoubtedly some crowd trouble initiated by *both* sides – but saw the Belgian Football Union as the guilty party given their poor ground standards and inadequate ticketing arrangements (Scraton 1999: 26).

[9] This was particularly the case in *The Sun* newspaper, which reported that not only were Liverpool fans to blame but also that they emptied the pockets of incapable and dead supporters.

Where Did Everyone Come From?

Andy Kerr

We were invited to a semi-formal meeting in Manchester town hall, which is on Albert Square, where one of the fan zones had been set up. Also in attendance were the mayor of Manchester, two senior police officers, council officers and various dignitaries. It was early in the afternoon and everything in the garden was rosy. It was a beautiful, sunny day and everyone in the room was simply awestruck by the sheer volume of Rangers fans and the atmosphere they were creating below us and all over the city. Jim Templeton, then president of the Rangers Assembly, and I, then vice president, were pleased with the way things were going.

It had been a short and frantic build-up to the UEFA Cup final, starting immediately after the memorable penalty-shoot-out win over Fiorentina. I cannot properly describe the tension when Nacho came forward to take his penalty but it was a magic moment when his shot hit the net. It was only at the point of going to Florence for the second leg of the semi-final, and as the possibility emerged of getting to Manchester, that there was talk of tickets. It was almost as if we didn't want to tempt fate.

Our group stayed in Pisa for the second leg of the semi-final and on the hour-and-a-half train journey back to our hotel after the game, we had time to chat about the practicalities of the ticket allocation for the final. The fans I was with were all Rangers Travel Club members and, given that there were around four thousand members, we felt confident of getting a brief for the final against Zenit St Petersburg.

So we were fairly relaxed about it but I knew that back in Scotland, a frantic search had begun. I was being bombarded with phone calls and texts about the allocation for Manchester. How many would Rangers get? How would the club allocate them? We would be playing a Russian side in the final, as we did in Barcelona in 1972, but circumstances had changed.

Then, we got as many tickets as we liked but Russians were now able to travel. Zenit were entitled to their share – fourteen thousand or whatever it was – and as it transpired they managed to have around nine thousand there on the night.

Rangers made a decision about ticket allocation immediately after the semi-final. Every person in the travel club would be guaranteed a ticket, and the remainder would be balloted among season-ticket holders. It was deemed to be the fairest way although, as always, some people were unhappy. I knew there would be people looking for tickets but the demand surprised me. I came under siege; dozens of people I knew – or barely knew – were on the phone to me. Again and again I heard the words, 'I know it's unlikely but. . . .' A friend asked me to get him a ticket at any price. I paid £450 but could have easily sold it to seven or eight other mates.

Jim Templeton and a few other fans representatives were quickly in discussions with the club and had a couple of formal meetings to set the ball rolling, one of which was a meeting with officials from Manchester City Council. The first sound bites suggested that Greater Manchester Police (GMP) only wanted those fans with match tickets to travel. We felt that was an impossible demand and that it was crazy to limit the number of people who wanted to enjoy a unique experience.

There seemed to be a change of attitude when the magnitude of what was to come dawned on them. The GMP then announced that all fans were welcome in Manchester. They knew they had a phenomenon on their hands but, like us, they underestimated its scale. Initially, the figure put on the likely number of Rangers fans travelling was one hundred thousand but as we know there was about double that on the day.

Along with Jim Templeton, I was invited to fly down to Manchester on an official trip with club sponsors. It was a dream come true for me because I knew it probably would never happen again. It wasn't the easy thirty-minute journey some people thought though: first of all I had to travel up to Glasgow from my home in Leeds. I grew up in Biggar but through my job I moved to Blackpool and then Leeds before joining the Harrogate Rangers supporters club in 1998. The club was well established by then. We run a coach to all home games and car-share to away games. For a trip to Ibrox, we leave at quarter to eight in the morning, pick up in a few places and get home around ten on a Saturday night. There are over

forty season-ticket holders, the majority are Scots and we have had something like five hundred different people travelling up to see games.

I had been to every European tie that season and this was the icing
on the cake. It had never crossed my mind that we would get to the final
and to be honest it seemed to be something of a distraction in the early
rounds. In fact, I remember wondering when we were losing 1–0 away to
Panathinaikos: 'Are we really bothered if we don't progress in this competition?' It was at an important stage in the league campaign and fans
were asking if the UEFA Cup was interfering with the title race.

At various stages of the cup run there were moments when we looked
like we were going out and I think a lot of people, especially early on in
the competition, wouldn't have been that bothered. There seemed to be
a 50–50 split. Some said that getting to a European final might never
happen again, and we could win the league in other years, while others
thought that winning the league was more important. I am in no doubt
that the European campaign cost us the league that season. It was an
arduous route to the final against good teams like Sporting Lisbon,
Werder Bremen and Fiorentina. However, the title race was put aside for
those few days in May.

Rangers fans arrived in Manchester from all over the world and by all
modes of transport. A friend who was working in Blackpool called me to
say the whole town was blue. Another was travelling up from the south
of England, meandering through places like Reading, and he said the
train was 90 per cent Rangers fans. I got another call at seven on the
morning of the game to say that traffic was nose-to-tail at Carlisle with
cars, buses and vans travelling south. The majority knew that they would
not get a ticket for the game but they accepted it and travelled just to be
there. As I stood overlooking Albert Square, I was thinking: 'Where did
everyone come from?'

All the meetings had gone well. We had been proactive, as had the club,
and we didn't think there was anything more that could be done. But
something was niggling me. My biggest fear was the amount of booze that
was being consumed. Some people were struggling to keep themselves
together for the game at night. I was wondering what might happen as
the day wore on. I also had a little concern about people from all around
the country turning up simply because it was a big event. They would no

doubt include people who had no loyalty to Rangers and who didn't care what effect any problems would bring.

We left the town-hall meeting and went to the cricket ground near Old Trafford for a pre-match reception and on the coach journey there, we watched Rangers fans swamp every road and street on their way back in to the city centre. It was amazing. We left for the game a few hours later and, ironically, the closer we got the stadium, the calmer it became. It was great to watch Rangers in a European final but of course the result didn't go our way. As long as the game remained goalless we were still in the hunt but when they scored the first goal the writing was on the wall and despite a valiant effort it was all over when they got the late second goal. It was just too much for the Rangers players, who looked shattered; they had been running on adrenalin and not much else in the previous weeks.

We hadn't heard anything about any trouble but on the way back to the coach after the game Jim got a call from a journalist, asking him to comment on the misbehaviour in the city centre. He was in no position to say anything. As we drove back to the Midland hotel we had to take a detour to allow emergency vehicles to use the main road. There was a menacing atmosphere in the air. We noticed a badly vandalised car and then our coach came under attack. A few missiles struck the windows and people were taking cover, genuinely scared.

Back in my hotel room watching the news, it was clear that the mayhem in the city centre was horrendous. Manchester had been a scary place after the game. The train stations were said to be particularly hairy as thousands of fans tried to get out of town. I was gutted and felt so empty. What should have been all about prestige had turned sour and it wasn't a few guys having a ruck, or one or two isolated instances. That said it was a small minority of the travelling fans who caused the problems and I've met many since who said they never encountered any trouble.

I knew what the outcome would be in terms of a negative media reaction. The club and fans had worked hard to make sure the occasion was special and had been largely successful, so this was a setback. I knew that Rangers fans would go their holidays that summer and people would be saying to them, 'A Rangers fan? You caused all the trouble in Manchester.' You might well ask what could have been done differently, and you could do all the planning you want, but you couldn't have foreseen those circumstances. An unprecedented number of fans had turned up in a busy city centre and the infrastructure couldn't cope. A small number of people – not necessarily all Rangers fans – had behaved in a manner we couldn't condone but the overwhelming majority had behaved themselves and enjoyed the occasion.

There was no formal debriefing in the aftermath of the final. The club issued a statement and the RSA largely agreed with it. The Manchester authorities and GMP seemed hell-bent on absolving themselves of any blame. There were lessons to be learned but it is unlikely that the circumstances surrounding the 2008 UEFA Cup final will ever be repeated.

There is undoubtedly a stigma surrounding the club with regards to Manchester and a lot of Rangers fans, unfortunately, were deemed by the media to be guilty by association. That is the great pity. In Manchester we showcased what we are as a club and the massive support we enjoy from all over the world. It was a true phenomenon. In fact, if every Rangers fan around on that day was to chip in a tenner then we would get rid of our debt instantly! Manchester aside, we have been praised by police forces in Newcastle, Ipswich and London in recent years and we were invited to the Emirates Cup and Portsmouth in the 2009/10 close season.

I am confident we will continue to be well-received and respected wherever we go in the future.

CONTROVERSIES

If We Keep Running, They Will Keep Chasing

David Edgar

The 'Famine Song', as it became known, had not been a huge thing among the Rangers support. People weren't belting it out at many matches. I had never heard it sung at a non-Old Firm game and it wasn't something you would hear at functions but it grew with its notoriety. The three lines that were sung emanated from one of those songs in the cassettes bought by hardcore fans that you see being sold outside Parkhead and Ibrox. The first time it really came into the public consciousness, even for most Rangers fans, was after the 4–2 win at Parkhead in August 2008.

It was all over the papers the next morning and was discussed in the media for days afterwards and there was a lot of cynicism among the Rangers support about that. It is amazing that when we lose to Celtic there is very little said about anything but when we win there always seems to be an issue that deflects from the game. Even then I don't think Rangers fans could believe the furore it caused. It was never aimed at Irish people and I think that is the important thing. It shouldn't be sung at Darren O'Dea or any other Irish players in Scotland because it would be offensive to tell them to go home. It was sung as a dig against those who had this fake, romantic ideal of what it means to be Irish. People, for instance, who call the phone-ins and claim to be fifth-generation Irish when they are Scottish with great-great-great grandparents who came from Ireland. In my view Aiden McGeady's decision to play for the Republic of Ireland rather than Scotland, the country of his birth, falls into the same category of mock Irishness.

It was no big deal but when certain parts of the media got into a flap it resulted in the formation of a siege mentality among the Rangers fans and the 'Famine Song' became popular. It was aimed at people who don't like it, in an attempt to put those people's backs up. Among the wider support there were those who said we should sing it whenever we wanted and those who said we shouldn't sing it, full stop. All the Rangers Supporters Trust said about it was that it was in poor taste and probably offensive but that it wasn't racist in the context in which it was being sung. It could be used in a racist way but we tried to place it in the context of singing at football matches. It was also aimed at people who, by this stage, had begun to get professionally offended at anything Rangers fans did.

It became like Pavlov's dog. People heard Rangers fans singing songs and they were offended. They didn't know why they were offended; they just knew that they were. The reaction from Celtic chairman John Reid, who called the song 'racist', was in my eyes simply grandstanding. Rangers chief executive Martin Bain publicly said it wasn't being sung in that context but asked for the song to be dropped. More interestingly, and for the first time, he said that it was noticed that it is always our supporters who were being examined. He echoed the RST's feeling that too often Rangers fans are scrutinised in isolation. Given that there had been nothing from the club along those lines before, Bain's statement was very welcome but there was a feeling that the horse had already bolted. People weren't looking at other chants, like the IRA stuff from some Celtic fans and the Aberdeen supporters with their song about the Ibrox disaster. It was obvious that Rangers fans were being singled out.

Rangers and the RST have done a lot to sort out the situation regarding songs. When the fans were told not to sing the 'Billy Boys' it was gone overnight from Ibrox. We had a meeting with the club and it became clear that the song had to go and the RST got behind the drive to get rid of it. We had to say to the fans who wanted to sing it because they didn't think it was offensive – don't sing it because it will hurt the club. We asked people why they were singing it and pointed out to them that the contentious word in the song was 'Fenian'. Some claimed and still do claim that it is a term for an Irish-Republican terror gang of the nineteenth century but we would reply: 'Are you using it in that context or do you really mean Catholic?'

You have to convince the majority that what you are doing is right. Tell them why it is right and it is amazing how many sensible people say: 'You're right. We see where you are coming from with that.' For those who didn't want to stop it was a case of telling them that they would get the club deducted points. So for some the carrot and for some the stick. It wasn't easy, and we are still working hard on the issue, but I was surprised how quickly it went from Ibrox. But the feeling among many of the fans was that it seemed like every time we did something to appease the critics, someone would come back with another demand. Colin Glass, former chairman of the RST, used to say:

'If we keep running, they will keep chasing.'

He was right. They were never going to stop.

When you go to away games and see the police going round with video cameras trying to find some drunk 18-year-olds singing a naughty song then you think it's a case of taking a sledgehammer to crack a nut. I am glad that we listened to the people who wanted songs eradicated for the right reasons but there were those who were only interested in using anything they could lay their hands on as a stick to beat Rangers. To those people you have to say 'enough'. Some people were also arguing that 'The Sash' was anti-Catholic, which is clearly wrong. It is pro-Protestant and what is wrong with that? Going too far back in history? 'Let the People Sing' is not relevant to twenty-first century Scotland yet no one mentions that when it is sung by fans at Celtic Park.

There has always been a dialogue between the RST and the club but I think it has got to the stage where the fans have gone as far as they are likely to go. There were, and still are, people making money out of what we in the Trust call the sectarianism industry. People are earning a living from it and in my view they don't want to see sectarianism being stamped out. It got to the ludicrous stage, where every time you tried to have a sensible debate, the word sectarian would be thrown in to the equation. I was on the radio and used the phrase 'we are the people' and there were floods of complaints about that term being sectarian.

Football is not the reason for sectarianism in Scotland. It might be a symptom of it but it is not the reason and until people look at the wider social context it will never go away. For many, it is easier to say 'this evil football club needs to be gagged'. Like many people in Scotland, if not most, I get bored with the tit-for-tat but you can't keep punishing one club and not saying anything to anyone else. Let's sit down and go through all the song books. If you want to be grown up and leave out the racist, sectarian

RANGERS: TRIUMPHS, TROUBLES, TRADITIONS

and homophobic stuff then that is great, but let's stop the songs about the IRA and the Ibrox disaster while we are at it. Or do we say that if there is just one person in a stadium who is offended by a particular song then that song has to go? We have to be sensible. It is opposing fans singing songs at each other. If you look at Liverpool versus Manchester United or Arsenal versus Tottenham then you will find offensive songs about the Munich air disaster or Heysel or gas chambers. In Italy, fans research the history of their opponents to look for things to sing about them. And on top of that, you can't have a Champions League game in Rome without someone being stabbed. You would think it was a purely Scottish problem but it's not. It is a problem among all football fans.

The RST, the Blue Order and the Rangers Supporters Assembly have encouraged the singing of traditional Rangers songs – for example 'The Blue Sea of Ibrox' and 'Wolverhampton Town' – but there is a generation of young fans at Ibrox who don't know these songs and so it is difficult. In addition, the atmosphere at Ibrox is generally flat and anyone who tells you different is a liar. The fans don't want to sing. I have known about three or four times in the last few years where the atmosphere has been fantastic and it has been the Rangers songs that were belted out that livened the place up. Modern stadia have something to do with this but what has happened over recent years at Ibrox is that a fear factor has developed. It is not that much fun going to the home games. Fans are not sure of what is and what is not acceptable. There is a Big Brother attitude. The club in my view are scared and the philosophy is very much, 'sit down, shut up, buy a pie and don't do anything'. It has massively affected the atmosphere at games. You need the club to be more innovative than sending Andy Cameron, God love him, out in a blue suit with a micro-phone.

There are great Rangers songs and they should be sung but I also think it is important to protect the fans' identity. Celtic are told they can be proud of their Irish-Catholic history but Rangers are told they can't be proud of their Scottish-Protestant-Unionist history. Celtic have embraced their Irishness. When they score a goal at Parkhead they couldn't be any more Irish if they brought on Paddy McGinty's goat. At the same time Rangers have been told to reject everything from their history and it sticks in the craw of many fans. And despite Bain backing the fans to an extent with his comments about the 'Famine Song', we feel the club should be doing more to protect its image.

Six or seven years ago there was an article claiming that Rangers launching an orange-coloured second strip had contributed to a Catholic boy being stabbed in Ireland. No other club in the world would have that rubbish written about them. There were also articles about the Ibrox pitch being cut in the pattern of a Sash and Pepperami being banned from the stadium because its packaging is green. I am pretty sure Celtic would say to journalists, 'That's just stupid, don't jeopardise your press pass by writing that' but I think they feel they should rise above that at Ibrox.

But what they have to understand is that Rangers fans go to work and people call them bigots because of what they have read in the papers. There is an ongoing debate about Rangers' identity and it needs to be encouraged, not shut down. This identity debate has spilled over in to the arena of the Scotland national team, where there is now a lot of tension. It has been coming for years and it is really all to do with the Tartan Army. There was a time when the anti-Rangers element among the Tartan Army would leave their club loyalties in the car park but not now. When I was younger you wanted the best players playing for Scotland, regardless of which club they played for, but that has gone. I have been at Scotland games when Rangers players have made a mistake and I've heard the word Hun used – and not in isolation. When Barry Ferguson played, he was criticised simply for being a Rangers player.

The Tartan Army deserves praise for its behaviour but what they do is hold themselves up and say, 'we are not Rangers'. There are many more fans in the Tartan Army who are anti-Rangers than anti-Celtic. For instance, many Aberdeen, Dundee United and Hibs fans, if their team don't win the league, would rather Celtic won it than Rangers. Attitudes are hardening all around. For years Rangers have been an elephant being poked by a mouse and we put up with it but the fans are now having a go back. The feeling among a section of the Rangers support now is: 'You know what? If you don't want me here then I won't come.' In consequence, there are a lot of Rangers fans who either don't care about Scotland or don't like the team. It is a shame but I don't know what we can do about it. I can see the chasm growing in years to come and people not being able to reconcile being a Rangers fan with being a member of the Tartan Army.

Some of the fans are starting to believe it is Rangers and Rangers only. You didn't used to get that. Someone even asked me: 'Do you know these people who only like Rangers and Rangers reserves? Well, I don't even like Rangers reserves.' There are parallels to be drawn with Manchester United fans and their relationship with England. I was speaking to some United fans and they told me that they got it in the neck for years about being arrogant, not caring about England and lording it over the rest of English football. They told me the attitude changed to, 'if that's how you think we feel then that's how we will behave' and that's why you've got 'Republic of Mancunia' banners and all that sort of thing.

Of course, tied up in all this is the fact that there has never been a monoculture at Ibrox. Some fans feel 100 per cent Scottish and not British at all, while you get some who feel Scottish and British and others who are British and not Scottish. The Protestant-Conservative-Unionist-Orange-Masonic Rangers fan, which is how most Celtic fans would describe us, does exist but it doesn't apply to everyone, nowhere near it. It is partly mythical and you only have to look at political polls over the years in places like Bridgeton and Larkhall to see that is the case. On the other hand, I know Celtic fans who are lifetime Tories and Unionists.

Where the two Old Firm clubs differ, in my opinion, is that Rangers fans have a problem with their club that is not replicated at Celtic. I don't think Rangers identify with their fans or know how to speak to them. I think they would rather the punters just turned up, cheered the goals and that's it. But despite the ongoing issues, there is a lot to be positive about in an Old Firm context. We have a tendency to make thing worse than they are. If you read some newspaper articles you would think Glasgow is like Belfast circa 1974 but it is not like that at all. People work together, play together and are friendly with each other. But you will never totally sanitise an Old Firm game. You will get an otherwise sensible person like a doctor, a lawyer or an accountant, who, with a few beers in them, will stand up and call someone a dirty Orange bastard or a dirty Fenian bastard. Is it right? No, but it doesn't mean they are bigots.

The problems we have won't go away overnight but it's getting better and that is all you can ask.

The 'Famine Song'

Roddy Forsyth

The 'Famine Song' was at the heart of one of the most peculiar and trouble-some problems ever to confront Rangers, an episode that took on a con-torted life of its own, which stretched on for the better part of a year and engaged two governments and the police plus, of course, the club itself. It provoked anger and resentment on both sides of the Old Firm divide and at one stage had the chairmen of both Celtic and Rangers snarling at each other publicly.

In Scotland the public response to the appearance of this lyric was largely a weary, 'Here we go again.' In Ireland, there was general bemuse-ment that the mid-nineteenth-century potato famines, which killed over a million people – overwhelmingly in that country, but also in the Highlands of Scotland – could become the subject of a jeering chorus heard at a football match.

The row raised questions, many of which were never explored to any sort of satisfactory conclusion. Probably the most basic was whether or not there is any subject so sensitive that it cannot be incorporated into the taunts of football fans intent on antagonising their rivals. It is, after all, entirely routine to hear songs and chants deriding opposing players or supporters as paedophiles, practitioners of incest or of sexual relations with animals, or as rat-eating slum dwellers – to take only a random sample of the charming choruses that echo around Scottish football grounds.

Transpose any of those lyrics into a spoken jibe in the pub or street and you are liable to be arrested and charged with behaviour likely to provoke a breach of the peace, but there has been a tolerance of the same thing practised en masse. On another level there have been songs which target human tragedies and calamities if they can be associated with a rival club.

In England, the Munich disaster of 1958 is the subject of a chorus which has been directed frequently at Manchester United. Jewish supporters of Tottenham Hotspur have seen rival fans making the 'Heil Hitler' salute or hissing in imitation of the Nazi gas chambers. As for Rangers, the 1971 Ibrox Disaster – which left sixty-six dead and hundreds injured amongst the mangled barriers of Stairway 13 – has featured in a mocking, nursery-rhyme parody sung by rival supporters. Similar verses were aimed at Liverpool after the Heysel disaster.

Sporadic attempts have been made by football administrators to address the most vicious occurrences of supporters' bile, mainly in respect of obviously racist outbreaks. Application of this policy varies from one jurisdiction to another, however, with wide variations in toleration across Europe.

In these contexts, how did the singing of the 'Famine Song' by Rangers supporters put it at the heart of a diplomatic exchange between the Irish government and its Scottish counterpart? It seems to me that it is worth beginning by asking if there is a stage in the contemplation of a catastrophe when it is possible – in fact, desirable – to laugh at it.

Black humour, after all, is recognised as a psychological mechanism that allows humans to deal with calamity by effectively declaring, 'Well, this happened, but we're still standing and the fact that we can joke about this subject is proof of our spirit.'

When Woody Allen was doing stand-up comedy on the New York circuit in the 1960s he could say, 'My family are not Orthodox Jews. In fact, my grandfather was a very Unorthodox Jew. He was a Nazi.' Of course, Allen is Jewish, but that did not shield him from criticism from some Jews, who felt that he was trivialising the Holocaust. On the other hand, he was performing his act in the liberal atmosphere of Greenwich Village comedy clubs where a new generation – including children of Holocaust survivors – saw the gag as part of the process of moving on with their own lives.

In respect of the Great Famine, I have only once ever encountered what might be taken as a joke about the event. It appeared in a nineteenth-century copy of *Punch*, the now-defunct humorous magazine, and it went like this:

Q: 'How many potatoes does it take to kill an Irishman?'

A: 'None.'

The bear from Oz. The 2008 UEFA Cup final in Manchester attracted Rangers fans from all over the world, including this wonderfully attired gentleman from Down Under.

The 'Famine Song' first came to prominence during an Old Firm match in August 2008. It not only divided both sides of the Old Firm but also became an issue between the Irish and Scottish governments. Despite the fact that most Rangers fans viewed it as harmless banter, the sectarianism industry went into overdrive, creating an unstoppable momentum for criminal prosecutions.

Alex Totten – assistant manager at Rangers in the mid-1980s under Jock Wallace – puts Ibrox legend Davie Cooper through his paces on the sand dunes of Gullane.

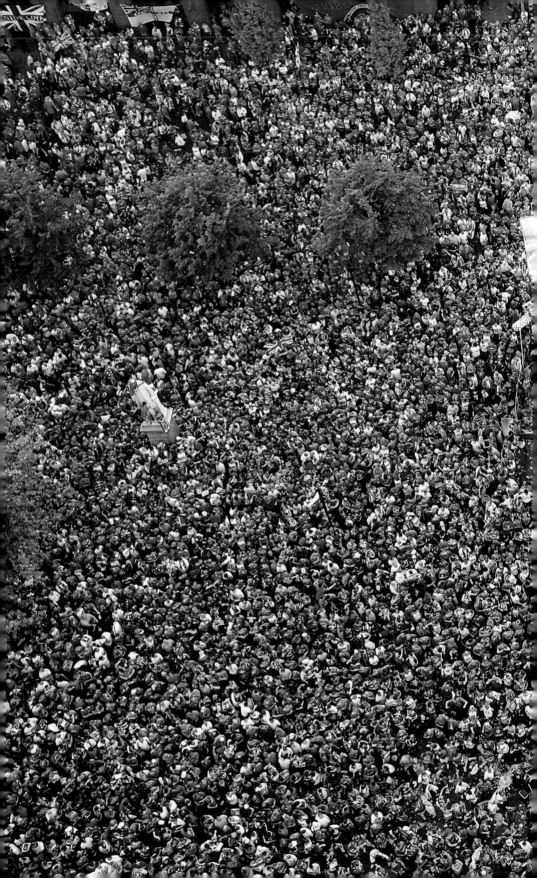

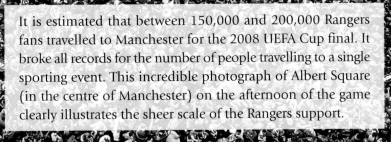

It is estimated that between 150,000 and 200,000 Rangers fans travelled to Manchester for the 2008 UEFA Cup final. It broke all records for the number of people travelling to a single sporting event. This incredible photograph of Albert Square (in the centre of Manchester) on the afternoon of the game clearly illustrates the sheer scale of the Rangers support.

Perhaps the most unlikely Rangers Supporters Club of all,
the Dublin RSC continues to follow on, often under the slogan
'Behind Enemy Lines'.

Rangers have long had a loyal fan base on the other side of the pond, even if demographic change has reduced its size. The photo of the Protestant Boys of Govan band – which has entertained delegates at the North American Rangers Supporters Association convention in Las Vegas – can be seen on the NARSA website and shows a firm determination to keep the club's proud traditions alive.

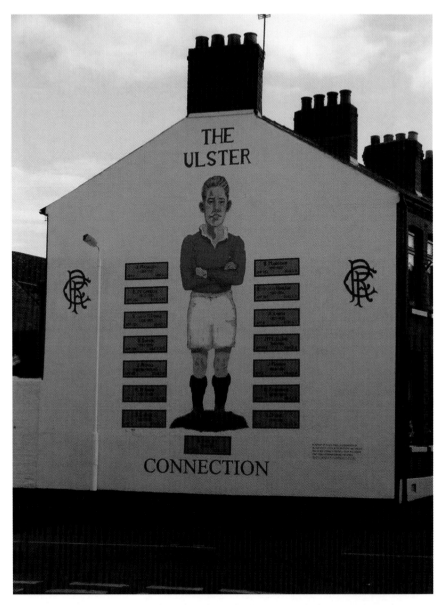

Sam English, a son of Ulster, was without doubt a Rangers great. But after the death of John Thomson in that fateful Old Firm game in 1931 he would never again be at peace. This mural (in a side street off Ravenhill Road, Belfast) on which English has pride of place, commemorates the close links between the Province and Rangers.

Was that meant as a penetrating comment on the fate of a people who became too dependent on a single, vulnerable crop, or was it just another Thick Mick joke of the sort common at the time – and for more than a century afterwards? To answer that, we would need to know the intent of the person who devised it and the response he thought it was likely to evoke amongst those who read it.

Steve Coogan, in his guise as thick-skinned radio host, Alan Partridge, visited the subject in an episode that featured two Irish broadcasting executives who are interested in syndicating his show but who are left gaping when he says: 'If it was just the potatoes that were affected, at the end of the day, you will pay the price if you're a fussy eater. If they could afford to emigrate then they could afford to eat in a modest restaurant.'

However, the thrust of that joke is directed at Partridge's own crass-ness. Likewise when Ricky Gervais – as the toe-curlingly insensitive boss, David Brent, in *The Office* – asks: 'Who says famine has to be depressing?' our laughter is prompted, not by the suffering of people who are starving to death – although it would be impossible to appreciate the joke if we were tormented by hunger pains – but by Brent's desperate attempt to launch himself as a comic on the back of any event that might afford him the opportunity.

The 'Famine Song' was definitely intended to annoy and provoke, although few Rangers supporters seemed to have heard about it before the Old Firm derby at Parkhead on 31 August 2008. On that occasion, the chorus – 'The Famine's over, Why don't you go home?' – was repeatedly sung to the tune of 'Sloop John B' as the Rangers fans celebrated their team's ascendancy in a 4–2 victory.

Although the chorus clearly antagonised the Celtic support, who tried to drown it out with jeers and their own anthems, there was not a great deal of public comment about the song at first. However, the issue was raised by callers to radio phone-ins, with Celtic fans declaring it racist and Rangers fans saying that it was no more than a wind-up of people whose families had been in Scotland for five or six generations but who insisted on considering themselves Irish.

As a journalist who comments on Scottish football for Irish newspapers and for Ireland's state broadcaster, RTE, I can testify that this attitude was not confined to Rangers fans. In Ireland, too, there is a degree of derision for the archetypical emigrant who cherishes romanticised connections with a country his forebears long ago quit. Hence the lyrics of 'Plastic Paddy', composed by the Scottish songwriter, Eric Bogle, but popular in Ireland thanks to a recording by that most Irish of Irish folksingers, Christy Moore. It talks about the eponymous Plastic Paddy drinking a well-known brand of stout and pseudo Irish beers.

Not that such mockery is confined to those of Irish descent. As the old joke has it: 'Have you heard about the Scottish boomerang? It never comes back. It only sings about coming back.' And as Billy Connolly once said of the Scots themselves: 'We're the only people who sing about coming home while we're still here.'

At first, in Ireland, the response to the chorus of the 'Famine Song' was a slightly bemused feeling that, yes, it was tasteless, but so what? For a while, even as the controversy gathered pace, that largely remained the attitude on the other side of the Irish Sea.

But it was a different matter in Scotland, as a variety of circumstances came together to generate significant trouble for Rangers. First, it became clear that while the Rangers fans might only have been singing the chorus of the 'Famine Song', online versions of the full lyrics revealed a nastier piece of work altogether. It was illiterate doggerel but also vehemently anti-Irish and directed, not light-heartedly at those of migrant descent who might be a touch precious about their heritage, nor towards all the descendants of Irish migrants – after all, some who fled from the potato failure were Ulster Protestants – but specifically at those of Irish Catholic extraction. Some of the references were coded, but anyone with more than a passing knowledge of sectarianism in the west of Scotland would recognise who was being targeted.

The song is inflammatory and, to many people, it is racist. It is certainly not the work of someone prepared to be a martyr for his (or her) contortion of history. Whoever wrote the 'Famine Song' has remained anonymous, presumably in the knowledge that to take responsibility for it would be to end up in court accused of a race-hate crime.

At any event, once the chorus had been sung repeatedly at Parkhead, and the full version could be accessed on the internet, it would have been astonishing if there had been no reaction. As it was, a Scottish Celtic supporter of Irish descent wrote to the Irish embassy in London, cited the lyrics and asked what they intended to do about it. The embassy replied that the Irish consul-general in Edinburgh would raise the matter with the Scottish administration at Holyrood. It was hardly a surprise that the embassy would wish to flag up its concern, given that the descendants of Irish emigrants were being indicted as paedophiles, thieves and ingrates.

To put it another way, if the same abuse was directed at Jews in something called the 'Holocaust Song' – with a chorus of 'The gassing's over, It's time to go home' – even the most slow-witted observer might reasonably expect the Israeli diplomatic corps to have something to say. The involvement of the consul-general, though, elevated the affair to another level altogether. Suddenly the issue of name calling between Old Firm fans had become an issue between governments.

The reality was more prosaic. Irish diplomats in London had passed the complaint along the chain of communication, as bureaucrats will do, so that it could be stamped with the words 'action taken'. Likewise, the Scottish government could reach for a ready-made response from the legislation that exists to deal with sectarian and racist behaviour and the monitoring system that goes with it.

Thus government speaks to government, in tidy fashion; it should be noted that the 'Famine Song' was not the subject of a formal protest from one administration to the other. Nevertheless, for many Celtic fans this represented a major symbolic and moral victory and Rangers, not for the first time in such matters, were caught off balance by the pace of events and the club's inability to take control of the narrative or, at least, get a comparable hearing for their own complaints.

Rangers had already proscribed the song and had asked the Glasgow police to issue a joint statement saying that anyone singing it would be liable to arrest, but at that stage the constabulary declined to do so without further consideration. Rangers were also under pressure from their own fans, angered that there was no equivalent condemnation of songs that were sung at a Motherwell–Celtic game at the same time as the diplomats were formulating their elegant exchanges. One of these ballads expressed hope that the Ibrox forward, Nacho Novo, would die in his sleep after taking 'a bullet from the IRA'. Another featured that staple character of the Irish songbook, the merry ploughboy, with a chorus of 'For we're all off to Dublin in the green, F*** the Queen.'

From this point on the issue splintered into a prolonged game of tit-for-tat with both Old Firm clubs playing to their own galleries, while the rest of Scotland – if it paid any attention at all – yawned with boredom or was anxious not to be tainted by association.

John Reid, the Celtic chairman – and former home secretary and secretary of state for Northern Ireland – weighed in with a public rebuke to the Rangers fans who had sung the 'Famine Song'. He said: 'There is offensive chanting and singing going on and I encourage anyone who has not read the song, however distasteful it is, to read it so they can see that we are not overreacting.' He added that the song was 'vile, racist and sectarian'.

Sir David Murray, stung by Reid's breach of the supposed protocol (by no means always observed in the past) that one Old Firm club should not comment on the behaviour of the other's support, retorted.

> I was maybe guilty of doing the same in my early days when I was naïve, but there has been an unwritten rule between Rangers and Celtic that you show respect for each other. I will continue to do that, but I'm disappointed in what John has said. I know that members of his political party encouraged the 'Famine Song' to become a public item in the agenda. I received letters from Labour MPs and Scottish Office ministers which backed John and made it a bigger story than it would have been.
>
> We don't want to enter that argument because I think when you are the chairman of Rangers or Celtic you have to be very, very careful. We're not denying that the 'Famine Song' is wrong, but so are many other things in society and I think that John must agree he's not in the House of Commons now, barracking people across the chamber.
>
> We're now in the west of Scotland world of Rangers and Celtic and I think we all have a responsibility to act in a sensible manner. The fact of the matter is that he can afford to be brave because he doesn't have to be elected again and I think there's a strong argument, especially in the west of Scotland, that to have a politician in charge of a football club is verging on the dangerous.

By way of a parting salvo, Murray trained his guns on another target when he said: 'I think Celtic are – and have been – good at managing you people, the media. They're on the phone all the time complaining.'

Thereafter, the 'Famine Song' slipped out of the headlines, although a few politicians did their best to pour petrol on the dying flames. In

Ireland, the representative for the Dublin South constituency, Alan Shatter, laid a question before the Dail, as follows.

> To ask the Minister for Foreign Affairs if his attention has been drawn to the fact that offensive anti-Irish songs were sung by supporters of Glasgow Rangers Football Club attending the match that took place between Glasgow Celtic and Glasgow Rangers on 31 August 2008 and that the singing of such songs is a regular event and has caused both fear and concern to Irish residents and their children who on occasion visit Glasgow for such football matches; if he will take an initiative with the relevant authorities in Scotland in the interest of Irish/Scottish relations to bring this behaviour to an end; and if he will make a statement on the matter.

The irate section of the Rangers support did not have a conveniently placed foreign government on hand. They fastened upon Gregory Campbell, DUP MP and sports minister for Northern Ireland, who had been invited to Celtic Park to see their anti-sectarian measures in action. Mr Campbell's retaliatory strike came with a statement that suggested that he hadn't planned to visit Celtic any time soon and was now in even less of a hurry to go. But by this stage, three months after the main event, the debate had lost its impetus and had become generally wearisome, even to most Old Firm fans.

Still, there was room for a bizarre sideshow briefly to pitch its tent. A previously obscure Scottish National Party MSP by the name of Michael Mathieson startled breakfast readers of the daily papers with his warning that choruses of the 'Hokey-Cokey' were suffused with bigoted undertones. He agreed that to most people it was an innocent song and dance, but declared: 'Its origins are more sinister and are essentially anti-Catholic. It is important that the police and clubs are aware of the sinister background and take appropriate action against individuals and groups who may use it at matches.'

A spokesman for the Roman Catholic Church in Scotland agreed: 'This song, though apparently innocuous, does have quite disturbing origins.' He added that if it was used malevolently, its status as an innocent party dance should be reconsidered.

At the time of writing, the most recent flicker of the 'Famine Song' controversy had burnt itself out in the Scottish Justiciary Appeal Court, when the case of William Walls was heard. The 20-year-old Walls had been arrested for singing the 'Famine Song' at a Kilmarnock–Rangers game in November 2008 and was convicted of breach of the peace, aggravated by religious and racial prejudice. Rejecting Walls's appeal – and the accompanying defence by Donald Findlay, QC, former vice-chairman of Rangers – Lord Carloway stated, in June 2009.

> Presence inside a football stadium does not give a spectator a free hand to behave as he pleases. There are limits and the appellant's conduct went well beyond those limits.
>
> The court does not consider that the lyrics of this refrain bear any reasonable comparison to those of 'Flower of Scotland' or indeed 'God Save the Queen'. Rather they are racist in calling upon people native to Scotland to leave the country because of their racial origins. This is a sentiment which many persons will find offensive.

Lord Carloway added that the 'Famine Song', 'displays malice and ill-will towards people of Irish descent living in Scotland'.

That more or less put the tin lid on the 'Famine Song' controversy, one might think. On the other hand, the Carloway judgement was handed down just three weeks short of the twentieth anniversary of the signing of Mo Johnston by Rangers in what was then a deliberate attempt by Murray and Graeme Souness to free the club from the shackles of sectarianism. Ten years after that event – utterly parochial to the wider world but epochal for Scottish football – Neil McCann, a Roman Catholic of Irish descent from Greenock, scored twice for Rangers in a 3–0 victory at Celtic Park as the Light Blues won the championship at the home of their rivals for the first time ever. Lorenzo Amoruso, a popular Rangers captain, was a co-religionist of McCann.

Another well-liked figure, whose Ibrox career was truncated by injury, was Sebastian Rozental. As his name might suggest, Rozental is Jewish, but he was signed from the Chilean club, Catholic University. Some of his female admirers at the Santiago club declared that they would form the first Catholic University Rangers supporters club, news that prompted the Ibrox fanzine, *Follow, Follow,* to comment: 'Should somebody no' tell them?'

Yet, throughout these events – which were, for all intents and purposes, unimaginable thirty years ago – many Rangers fans have felt cast adrift, no longer sure what their club stands for. Well, then, what exactly did Rangers stand for in – as they like to say down Ibrox way – the bygone days of yore? When Moses McNeil, his brother, Peter, and a couple of friends, founded Rangers in 1872, they had not the slightest intention of establishing a sporting bastion of the Scottish Protestant and Unionist establishment. They were a bunch of young lads from the Gareloch who had come to the big city and were amusing themselves on the banks of the river Clyde when they noticed some other youths playing football, a game that took their fancy. They decided to form a team and, if they had settled on their first choice, the oldest rivalry in football would be known as Argyle versus Celtic. But they preferred a title borrowed from an English rugby club and Rangers were born.

For the next thirty years, Rangers were not associated with Protestantism. Celtic, though, were a Roman Catholic club in heart and soul from the club's foundation in 1888 – and, more specifically, a club that depended for its survival on support from Glasgow's expanding Irish Catholic community. Had Celtic not been a notably successful team from the beginning, there might never have been a sectarian rivalry in Glasgow football. But they were swiftly triumphant and many amongst the native population sought a club who could match them.

Again, we can contemplate tantalising ifs and buts. Queen's Park were the dominant Scottish club of the day and had they been able to joust on equal terms with the newcomers, we might be talking today of volcanic Spiders–Hoops clashes. However, Queen's Park refused to embrace professionalism and Rangers became Celtic's rivals of choice – quite literally, because they were invited to inaugurate Celtic Park – and, at the beginning of the twentieth century, a Scottish sporting journal observed: 'The Light Blues are firm favourites with the Parkhead crowd.'

Why was this friendly competition between two municipal neighbours replaced by a poisonous schism? The details can be debated endlessly, but an overspill from Irish politics was surely the decisive factor, partly because of the establishment of Harland and Wolff shipyard at Govan, close to Ibrox, but also because of bitter feelings that washed over both communities after the outbreak of the First World War.

The disproportionate losses suffered by Scottish and Ulster regiments at the Somme were compared with the refusal to impose conscription in Ireland and the Easter Rising in Dublin, which occurred in the same year as the horrific slaughter on the Western Front. Ill feeling generated by these events persisted for generations and found a ready outlet in the Old Firm rivalry.

If Rangers were effectively commandeered to oppose Celtic around one hundred years ago, they have been left behind by the tendency to come together in the last thirty years. Who could ever have guessed that Ian Paisley and Martin McGuinness would join forces in a joint administration at Stormont? Who, in 1980, foresaw the emergence of the Celtic Tiger – even if it looked more like a neutered kitten during the global economic crisis of 2008/09 – and who predicted that the Scottish National Party would hold power in a government based in Edinburgh? Who could know that the communist bloc would collapse, the European Union double in size and that human-rights legislation would be dictated by Brussels?

What matters for Rangers, in the context of the Old Firm rivalry, is that Celtic grasped the potential of some of these developments much more astutely. Under Fergus McCann, Celtic tapped into the new global perception of Ireland as a young, energetic nation at ease with its past. Who cared if Irish theme pubs were hokum? They were as pervasive and lucrative as Starbucks. And where was the Scottish equivalent?

Scotland was moving more slowly, but it was on the march towards Holyrood. Unionism, that pillar of Rangers' identity for a century, was imploding. Rangers fans might wave the Union Jack, but in England it was replaced by the cross of St George and in Scotland the Saltire was the flag of choice. More and more, the diminishing but persistent group of diehard Rangers supporters resembled those Confederate rebels who fought on, raggedly and forlornly, for years after the Civil War. Yes, Celtic have equivalents who can't shut up about the Boys of the Old Brigade, but their impact has been marginalised.

Celtic won a Fair Play award for the conduct of their supporters at the 2003 UEFA Cup final in Seville. Rangers fans were excoriated for the disorder of their fans at the 2008 UEFA Cup final in Manchester (the city council's detailed report reads like a mediaeval account of a Viking pillage). Sure, many of those who went on the rampage in Manchester city centre on the evening of the game were – to judge by age of their replica shirts – throwbacks to a previous era. The point is that Rangers are persistently put in peril by a hardcore of recidivists and the club has only escaped severe sanctions by UEFA because it has made strenuous attempts to curtail them and because it has employed ingenious arguments to sanitise their outrages when the evidence looked incontestable.

Thus the Nazi-style raised arms seen in Tel Aviv when Rangers played Hapoel in 2007 were parlayed into something called the 'Red Hand of Ulster salute', a gesture which – curiously, wouldn't you think? – has never been seen at Ibrox, even during the white heat of an Old Firm derby. But then, neither has the song which accompanied it in Tel Aviv, a ditty to the tune of 'Chirpy, Chirpy, Cheep, Cheep', with a lyric that went: 'Where's your foreskin gone, where's your foreskin gone?'

For some, that might count as 'the banter' but it doesn't take an advanced intellect to see that if this persists, sooner or later, Rangers are going to be indicted and convicted by the football authorities, with serious consequences. In the meantime, as a matter of urgency, the club needs to find someone who can write a catchy piece of schlock, something to get the stadium bouncing again without causing offence – the Rangers equivalent of 'Fields of Athenry'. Maybe it could feature Moses McNeil coming down from the mountains to lead his people to glory.

Oh, and by the way, we should not confuse Moses's birthplace on the Gareloch with the Gairloch. If Rangers' founding father had been born on the shores of the more northerly loch, he would have been familiar with the Destitution Road. That was a route carved out of the rock by desperate Highlanders, who were paid for their labours by a board set up to relieve distress in the region in the 1840s. The crisis was caused by the failure of the potato crop. What an irony it is that, but for the difference of a syllable in a place name and an accident of birth on the Gaelic-speaking fringes of Britain, the descendants of Rangers' founders might today be warned by rival fans that – since the Famine is long since done – they should get themselves on the bus back to his croft on the Ullapool road.

The 'Famine Song': a Case Study in Football Rivalry

Daniel Taylor

As a sport with humble beginnings, football has developed from a rural folk game to a codified sport. In the Middle Ages, ball games were contested between two local communities and intense rivalries developed. Over time, football has become an arena in which national, religious, political and ethnic antagonisms are displayed.

Since the late nineteenth century, Rangers and Celtic have dominated Scottish football and have become an integral part of Scottish society. Their influence on Scotland in terms of economics cannot be underestimated. The Old Firm generates £120 million per year for the Scottish economy.[1]

In Scotland, football is said to provide a stage for an argument over ethnic and religious identity. Celtic and Rangers are said to have distinct religious and political identities. The rivalry between these two clubs and their supporters, and their conflicting ideologies, has been the source of much controversy.

This chapter investigates the rivalry and will examine these conflicting identities. It will also question whether the rivalry, in its current context, is about political or religious conflict. It could be argued that, despite media and academic obsession with the Old Firm and sectarianism, the nature of their rivalry is not a rare phenomenon in football. Though there have been songs sung by both groups of supporters that have caused offence, they are designed to offend local rivals, and this occurs in many countries. This case study concerns the recent controversy over the 'Famine Song' and it analyses the rationale behind the song.

The 'Famine Song' was a major talking point off the field in the 2008/09 Scottish Premier League season, discussed by fans, media and major figures in society, all with conflicting opinions. This study will look at differing views of the song from newspapers, Rangers Football Club, Rangers Supporters Club, the *Follow, Follow* fanzine and a select group of Rangers supporters. These sources have been selected as illustrative examples to aid discussion of the 'Famine Song' and to provide some insight into whether it is sung as an act of political and religious expression or as a means of baiting Celtic fans.

The 'Famine Song', as it has become known, is more of a chant than a song, at least in a football context. In fact Rangers fans use only one line:

'The Famine's over, why don't you go home?'

This refers to the Great Irish Famine of 1845–9, which caused massive devastation in Ireland. Celtic chairman, John Reid, said it made light of, 'a human tragedy of immense proportion'. Reid also spoke of other verses of the song, which he said he had discovered. However, these lyrics are familiar only to a very small number of people and are not sung in the football context. At matches it is only the chorus, as described above, which is sung.

This song, or chant, has been the focus of much media attention and there has been strong condemnation of the Rangers supporters who have sung it. One such journalist is Graham Spiers. In his newspaper column, he took the opportunity to criticise the Rangers supporters in the following terms.

> With its racist and bigoted content, it is the latest in a long line of supporters' anthems which have made the Rangers hierarchy cringe. Commendably, Rangers plug away behind the scenes trying to root out such themes among their support, but so far with limited success. There is a Rangers hardcore who remain agitated by Celtic's Irish heritage. (*The Times*, 6 October 2008)

However, not all commentators have castigated Rangers supporters. For example, leading Scottish sports journalist James Traynor suggests that media coverage of the song and the offence it is said to cause have been blown out of all proportion.

> This line is not inciting violence . . . it isn't celebrating the fact that one million people died because of potato blight . . . the line is mocking the often cloyingly sentimental longing of Celtic fans for the old country

and if you accept that's all it is then it might even border on humorous. (*Daily Record*, 22 September 2008)

Already, contrasting opinions are evident. On a BBC Radio 4 programme, Revd Stuart McQuarrie of the University of Glasgow argued that the 'Famine Song', though offensive, was simply a retort from the Rangers support to 'The Fields of Athenry', which McQuarrie believes is 'vile, vicious and racist'. However, Robert Davis, also of the University of Glasgow, condemned this opinion.

> Rev MacQuarrie's baffling attempt to draw a political and ethical equivalence between a football stadium chant calling for people of Irish descent to leave Scotland and 'The Fields of Athenry', an Irish ballad sung internationally by folksingers of myriad ethnic and religious affiliations, is very difficult to reconcile with his reputation as a distinguished Glasgow ecumenist. (*The Herald* website, 10 January 2009)

Rangers Football Club, perhaps inevitably, has also become embroiled in the controversy over this chant. Prior to a league match at Ibrox on Sunday, 21 September 2008, Rangers sent letters to all supporters urging them not to sing the 'Famine Song'. However, the club was also aware that for many supporters it was not a straightforward issue.

> Some supporters feel aggrieved that a song they believe to be no more than a 'tit-for tat' wind up of Celtic supporters should be singled out in this way and merit the attention of police, governments and anti-racism organisations. . . . The Club shares that offence and [notes that] wholly unacceptable songs . . . are sung by supporters of other clubs on a regular basis with little or no comment or reprimand from any quarter.

That said, the Rangers chief executive, Martin Bain, was anxious to point out that for the sake of the club and the fans' reputations, it would be best if they would refrain from singing the 'Famine Song'.

> The Club has a duty to ensure the interests of our supporters are protected. It is not in the interest of any supporter to stand accused of racism or sectarianism or face the prospect of being arrested.

Clearly, Rangers felt that the issue of the song was important enough for a letter to be sent to fans urging them not to use it. However, the club, on the basis of the letter referred to, was also concerned to acknowledge the feeling that exists among the supporters that Rangers are continually singled out for condemnation.

Following the initial debate over the 'Famine Song', the Rangers Supporters Trust (RST) released a statement. In it the RST takes the view that Celtic's criticism of the song was largely based on misinformation and was driven by a political agenda.[2] The statement questions the validity of the comments of Celtic chairman, Dr John Reid.

> Celtic FC choose to play two songs over the stadium PA on home match days referring to the Famine: 'The Fields of Athenry' and 'Let the People Sing' . . . Dr Reid's inflated rhetoric condemns a song which, far from being some sick 'celebration' of human tragedy is actually a mocking response to Celtic fans' tenuous, borderline-obsessive, affiliations with the Republic of Ireland.

The RST also lists examples of where they believe Celtic fans have behaved in a sectarian manner and questions why they have not had the same level of criticism.

> This behaviour would, in any normal society, be worthy of at least the same level of political comment and sustained media scrutiny as the song at issue. Despite the best efforts of Messrs Reid, Lawwell and their cheerleaders, these are far from the actions of a small minority and the Rangers support wishes Dr Reid every success in taking the 'stringent action' needed to tackle this abhorrent behaviour.

The main thrust of this statement from the RST is the refusal to take lectures from Celtic Football Club over the singing of controversial songs.

Follow, Follow is one of the most popular fanzines amongst Rangers supporters. The fanzine discussed the issue of the 'Famine Song' in great detail in the months from September to November 2008. Contributors were generally unhappy with the complaints made about the song and about the person who reported Rangers supporters to the Irish embassy in London.

> From lowbrows to highbrows the guff has continued apace. A political correspondent for the *Sunday Times* . . . eked out a page of nonsense telling us that the 'Famine Song' complainer was living in fear. Yeah right. He was prepared to come on national TV but is now in fear of his life? (*Follow Follow*, 203, p.31)

The fanzine went onto to accuse Celtic chairman, John Reid, of being hypocritical by criticising the 'Famine Song' while 'The Fields of Athenry' continues to be played at Celtic Park.

> As for singing, if Reid is so reviled [sic] by wind up songs such as 'The Famine's Over' perhaps he should explain why is [sic] club still feel the need to play two songs referring to the days of the potato blight at Celtic Park prior to matches. (*Follow Follow*, 203, p.7)

In addition, another article tries to rally the fans to, 'tell Celtic to get stuffed, stand up to the Tim-loving media . . . stop blaming Rangers for the woes of the world'. The fanzine writers clearly believe that such fervent interest in the 'Famine Song' is unique to Scotland, as one fan from Dublin notes.

> In my workplace I was telling the non-Tims about the furore over the song and I kid you not they actually laughed when I told them the Irish govt had got involved and [they] couldn't believe this was headline news in Scotland. (*Follow, Follow*, 203, pp.41–2)

What is evident from reading *Follow, Follow* is that fans regard the song as a wind-up and not an expression of religious or political protest against the Irish-Catholic community of Scotland. The article penned by a supporter from the Rangers supporters club of Dublin notes the apparent lack of offence taken by the indigenous Irish in the Republic of Ireland to the song: 'If your average Irish person doesn't care about the song then who does?'

The position of mainstream Rangers fans must also be considered. Three supporters were interviewed as a group prior to a match at Ibrox in season 2008/09. When asked why Rangers supporters sang the 'Famine Song', they suggested it was a tit-for-tat song, common in Old Firm rivalry and indeed in other football rivalries.

> It's a simple answer. [It is to] wind up them Celtic idiots. To see them squirm. They sing their songs that wind us up, we sing some back. Most fans, both Rangers and Celtic, realise it's just a wee bit of banter, but some of them just can't take the banter.

The supporters in question insisted that neither the song, nor their hatred of Celtic, was anything to do with religion or politics.

> AC: Nah, that's in the past like. I couldn't give a toss about religion or politics with football. This whole religious stuff is a myth. We hate Celtic like how Arsenal hate Tottenham or [Aston] Villa hate Birmingham. It's all football.

> AMcD: The lyrics say 'famine', but we ain't mocking the famine nah, we're mocking Celtic.

One point of interest that arose from the interviews was the fans' use of terms such as 'Fenian', which has been widely been acknowledged as a sectarian term. The Rangers fans questioned argued that their words were used as an expression of disdain for the Celtic support, rather than a direct attack on the Irish-Catholic community in Scotland. One supporter from the interview said, 'The word Fenian to me means Celtic fan. It's meant to be offensive, but not in a sectarian way.'

In addition, with the banning of certain songs from the Rangers repertoire, and the continuation of others, some fans are confused about what they can or cannot sing at Rangers matches anymore, adding more weight to the argument that opinions of the relevance of sectarianism in Scotland are highly subjective.

> I dunno what is sectarian or not. I can sing 'I Was Born Under a Union Jack', but not 'The Billy Boys'. I can sing 'If we go to Dublin we will follow on' in 'Follow Follow', but I can't sing the 'Famine Song'.

The Rangers supporters believe the 'Famine Song', and indeed other songs or terms associated with sectarianism, are about football rivalry. Though they acknowledge that Rangers Football Club has a Protestant and British identity, their hatred of Celtic Football Club is not one born of anti-Catholic or anti-Irish sentiment. They feel that Scottish society has been focusing too much attention on sectarianism in Scotland, and that Rangers supporters have been subjected to unfair criticism.

Taking all the evidence into account it is clear there are sharply conflicting opinions regarding the song's intent and its effects. This demonstrates the ambiguity surrounding the sectarian debate in Scotland.

The statement from Rangers Football Club seems to suggest that although the intent of the song is to wind-up opposition fans, the club is fully aware of how the song has been interpreted and to avoid further negative press has discouraged supporters from singing it. The supporters themselves, some of their official organisations and *Follow, Follow* are unhappy with the accusations that the song is sung with sectarian intent. There is some acknowledgement that the desired affect is to cause offence, but not in reference to any political or religious debate.

What we can say is that most Rangers supporters are singing this song to wind-up Celtic fans in a non-sectarian manner. Some may argue that the lyrics are badly chosen, given the social context of a group of supporters who are known to have a British-Protestant identity and, whether it is justified or not, have been accused of being anti-Irish. Given the historical context, one might argue that a song that refers to the Great Irish Famine may indeed be interpreted by the Irish diaspora in Scotland as sectarian. Here of course is the dilemma regarding sectarianism, as the two groups on either side of the divide disagree fundamentally as to what constitutes a legitimate taunt.

The 'Famine Song' is offensive, but offensive songs are evident in football rivalries across the world. Indeed, the celebration of disaster has occurred in Scottish football rivalries for a significant period of time. In 1971, sixty-six Rangers fans lost their lives due to a crush of fans leaving Ibrox. Though the Ibrox disaster upset most of Scottish society, it wasn't long before some Celtic supporters decided to chant songs that mocked the victims.[3]

In England, supporters of Manchester City, Liverpool and Leeds United regularly belt out songs that celebrate the death of eight Manchester United players on 6 February 1958 in the Munich Disaster. In reply, Manchester United supporters have sung songs taunting Leeds United fans about events in Istanbul where two fans were stabbed in 2000 before a UEFA Cup game versus Galatasaray.[4] Blood-curdling sentiments are a routine feature of songs and chants among rival fans in countries such as Italy, Spain, Greece and Turkey.

In conclusion, this article will not condone the singing of the 'Famine Song', nor any other song that causes genuine offence to others. However, this song, and indeed others chanted by Celtic and Rangers fans, may not have a political or religious intent, even if the lyrics suggest otherwise. Historically, when there was antagonism directed towards Irish Catholics in Scottish society and religious and political tensions were high in Northern Ireland, Ibrox, Celtic Park and other football grounds in Scotland became arenas for political and ethno-religious expression. However, in today's more secular Scotland, the Irish-Catholic community has been broadly recognised as an integral part of society for several generations and, after a decade of relative peace in Northern Ireland, it would be unjustifiable to interpret these songs as representing religious or political protest.

Notes

1   BBC News website: 'Old Firm on the ball for economy' (Wednesday, 29 June 2005)
2   Rangers Supporters Trust: 'Position Statement on the 'Famine Song'. (3 October 2008)
3   Walker, G. (2004) 'The Ibrox Stadium Disaster of 1971', in *Soccer and Society*, pp. 169–182
4   At a match between Leeds United and Manchester United on 18 October 2003, the Manchester United fans sang 'Always look out for Turks carrying knives', to the tune 'Always Look on the Bright Side of Life', from Monty Python's *Life of Brian*.

'No Pope of Rome': Football Fans Wearing False Noses

Steve Bruce

Chanting

Thirty years ago I worked at the Queen's University in Belfast and regularly travelled back to Scotland on the Stranraer–Larne ferry. It was on one such journey that I heard a group of Rangers fans singing a little ditty entitled 'No Pope of Rome', which in essence is an encomium to an imaginary world in which there are no Catholic churches, clergy or icons. The first verse stuck in my mind and indeed the opening line became the title of my first book about sectarianism in Scotland. To give the context I reproduced the whole of the opening verse on the book's title page, which turned out to be an expensive mistake. I had assumed that football fan songs were, like folk songs, 'traditional', common property that developed spontaneously on the terraces.

I was wrong.

Someone, registered as Mavis Music, had actually composed 'No Pope of Rome' and because I had inadvertently infringed his copyright, I had to pay him a small sum not to sue me and in addition the publishers had to blank out the verse with little white stickers. As the royalties I earned from the book were so small that they could have been covered by the same little white sticker, the payment to Mavis Music was painful but I now regret more that my annoyance prevented me investigating the Jerome Kern of the terraces. Did Mavis Music have an office in a Glasgow equivalent of New York's Brill building? Did B. A. Robertson or Sydney Devine work in the office next door? Did Mavis Music write conventional pop or were all his compositions in the key of Spleen Major? Did he pitch only at Rangers fans or did he write catchy ditties for the fans of all the major clubs? And, as I cannot imagine 'No Pope of Rome' got a lot of needle time on Radio Clyde, how did the Rangers fans learn the song? There are so many things I now want to know but sadly web and directory searches throw up no mention of Mavis Music so my chance seems to have gone.

Had the book been about football, I would not have used the title because it would have been misleading. It is a pretty safe guess that very few of the people who sing 'No Pope of Rome' really care about popes, priests or rosary beads. The pleasure presumably lies in the potential to annoy the opposition. Some football-fan taunts are witty and elegant. The prize for the most erudite abuse must go to the Napoli fans who taunted the Verona opposition (the clue here is Shakespeare's *Romeo and Juliet*) with a banner that read – in Italian, of course – 'Juliet's a slag'. More often the abuse is just mean. During the recession of the 1980s, fans of London teams used to annoy fans of teams from the north of England, where unemployment was much more severe, by waving wads of money at them or singing 'He's fat/he's Scouse/he'll rob your fucking house/ Steve McMahon, Steve McMahon': a chant still used for Wayne Rooney.

Chants are topical because they have become the focus of an attempt to civilise football fans. Lord Carloway of the Justiciary Appeal Court is undoubtedly right that the 'Famine Song', which Rangers fans now use to wind-up Celtic, 'displays malice and ill-will towards people of Irish descent living in Scotland'. That is the point. If it did not irritate Celtic fans, Rangers fans would not sing it, just as Celtic fans would not sing the 'Soldiers Song' if it did not antagonise Rangers fans. Carloway is also right that 'Presence inside a football stadium does not give a spectator a free hand to behave as he pleases' but unless he is planning an unprecedented campaign of social engineering that will cause football fans to like the opposition and will prevent what was once euphemistically called 'industrial language', then preventing fans abusing any one perceived characteristic of the opposition will simply cause them to find another feature that can become the focus of abuse.

As all football fans devote a great deal of energy to abusing the opposing team and its fans, and as that activity seems to be one of the main attractions of being a football fan, I see little point in trying to rank such chants in a hierarchy of acceptability and outlawing the most unpleasant. So long as the desire to abuse is there, trying to legislate its terms is like devising a new euphemism every time the technical term for an unpleasant, unfortunate or undesirable characteristic becomes a popular term of abuse. When I was at school the once respectable term 'cripple', because it was being used as an insult, was replaced by 'spastic' and the new word immediately became a playground staple of abuse. A few years ago I heard one young boy sneer that another was 'special': not an endearment but a reference to 'special needs'.

Given the centrality to football fandom of mutual loathing, there is something frankly silly about one group of fans pretending to be sensitive souls in need of the protection of the courts from verbal abuse. There is something equally ridiculous about another lot defending their insults under the banner of the right to free speech. I am pretty sure that when my father and his contemporaries fought in the 1939–45 People's War Against Fascism – a cause apparently rejected by some Celtic fans – they did not think they were fighting to defend the right of Rangers fans to insult the descendents of Irish migrants. Old Firm fans would be a lot more impressive if they were honest about their motives. Each set of fans is playing a political game of trying to make the other lot look worse.

That Lord Carloway now knows the words of a football fan song is a consequence of the unusual status of the Old Firm and it is to this I now turn.

The Death of Protestant Scotland

1955 was a watershed year for two major Scottish institutions. In the general election that year, the Conservative and Unionist Party won 50.1 per cent of the vote. It was also the point at which the communicant membership of the Church of Scotland started its long and steady slide. The ideal Rangers fan of the post-war era was a skilled working-class man, a Conservative and Unionist voter, a member of the Orange Order and a church-attending, evangelical, Protestant Christian. While most Rangers fans fell short of this ideal – many voted Labour and many more rarely attended church – the image was an effective one because it mirrored the image of the opposition.

The ideal Celtic fan was unskilled or semi-skilled working class, a confirmed Labour voter, a mass-attending Roman Catholic, perhaps a member of the Ancient Order of Hibernians, with strong Irish roots.

When the Ulster Troubles came along in the 1970s, the Irish dimension gained a new lease of life. Rangers fans tended to support the Ulster Unionist cause and the fans who travelled from Ulster were a small but vocal presence. A very small number pretended to support Loyalist para-military organisations and a tiny number actually did. Again Celtic fans were the mirror image: many supported the Irish nationalist cause, a few became Republicans and a tiny few supported the IRA. So Old Firm games became a venue for the symbolic demonstration of important social, religious and political divisions, often abbreviated to the catch-all term 'sectarianism'.

Half a century later, all of those props of Rangers and Celtic identity have collapsed. The manual working class has all but disappeared, as have most of the residential areas that its various fractions inhabited. Whatever being British meant in 1955 it means a lot less now. The combined effects of ceding power to the European Union and devolving power from Westminster to Edinburgh, Cardiff and Belfast means that there is a lot less of Britain to be British about. Most Scots are still (somewhat grudgingly) in favour of the Union but Unionism as a philosophy is hardly popular with Scottish Conservatives, and the Scottish Conservatives are hardly popular with the Scottish electorate. Margaret Thatcher had so little interest in the Union that she had the word removed from the title of the party in Scotland. Scots Tories have recently restored it but in the context of devolved politics and the need to distinguish themselves from the other pro-Union parties, the Tories now stress their liberal-economic, anti-statist policies far more than their strong emotional ties to the romance of the Union.

The power and influence of the Orange Order has always been exag-gerated: at its peak the Order had less than 2 per cent of adult male Protestants in west central Scotland in membership. The growing popu-larity of Scottish nationalism has given a new salience to the Order's unionism but the twelve thousand Orangemen and women who marched in Edinburgh in March 2007 to celebrate the Act of Union is still a tiny minority of Scots and it now recruits from a base far narrower than that which supports Glasgow Rangers. In the 1920s the Order still had great men in its ranks. A good example is Sir John Gilmour. A Unionist MP from 1910 to his death in 1940, he was the first secretary of state for Scotland, in which office, incidentally, he rudely dismissed the attempts of some

Church of Scotland clergy to campaign against the Irish in Scotland. It is difficult now to imagine any serious Scottish politician being a member of the Orange Order. It is equally difficult to imagine the Church of Scotland campaigning to repatriate the Irish. As far as I can tell no Church of Scotland minister is a member of the Order. The very few clergy who have served as chaplains since the 1960s have been independents or members of peripheral denominations.

Even the Ulster part of a popular Protestant identity has gone. All Ulster unionist parties actively support the devolution settlement. The most popular – the Democratic Unionist Party – is in government with Sinn Fein. And the Loyalist organisations have disarmed and disbanded. It is hard to imagine that the views of Northern Ireland held by most Rangers fans (in so far as they hold any) differ at all from the Scottish consensus, which is to be glad not to have to think about the place again.

The elements that form the ideal Celtic fan of the 1950s have changed in much the same way. Despite the majority of lowland Catholics being educated in Catholic schools, the Catholic Church has followed the Protestant churches in precipitous decline. Between 1994 and 2002, Catholic mass attendance fell by 20 per cent. Catholics are no longer concentrated in small, distinct areas. Apart from the state-funding of Catholic schools there is no distinct Catholic political agenda, and even that support has declined in recent decades, with recent surveys showing only a minority of Scots Catholics in favour of a separate school system.

Even Irishness has gone. A large 2001 Glasgow survey allowed respondents to choose as many national or ethnic identities that they felt best represented them, and while 81 per cent of Catholics chose Scottish and 23 per cent chose British, only 8 per cent chose an Irish identity (and many of them may actually have been Irish!). For Scotland as a whole, Catholics were more likely than Church of Scotland identifiers or people who claimed no religion to describe themselves as 'Scottish not British'. They were less likely than Church of Scotland identifiers to describe themselves as 'Equally Scottish and British' but in this they were no different from those people who claimed no religious identity. What is crucial is 'other description' figure. The survey allowed respondents to claim another identity. It was thus open to those who felt Irish rather than Scottish or British to say that. They did not.

In the run-up to the 2001 Census adverts were taken out in places such as the *Irish Post* and *Celtic View* encouraging people of Irish descent to give their ethnicity as Irish. The campaign did not produce the desired effect. At 40,000 the number of people resident in Scotland at the time of the census who choose to describe themselves as Irish was less than the 55,000 who had been born in Ireland. That is, they were not Scots Catholics reacting to their oppressive environment by thinking of themselves as Irish. They were simply Irish in the sense that the people who said they were Swedes were Swedish. Even before the census, a convenient explanation for this failure of reality was being composed. It was asserted that 'people born in Scotland with Irish parents or grandparents frequently hide their roots because they fear hostility' and hence 'the "Irish" box will not be fully used by those who feel they have an Irish cultural background'. This seems implausible. When respondents to anonymous surveys routinely declare their income and their views on controversial subjects such as abortion and capital punishment, it is not likely that they become coy over ethnic identity.

To summarise, the last half-century has seen a major decline in the social characteristics from which Rangers and Celtic fans traditionally constructed shared identities of themselves and each other. There is now little – apart from football – which divides the fans of the Old Firm.

Reasons to be Cheerful

It may be possible for animosities based on trivia to be become widely shared and to pass intact from generation to generation but serious social divisions, like recessive genes such as those that produce blue eyes, are best maintained by marriage selection. Religion, social class and national identity are most likely to pass from one generation to the next if adults who 'carry' the relevant quality make a point of marrying someone who is the same and thinks the same. Marriage patterns are also a good indicator of what really matters to people. If race is important to people then interracial marriage will be rare, as is still the case in the United States where less than 5 per cent of marriages are racially mixed. If religio-ethnic identity is important then marriage across the religious divide will be rare, as is the case in Northern Ireland, where in 1991 only 2 per cent of marriages were religiously mixed.

One of the clearest signs that religion is increasingly a matter of indifference to most Scots is that mixed-religion marriage is now commonplace. Two big surveys in 2001 asked people if they would mind if a close relative married someone of a different religion. For Scotland as a whole only 3 per cent minded a great deal, a further 7 per cent minded a little; the rest either had no view or did not mind. Remarkably, Glasgow, supposedly the hotbed of sectarianism, was more tolerant than Scotland as a whole: over 80 per cent of Glaswegians did not mind at all. Now that might just be polite talk but we do have some firm evidence from the 2001 census, which asked for the religion of each adult in the household. We should make allowance for density. Even if they did not differ in their preference for marrying a co-religionist, a Glasgow Catholic is more likely than an Aberdeen Catholic to marry another Catholic simply because there are relatively more Catholics in Glasgow than in Aberdeen. Nonetheless, it is significant that almost a third of Glasgow's Catholics and almost half of Scotland's Catholics are married to non-Catholics. Even more important, given that getting married is increasingly rare, are the figures for what we used to call 'living in sin'. Two-thirds of unmarried Catholics who are co-habiting are doing so with non-Catholics.

Considering that many young Scots are segregated by religion at school and so are more likely to socialise with their own nominal religion than with the other side, the extent of inter-marriage is remarkable. What it tells us is that in the most important decision they get to make in their lives, young Scots are proving that they do not care about religion.

Two things have made this possible. One is the general decline in the power and popularity of religion. The other is the upward social mobility of the descendants of the Irish immigrants.

As the Scottish churches have shrunk so has the importance of the old arguments that divided them. Forms of church government, age of baptism, the number of sacraments, the propriety of 'man-made' hymns in worship; very few people know or care about these disputes. As they have declined, the major churches have become more tolerant and ecumenical. They can still sometimes act in a self-interested manner but the Catholic Church and the major Protestant denominations are now on the same side: a small Christian minority surrounded by a mass of indifference. Of those Scots who attend church, only a tiny fraction – at the most thirty thousand people – belong to sects that have anything much against Catholicism or believe that popery represents any great threat and most of them live in the Highlands and Islands.

Even if religion did not matter much, the division between Protestants and Catholics could still be reproduced if it was a surrogate for social class. Are Catholics of markedly lower socio-economic status than Protestants? It is certainly widely believed that sectarian discrimination in the workplace is common and as Protestants are in a majority that would mean Protestants colluding to protect their privileges. In one Glasgow survey a majority of both Protestants and Catholics said that they thought it common for people to be turned down for a job because of their religion. But when they were asked if they personally had suffered this, almost none had. That paradox tells us something very interesting about myths and stereotypes but we do not need to rely on rumour and gossip; we now have good objective evidence.

Like most migrants, the Irish entered the Scottish labour market at the bottom: relatively short of capital, industrial labour skills and useful networks. If discrimination was widespread, Catholics would still be con-centrated at the bottom of the socio-economic ladder. There are a few complexities: not all the Irish migrants were Catholic and not all current Catholics are descended from Irish migrants but the Protestant Irish and the old Scots Catholics populations were both too small to much distort the evidence. We can also leave aside the very real possibility that the descendants of Catholic Irish migrants to Scotland suffered disabilities that were not the result of discrimination: for example the Catholic Church's refusal to join the state-school system from 1872 to 1918. If we find that Catholics and Protestants are now very similar in socio-economic status then, unless we assume that Catholics are innately superior, we have demonstrated an absence of disadvantage and hence an absence of dis-crimination. What two major surveys and the national census in 2001 show is that there are marked differences in the social class of Catholics and other Scots for those aged 65 and over but for those 34 and under there is very little difference. That is, there has been a gradual levelling of status. Bizarrely, and I have no idea why this is the case, the one 'religious' group that does stand as clearly disadvantaged is that formed by people who say they were raised with 'no religion'. Why atheists and agnostics should be the losers in the economy is anyone's guess but the evidence is clear that whatever explains the relative disadvantage shown by elderly Catholics has now gone.

In brief, growing indifference to religion and increased social levelling has permitted a very high degree of inter-marriage, which in turn is a levelling device because it makes sectarian discrimination ever less likely. However strong (or weak) the desire to persecute a minority, one needs the opportunity and inter-marriage reduces that opportunity far more effectively than any government equal-opportunities policy. In a context where religious identity is already weak, loyalty to actual family members generally wins out over loyalty to an imaginary community.

Though the divisions were never as deep as the oft-told anecdotes imply, in the 1950s Old Firm rivalry could be taken as a symptom of something bigger. Now it signifies nothing but itself: a competition between two teams that is more bitter than most because no other teams in their league pose any serious threat to their domination. Liverpool fans can share their animus around the fans of Arsenal, Chelsea, Tottenham and Manchester United. The Old Firm have only each other to hate.

False Noses

The great Argentine poet Jose Louis Borges famously described the Falklands/Malvinas War as being like two bald men fighting over a comb. I am minded of that when I think about the 'Famine Song' and the 'Soldiers Song', the IRA chants and the inflatable Red Hands of Ulster. The vast majority of fans of Rangers and of Celtic do not actually care about religion, about ethnic origins, about the Troubles in Northern Ireland or about the constitutional future of the British Isles. They only pretend to care in order to maintain an identity that offends the other side and in order to have an excuse to offend the other side.

The issue at stake is not actual shared social identities built on real differences but pantomime costumes. The fans of both teams wear false noses. Each lot pretends to find the noses of the other ugly and grotesque while claiming to be deeply hurt by the cruel remarks that those scumbags have made about our noses.

Scapegoats in Scotland's Blame Game

Alan Truman

In the not too distant past, the media portrayal of the Old Firm and its accompanying 'baggage' essentially reflected Scottish public opinion in being fairly even-handed if somewhat aloof. By and large, football reporters and pundits stuck to matters on the pitch while serious journalists and columnists steered well clear of Rangers and Celtic. Politicians and academics too seldom broached the subject and the embodiment of Scotland's religious divide through allegiance to two football clubs was construed as a simple, if regrettable, fact of life. Songs and chants were viewed solely as ritualistic demonstrations of solidarity and never interpreted literally, distasteful though some may be. Most importantly, neither support was held to be 'worse than' the other; the axiom that there was good and bad in all communities still applied.

This analysis of Old Firm rivalry has been radically revised within the past decade. For example, the book *It's Rangers For Me?*[1] provoked an inquisitorial response from BBC Scotland's flagship current-affairs programme *Newsnight*, with guests asked in a sombre tone whether they had ever sung 'The Sash'. Football writers have likened Ibrox stadium to a 'Nuremberg rally' and smeared Rangers supporters as a 'white underclass'. A radio-news bulletin broadcasted a listener's email, which asserted that Rangers fans originated from human-animal hybrid embryos[2] while a popular television comedy and a radio sketch have used the sectarian slur 'hun' in reference to a follower of the club.[3]

In effect, Rangers FC – or, more accurately, its support – has been blamed for the social problem known as sectarianism and maligned with impunity. By contrast, Celtic FC is rarely taken to task over the issue. If mentioned at all, contentious songs sung by Celtic supporters are routinely excused on the basis they are political. That the politics involved is openly supportive of Irish Republican terrorist groups and contemptuous of the British state is left unsaid.

While some within the Scottish press increasingly disdained the hard-line Unionist/Loyalist stance of many Rangers fans, it can be argued that the determining factor behind the sea change in the consensus view was the advent of devolved government. Indeed, Donald Findlay – then Rangers vice chairman and a leading figure in the No, No campaign against devolution – was subjected to a metaphorical kicking from the Scottish media after being caught on a camcorder at a private function in 1999 singing 'party songs'. Only a few years previously such press intrusion was universally frowned upon and the suspicion arises that Findlay was hounded because he ticked all the wrong boxes. The late Cardinal Winning had already established a high profile in advancing the interests of his flock when, in the wake of devolution, the composer James MacMillan exploited the occasion of a speech attended by an international audience at the Edinburgh Festival to allege that Scotland was guilty of 'sleep-walking bigotry' and 'visceral anti-Catholicism'.[4] Despite a failure to substantiate his claims by providing non-anecdotal evidence and, as exemplified by a comparison of John Knox with Pol Pot, a propensity to indulge in polemic which, in my view, revealed zealotry, MacMillan succeeded in establishing an agenda that was ultimately appropriated by politicians.

Donald Gorrie set the ball rolling in the political domain with a much-publicised bill in the Scottish parliament, which sought to criminalise sectarian behaviour, though police and MSPs expressed doubts that this approach was workable. In what was to become a consistent theme, the examples Gorrie used to highlight the problem of religious bigotry in Scotland invariably placed Protestants/Rangers fans as the perpetrators and Roman Catholics/Celtic fans as the victims. After becoming First Minister, Jack McConnell effectively commandeered Gorrie's proposed measure, forcing through section 74 of the Criminal Justice Act (2003) which addressed offences 'aggravated by religious prejudice'. Deploying the slogan 'Scotland's secret shame', it soon became apparent that McConnell – in common with many other Labour politicians in west-central Scotland, a Celtic supporter – had identified football as lying at the root of the problem, although Orange parades were later targeted in the Orr Report (2005).

Consequentially, Scotland has witnessed a torrent of news stories and opinion pieces concerning religious bigotry and, in what has become a burgeoning cottage industry, the concomitant establishment of 'anti-sectarianism' groups funded mainly by government. The contribution of Bruce et al[5] (which found sectarian intolerance to be relatively insignificant, in decline and distributed commensurately within both denominations) and David McLetchie's argument[6] that the McConnell/Gorrie legislation and its implementation by police unfairly targeted one half of Scotland's religious divide challenged the new orthodoxy and were largely disregarded. The Scottish political-media complex had its bogeyman and there was no room for debate. Lest there be any uncertainty, one of Scotland's most influential and politically connected academics, Tom Devine, spelled out the message: 'We should be calling this for what it is: it isn't sectarianism, it is anti-Catholicism.' [7]

Devine's outburst notwithstanding, 'sectarianism' is rarely defined unambiguously and is most often used in relation to singing at football – invariably Rangers – games, surely a symptom of an underlying problem and not its cause. It is perfectly reasonable to assert that certain chants are offensive and might dissuade some people from going to matches; it is not tenable to maintain that such behaviour inevitably leads to violence (absolutely no evidence has ever been produced to support this theory) or that its removal will have an appreciable impact on sectarianism in general.

Even within this narrow context, there has been no recognition that judgment of offence is essentially subjective and the only logically sustainable positions are to either permit or ban outright all partisan songs at football games. A corollary of the foregoing points is that the extent or level of sectarianism in society cannot be gauged by selectively citing certain football chants. However, of possibly greater concern is that the failure to specify definitively what is meant by sectarianism facilitates the marginalisation of certain beliefs (pejoratively branded 'attitudes' by opponents) relating to Scotland's historical schism, which in a modern context primarily involves identity politics rather than religion per se.

The contention that sectarianism results from a fundamental divide in society – which is perpetuated by a generational cycle induced by Scotland's segregated schooling system – is now seldom articulated by public figures, presumably due to fear of the inevitable backlash from the Roman Catholic Church. However, Joseph Devine, the Roman Catholic

Bishop of Motherwell, admitted that 'denominational education is an enabler of sectarianism' and 'Roman Catholic schooling is divisive – sometimes it's a price worth paying.'[8] Although a large majority of the Scottish public concurs with the statement 'Catholic schools should be phased out' (81 per cent in favour, with 15 per cent opposed)[9], the Church is evidently most reluctant that any debate on the future of religious segregation in education should take place. In part of a press release that was not reported, Cardinal Keith O'Brien in my opinion effectively called for censorship when he urged the First Minister to join him in 'asking the Scottish media to adopt a far more cautious and measured approach in future to the topic of Catholic schools' since 'each time a newspaper or broadcaster decides . . . to raise, promote or advance these arguments [against denominational schooling], they fan the flames of religious hatred.'[10]

One outcome of McConnell's initiative is that much relevant discussion now takes place within the de-intellectualised framework of radio football programmes and the pages of tabloid newspapers. Indeed, if the aim of Rangers' adversaries was to dumb-down debate to the most superficial level imaginable, and to use the current attention devoted to sectarianism as a vehicle to damage the club, then they have thoroughly succeeded. Rangers fans now complain bitterly of the double standards adopted by the media and football authorities whereby a deaf ear is turned to chants of 'soon there'll be no Protestants at all' from the Celtic support and ditties celebrating the Ibrox Disaster sung by followers of Aberdeen. In a similar vein, whereas the press had no qualms about liberally using the term sectarian following an attack on Neil Lennon (significantly, the element of 'aggravation by religious prejudice' was withdrawn from the consequent charge) the more serious and prolonged assault on a Rangers fan a few hours earlier was dismissed as 'football-related'.[11]

The mounting pressure on Rangers manifested itself most noticeably in the increasingly draconian tactics employed against the club's supporters by police and stewards. However, a more serious threat came from outside Scotland in the form of a UEFA charge against Rangers for discriminatory chanting by its support. Although the fine meted out was less than the club's critics expected (and, in some instances, undoubtedly hoped for), the prospect of stand closures and even a ban from European competition in the event of further infractions worried the board of directors. All the complaints received by UEFA came from sources within Scotland and it was reported that the 'anti-sectarianism' organisation Nil by Mouth, a retired Episcopalian bishop, 'at least' two academics and 'at least' one politician provided evidence in the case against Rangers.[12] The charge related chiefly to the song known as 'The Billy Boys' and, in particular, the definition of the word Fenian, which UEFA was misled into believing is synonymous with Roman Catholic.

More recently, the goalposts were widened when Rangers fans were accused of anti-Irish racism in connection with the chant 'the Famine's over, why don't you go home?' Disingenuously labelled a song by most media sources, this pungent barb provoked a hostile reaction from Scotland's moral guardians. In fact it was designed to mock what in my eyes are the theme-park Irishness and sense of victimhood which have all too often been espoused by Celtic FC and its followers: for example the maudlin 'Fields Of Athenry' and 'Let The People Sing' (which to me is also a rebel song) are played over the tannoy at Celtic Park and both allude to the Irish famine. In the midst of a banking crisis that had the most serious implications for the country, twice within days the chant was the lead news item and an increasingly politicised police force warned fans that they could be arrested for singing it.[13]

The unscrupulous manipulation of news stories has become the favoured modus operandi of Rangers' enemies as a means of traducing the support. A classic example of the nature of the forces directed against the club came in 2006 via the propagation of the 'news' that Celtic goal-keeper Artur Boruc was cautioned by police for making the sign of the cross in front of Rangers fans at Ibrox. Enthusiastically exploited by the SNP, a story that had originally appeared on the pages of the *Scottish Catholic Observer* was taken at face value by the Scottish media and used to demonstrate how 'backward' the country was. The affair received global attention and inevitably cast a huge cloud over the Rangers support. When the truth emerged three days later that in reality Boruc had been warned for making obscene gestures[14], there were few apologies and precious little publicity was given to the letter from the Crown Office to First Minister Alex Salmond which complained of 'wholly unfounded reporting and comment'.[15] From the Machiavellian perspective of those behind the story, though, it was very much a case of mission accomplished – most of the Scottish public had been duped and Rangers' image further tarnished.

Moreover, Rangers supporters with access to the internet are familiar with many stories that show the Celtic support in a poor light being apparently censored or downplayed. These range from the vandalism of thousands of seats at Kilmarnock and arrests made on Celtic's European trips to the disruption of memorial silences.

Would it be overly cynical to suggest that Rangers supporters have become scapegoats in a battle being fought between Labour and the SNP for Scotland's Catholic vote, while sections of the media have exploited the latitude ensuing from the sectarianism issue to pour opprobrium on a club they loathe? Indeed, has the crusade against religious bigotry not degenerated into a blame game which is palpably failing to alleviate the problem and in certain cases seems largely motivated by the very prejudice it purports to condemn? The revelation that a co-author of a one-sided, pseudo-academic, sham report professedly examining sectarianism in the workplace – and eagerly embraced by both the STUC and the Executive – was a member of a pro-IRA fanzine surely encapsulates the current travesty.[16]

There can, of course, be no justification of anti-social behaviour on the part of a minority of Rangers fans. Nevertheless, it is reasonable to insist that the support as a whole is accorded equitable and proportionate treatment. Under the stewardship of Sir David Murray, the club was, in the view of many of its staunchest followers, unfathomably reluctant to demand a level playing field. The danger consequently arises that some fans may adopt a myopic, no-one-likes-us-we-don't-care posture, cocking a snook at their most trenchant critics but correspondingly alienating potential supporters and causing problems for the club. Those of us with Rangers' interests at heart must hope the support acknowledges the realpolitik of the situation and that the board in the post-Murray era faces up to the challenge that lies ahead in relation to countering the propaganda onslaught from powerful and influential antagonists.

Notes

1   *It's Rangers For Me?* R. Esplin and G. Walker (eds), (Fort Publishing, 2007)
2   *Newsdrive*, BBC Radio Scotland, 21/3/08
3   *Rab C. Nesbitt*, BBC 1 Scotland, 31/12/08; *Off the Ball*, BBC Radio Scotland, 23/1/10
4   *Guardian*, 9/8/99.
5   *Sectarianism in Scotland*, S. Bruce, T. Glendinning, I. Patterson and M. Rosie. (Edinburgh University Press, 2004)
6   *The Herald*, 18/3/09.
7   *Scotland on Sunday*, 14/9/08
8   BBC website, 22/2/02. (http://news.bbc.co.uk/1/hi/scotland/2274383.stm)
9   Scottish Social Attitudes Survey, 2000. (http://www.ccsr.ac.uk/esds/variables/ssa/ssa4503/mxrlgsc1)
10 Scottish Catholic Media Office press release, 27/11/06. (http://scmo.org/articles/421/1/Cardinal-responds-to-sectarianism-statistics/Page1.html)
11 *Daily Record*, 2/9/08.
12 *The Herald*, 26/5/06.
13 BBC website, 29/10/08. (http://news.bbc.co.uk/sport1/hi/football/scot_prem/7696302.stm)
14 Crown Office and Procurator Fiscal Service press release, 28/8/06. (http://www.copfs.gov.uk/News/Releases/2006/08/28140026)
15 Crown Office and Procurator Fiscal Service press release, 29/8/06. (http://www.copfs.gov.uk/Resource/Doc/13547/0000188.pdf)
16 *Sunday Herald*, 13/12/09.

HOME AND AWAY FANS

A Lifetime Following Rangers

Gregory Campbell MP

The Early Years

I was born and raised in Londonderry, Northern Ireland. During my time in secondary education I had developed a love of football and became a passionate follower of my favourite team, the famous Glasgow Rangers. I can well recall how I first became so interested. I was always a football fan and a friend of our family was a Rangers fanatic with plenty of para-phernalia, including pictures, scrapbooks, mementoes and so on. Hearing stories of the great players probably did it for me and like most young people the more vivid and colourful the stories were, the more you wanted to know.

School and Starting to Support Rangers

In the mid 1960s, which was even before *Match of the Day* highlights were being screened on a Saturday night never mind live coverage, the only pictorial element available of football was the newspapers. I would pore over every detail of the match reports and as I set off for school on a Monday morning I took to wearing my Rangers scarf and lapel badge only to hear my teacher at the local technical college shout at me in class:

'Campbell! Get on with your work. Do you think yer heading for a match coming to school dressed like that?'

I became enthralled by the exploits of Willie Henderson and Jim Baxter and like virtually every other teenage supporter my own attempts to replicate the skills of my heroes were doomed to failure as I took to one of the bumpy pitches in St Columb's park, Waterside, which in my dreams was transformed into the silky-smooth surface of Ibrox stadium.

The First Follow Follow

As I became a teenager I became more and more interested in the mystique of this famous football team. I was still only able to follow them through the pages of the newspapers, by listening to radio reports and by catching the occasional television clip of the winning goal in a cup final. Hearing stories of how they played and how the supporters sang was all still second hand. The more I heard the more determined I became to get to a game.

Then in the autumn of 1968 I read of the draw for the European competition that was the forerunner of the UEFA Cup. Rangers had drawn Dundalk from the Irish Republic. Dundalk was still about a hundred miles away but it didn't mean a ferry crossing and I pestered my mother to let me go to the game. The Troubles in Northern Ireland had only just begun to smoulder so my mum was very reluctant as I was only fifteen and had never been as far away on my own before. I found out that a local supporters club was taking a bus to the match so I made sure that one of the older men on the bus agreed to be my minder to try and keep my mum content. I would not be put off and just kept pestering her until she agreed that I could go. The build up was incredible as I was finally going to see the Gers play live.

I still recall the bus journey down to Dundalk and then after our arrival having my first sight of thousands of Rangers fans arriving in the border town for the game. What made the prospect even more exciting was the fact that the Gers had just signed a new striker called Colin Stein and he had scored a hat trick on his debut. He scored another hat trick in his next game and I was ecstatic at the thought of seeing my first ever Rangers game and what had they done? They had just signed a real-life version of Roy of the Rovers!

The ground at Oriel Park, Dundalk, where I saw that first match, was pretty mediocre. The surroundings were drab and dreary but it didn't matter. It's over forty years ago and I still recall the Rangers team standing in the middle of the pitch before kick off applauding the travelling thousands in the stands. My beloved team were applauding me! Colin Stein scored twice and any possibility of my doing cold turkey to get off the Rangers drug was banished forever with Roy of the Rovers having scored *eight* goals in his first three games for the team. The bus journey home was sheer bliss as we recounted the game and of course Stein's goals.

Beautiful Seat and Birthplace of a Legend

As I became interested in politics in Northern Ireland later on in the 1970s as a canvasser and then eventually in the 1980s as a candidate for my party, the Democratic Unionists, I stood for election initially unsuccessfully, and then won my present Parliamentary seat of East Londonderry in 2001. It has one of the most beautiful coastlines in these islands and includes the seaside resorts of Portrush, Portstewart and Castlerock.

But not long after I was elected I discovered something else that was beautiful about the area I had the privilege to represent. The player who was the greatest ever single-league-season goalscorer in the history of Rangers Football Club was born in a townland called Aghadowey near Coleraine, which is the main town in my constituency. I have family connections in this area and to discover that the famous Sam English also came from here filled me with immense pride. When I then discovered that 2008 was to be the centenary of Sam's birth I decided the occasion was too significant to let pass at the Mother of Parliaments when the birth of this Father of all goalscorers was about to be commemorated. I tabled a Parliamentary Motion, numbered1232, which was entitled:

CENTENARY OF THE BIRTH OF SAM ENGLISH
Dated19.03.2008

Campbell, Gregory

That this House notes that 2008 marks the centenary of the birth of Sam English, born near Coleraine, who became the highest goal scorer for Glasgow Rangers in a single season, with a total of 44, a record still held to the present day; acknowledges the tragedy that occurred during a Rangers versus Celtic game in 1931 when English was involved in an accidental on-field collision with Celtic player, John Thomson, resulting in Thomson's death; notes that this deeply tragic death overshadowed English's playing career from that game onwards; and welcomes the efforts those involved with Glasgow Rangers FC are undertaking to ensure that this Ulsterman will be remembered for his goal scoring exploits rather than an accident from which an official inquiry at the time cleared him of any malicious intent.

One very pleasing aspect of this Motion was that MPs from all sides of the House signed up to support it. Welsh Conservative and English Labour MPs joined with myself and my Ulster colleagues in paying this tribute to a man who was a football legend. Famous Rangers strikers seemed to be getting in my blood, from Colin Stein to Sam English, men who could score goals for fun and who seemed to have a second nature for setting records. This motion and other associated local publicity meant that the local council marked the spot where Sam was born and raised so that future generations will know the origins of the great man who set a record nearly eighty years ago that still stands and will probably never be surpassed.

Westminster Supporters and the UEFA Cup Final

About the same time that I had tabled the motion I was approached by another Westminster MP whom I knew to be a long time follower of the Gers: Adam Ingram. I had known Adam for some time as he had been a Northern Ireland Office minister for a while. He knew I was a bluenose, so he comes over to me in the House of Commons tearoom and says:

'Some of us are thinking of forming a Westminster Rangers supporters club Gregory, are ye up for it?'

Now this is a bit like asking a duck if he likes water. 'Count me in' says I to Adam and shortly after the supporters club was formed. There are people from all over the United Kingdom as members; anyone working in the precincts of the House can join, many have, and of course all shades of opinion are welcome. There are staff members, MPs and peers. English, Scottish and Ulster people all with one thing in common: supporting Rangers Football Club.

This of course happened in one of Rangers' best seasons in recent years. We not only won domestic trophies but also, in the undoubted highlight of the year, reached the final of the UEFA Cup. A local journalist who knew of my light-blue leanings contacted me a few weeks before the final asking if I was going to Manchester and at that stage I hadn't got a ticket. A story with a picture of me in my Rangers top appeared in the press, explaining that I was on the hunt for a ticket with me saying that as it was thirty-six years since our last European final I wasn't going to pass up the chance that I might be ninety-one years of age before the next one came along. Several days followed making phone calls, in between constituency business and parliamentary duties. Eventually I found a source and bought a ticket and on the day made preparations to go to Manchester for the final.

I will never ever forget it. Even by lunchtime when I arrived it became obvious the anticipated number of fifty thousand travelling fans was a massive underestimate. Most independent journalists and police estimates after the game gave the figure at between 150,000 and 200,000. The weather was good, the atmosphere and attitude of the fans was superb. Just after six o'clock I made my way to the ground. Rangers and St Petersburg fans went to the ground together with no animosity at all. Exchanging scarves and trying to understand the broken English of the Russians certainly kept the banter going right to the ground of Manchester City FC.

A greater contrast between Oriel Park, Dundalk and the City of Manchester stadium you couldn't imagine. I texted each of my family to let them know the build-up as they were watching on television and that never relays anything like the same atmosphere. The ground was almost completely full of Rangers supporters and each team had a presenter on the public-address system who introduced the respective club songs before the official proceedings got under way. The Russians had a few thousand supporters and made a bit of noise as they sang their tribute. When they had finished the Scottish presenter took over the microphone and really got the sound levels cranked up with his intro.

'Right the Russians have sung their song, now we're goin' tae show them how tae sing.'

Then came the most fantastic rendition of 'Follow Follow'. The noise and the occasion were both incredible, and while the score and the team performance were obviously disappointing the colour and commitment of 200,000 Rangers fans in the centre of Manchester could not be questioned. The team had to endure the most exhausting schedule of games in the run-up to the final, playing virtually every other day for about three weeks so the two-nil scoreline was hardly surprising. It was deeply regrettable that a few hooligans – who constituted about one-tenth of 1 per cent of those in Manchester – let the club down and denigrated the excellent behaviour of the 99.9 per cent. Nothing however will ever diminish the memories I have of that wonderful day in May 2008. Getting back at 3.30 a.m. for Parliamentary business at 9 a.m. was 'wee buns' after such a dramatic day.

Keep the Faith

From time to time the media, many of whom know my Rangers allegiances, make contact and pose questions on issues that arise. Sometimes if a journalist is asking a question about Rangers there is controversy in the air. I always try and deal with the issue in an even handed but honest fashion. The great club that so many millions of us have supported for so long should not be tarnished, particularly by those who would try to devalue the proud heritage and traditions it stands for. A British football institution with strong ties that bind both Scotland and Ulster is a fantastic sporting legacy that I trust everyone at the club will do all they can to see thrive in the exceptionally challenging economic times we are in.

To all those who support Rangers through good times and bad, I say walk tall as you follow in the footsteps of our team.

Behind Enemy Lines: the Story of the Dublin Loyal

Stevie Clark

Were we being mischievous starting up a Rangers supporters club in Dublin? Too right we were. It was the ultimate wind-up. I don't think Celtic fans over here took it too seriously at the time but now they hate the fact that there is a Rangers supporters club in the Republic of Ireland's capital. In 2001, after a year or so living just outside Dublin, I noticed that there were a lot of British people living in the city so it made sense that there would be some Rangers fans. I enquired on Rangers websites if any supporters in the Republic would like to start up an RSC. I met up with Ian Cox, who was a Dubliner, and Dave Nichol, who was from Arbroath, in Connolly station in Dublin to travel up to Belfast to see a Rangers Legends team playing Linfield. On the way back from the game we decided to form a supporters club and within six months we had fifty members.

In the beginning, it was all cloak and dagger. Our first meeting was in a pub in the middle of Dublin. There were about ten of us present, none of us with colours on and we talked about the usual things like organising travel and tickets. One of the guys knew someone who owned a private-members club and we moved there and since then that's where we have met although I would still rather not say where it is. Once it became known that we were starting the club we began to get feedback from Celtic fans in the Republic, mostly negative, with one person saying that if we started a Rangers club in Dublin we would be introducing bigotry into the city! We laughed at that but it showed the mindset of some of the Celtic fans. The more sensible supporters knew it would be reflect badly on them and the club if we were abused. The biggest Celtic club in Dublin is St Patrick's; it meets in a pub called Fraser's in O'Connell Street and they have around 150 members. We heard that one night they spent their whole meeting discussing the Dublin Loyal, which was amusing.

We put an advert in the *Dublin Evening Herald* but there was no phone number, only an e-mail address. There was the occasional dodgy e-mail trying to find out where we met but we soon learned to recognise genuine Rangers fans. Half of our members are from Scotland and the others are from Northern Ireland and the Republic. I presume that they are all Protestants but we never ask. As well as football, we use the meetings to let off steam about politics and religion. There are some members who are of a left-wing persuasion but there are no Nationalists and no Republicans.

The first time we displayed our 'Dublin Loyal' flag at a game was against Dundee at Ibrox. We had flagged it up, so to speak, on the internet and in the *Follow Follow* fanzine so people were expecting it. The night before the game we went on a tour of all the pubs down Paisley Road West and we got a great reception. We also have club polo shirts. People always do a double take when they see them and it's the same question every time.

'Do you get much hassle?'

And yes, we did get hassle at first. We fly over to the games and meeting Celtic fans in the airport is either funny or dangerous. The worst experience was after an Old Firm game at Parkhead when we unfurled our 'Dublin Loyal' banner at Prestwick airport. There were only two of us on the flight, which was full of Celtic fans, and we got a torrent of abuse from them. Airport security staff came over and sat with us, then told the Celtic fans that they would not get on the plane if the threats continued. At this point an official of one of the CSCs approached us and guaranteed that nothing would happen to us. He actually sat with us on the plane and made sure there were no problems when we arrived back in Dublin.

Usually we give as good as we get when it comes to banter with our friends from Parkhead, but we are not fooled; you can't go broadcasting it in Dublin. There are always groups of guys over in Dublin on stag weekends so nobody takes a blind bit of notice of people wearing club tops, even England strips, but if you walked down O'Connell Street with a Rangers top on it would be different. Some of our members were getting brave and wearing their polo shirts down Temple Bar and places like that but it had to be knocked on the head. Our feeling is that we know who we are; we don't have to shout about it.

We have gone from strength to strength since we first started. We organise St Patrick's Day bashes in Glasgow and they are a great success. It started when we were looking to organise a night in the city to coincide with a visit to a game. We didn't have a particular date in mind but when we realised we would be over on the seventeenth of March, we couldn't resist it. I ran the idea past a few Rangers supporters in Scotland and the feedback was highly positive. We sold every ticket and there were Rangers fans from every corner of Britain. We didn't get much reaction from Celtic supporters – I think they would have looked extremely foolish if they had objected.

I never thought that I would end up living in the Republic of Ireland. I have been a Rangers fan ever since I can remember; my first strip at five and my first game at seven, a year after I had moved to Forfar from Montrose. At seventeen I started going to games on the Dundee Loyal, had a spell with the Monifieth RSC before the Forfar True Blues were formed in the 1990s. In 1984 I made my first trip to Dublin with the Dundee Loyal to see Rangers playing Bohemians in the UEFA Cup. It was an experience never to be forgotten, and I swore that I would never set foot in the Republic again. Everyone from the bus stuck together in the city centre during the day and it had been very quiet, although we were told that a ferry carrying supporters over from Liverpool had been turned back. It was when we made our way to the ground that the atmosphere began to change and once we got there it all kicked off. The Gardai had been friendly enough at the beginning and there was plenty of banter but afterwards they were putting us on any bus to get us away from the ground as quickly as possible. I don't know if I'm being paranoid but, once out of Dublin, the Gardai escorted all the buses slowly through every town and village on the way back to the border. Every time one bus would stop, we would all stop and there was fighting with the locals. It was madness. Once we got to the border, the RUC took over and we sped all the way back to the port. I honestly didn't think that I would ever go back to the Republic of Ireland.

But, in 1996, I met the woman who would become my wife, in Dundee, where she was a nurse, and, after we got married, we moved back to her home village of Ardee, near Dublin. There was bit of banter with her brothers but I was made very welcome by all her family and friends. Living in the Republic has certainly opened my eyes. A lot of Rangers fans think everyone here is a Catholic who supports Celtic and the IRA but the reality is very different. Of course there are people like that and some in Dublin are staunch Republicans but it is only a minority. In general, people down here don't give two hoots what happens in Northern Ireland. The level of ignorance, especially towards the Unionist community, is breathtaking. We have developed a great friendship with a Linfield Rangers supporters club from the Shankill Road and when I mention to my workmates that I am going up to the Shankill, they seem to think I am going to the other side of the world.

I was actually surprised at how few football fans over here care about Celtic. Most people are only interested in the Premiership and when we are at the airport getting ready to fly over to Scotland, the place is full of Manchester United, Liverpool and Everton fans. You have to remember that football is not the number-one sport all over the Republic. In urban centres, it is the most popular, but, in the country, GAA is king and they get massive crowds at All-Ireland games that dwarf anything the Eircom League can muster, while in some areas, like South Dublin and Limerick, rugby is top.

I remember watching an Old Firm game for the first time in the village pub. I thought it would have been busy but there were only about ten customers. It was the game in which Bo Anderson scored a double to give Rangers a 3–1 win. I even cheered at the goals and nobody said a word.

At first, though, I wouldn't say who I supported but after a while I would admit it was Rangers and indeed the first time I did so, the guy I was speaking to replied, 'so do I'. I was stunned. Even my wife was shocked that someone from her village had a soft spot for Rangers. And when Rangers played Parma in the Champions League group stages in 1999 I told my gaffer that if we beat them then I would wear my Rangers top to work. Of course they did and the next day when I walked into the canteen with my top on the whole place came to a standstill.

If Rangers fans think that the Irish are all Celtic-supporting Republicans then in some ways the stereotype works the other way as well. Due to the popularity of *Braveheart*, people here think we hate the English and that anybody who supports the Queen must somehow be a traitor. They also seem to think everyone lives within a fifty-mile radius of Glasgow! Another thing I have noticed is that the Irish can't get their heads around a Scottish/British identity. Although English football teams are well liked in the Republic there is a great loathing of England. They can't believe that we don't all want independence and there are some work colleagues who believe that Scotland is part of the United Kingdom against our will. I keep telling them that Scottish people could vote for independence in any election but that the majority favours the status quo. I wear a poppy in the week leading up to Remembrance Sunday and I have lost count of the people who call it an 'English symbol' because they think being British and English is the same thing.

Although I have met many who are surprised to discover that some Orange parades in Scotland are as big as those in Northern Ireland, their perception of the Rangers support generally is that they are anti-Irish bigots. I always point out that Rangers fans have no anti-Irish songs. I constantly argue that just because the majority of Rangers fans are Unionist does not mean we are anti-Irish. 'The Sash' is not any more offensive than 'Flower of Scotland' but as soon as you put FTP on the end you are giving our enemies the stick with which to beat us. But simply telling the FTP brigade to stop won't work. We have to try if possible to educate these people to realise that if we stop the FTP add-ons then we are untouchable. Rangers could do so much more to help by making it clear that traditional songs such as 'The Sash' and 'Derry's Walls' are not the problem and that the club will defend the fans who sing them. Those songs represent the line in the sand for me. As long as we get rid of the 'FTP' and other add-ons we can defend songs like these to the hilt.

Instead, we have found ourselves at loggerheads with Rangers and Strathclyde Police over our Dublin Loyal banner. Before the Champions League game in Barcelona in 2007, we had the words 'Behind Enemy Lines' put on the banner. The words were taken from an Irish newspaper headline above an article written about our club. We found it funny and so put it on the new banner but in a home match against Falkirk the following February, the stewards confiscated it, saying that it was sectarian. We had a two-hour meeting with head of security Kenny Scott one Sunday at Ibrox to discuss the situation and we slapped down a suggestion from the club and police that the slogan was sectarian. Initially, we did make some headway with Rangers but when we met the match commander,

Robin Howe, just before the UEFA Cup final in Manchester, we were given what I thought were farcical reasons for the ban. He told us he had looked at Celtic internet message boards and consulted with Celtic fans who, surprise, surprise, claimed that the banner was offensive. So, in essence, we were told that our flag was banned because Celtic fans didn't like it. Ironically, Ibrox is the only place where the flag is banned. You couldn't make it up.

The level of support we subsequently received from the Rangers support worldwide was astonishing. We had a letter from Rangers saying they accepted that there were no sectarian overtones or intentions in the use of 'Behind Enemy Lines' but that they had to accept the advice given by the match commander. We've had to make two coverings: one has 'censored' written on it; the other has the inscription *faugh a ballagh* (clear the way), which is Irish and has been used by Irish regiments down through the years. At first the whole issue shocked everyone in the Dublin Loyal but it has made us more determined and we are now adamant that we will not change the flag.

Sadly, we have had more hassle from the club in recent years than we get in Dublin. We are well established now and our membership has really taken off. It includes two Polish members – and no, they don't like Boruc either. We also have a working relationship with the Dublin branch of the Royal British Legion branch and we took part in the annual remembrance service in July 2009 for all the Irishmen killed in service of the British armed forces. We felt real pride when the name of our club was read out as we laid our poppy wreath.

The Dublin Loyal will continue to give a voice to Rangers fans in Ireland. We will continue to buy season tickets and we will continue to travel to away games as well as to Ibrox. And we are determined that our Dublin Loyal flag will not just be seen at Ibrox, but all over Scotland and all over Europe.

We will follow on.

From Tradeston to Toronto

Bobby Smith

There is diminished sense of Scottishness in Toronto these days, no doubt about it. You don't hear many Scots accents when you are going about your business or walking around the mall. There was a huge influx of Scots in the 1960s and 1970s, and also lots from England and Ireland, but that has slowed to a trickle. People are not coming over from Britain in the same numbers while Toronto has experienced a different type of immigration in recent decades.

That is why the supporters clubs over here are dying although in comparison with others we are relatively healthy. My club, the Toronto Number One RSC, has about 280 members at the moment, whereas as at one time we had 450. The older ones are dropping off; we had three or four die this year and half a dozen in 2008, people who had been members for thirty or forty years. I think that only about 20 per cent of our members are under sixty. We just don't get so many young members any more. Like most supporters clubs we have our own website but we don't advertise for new members as such, relying instead on word of mouth. We get quite a few visitors in the summer, people over on holiday, but it's usually quiet from June until the league starts.

Like many Scots, I was attracted to Canada by the prospect of a better life. I'm from Tradeston originally, which is not far from Ibrox. But I was twenty years old and in a dead-end job so, in 1965 – having been over for a holiday in 1964 with my new wife – I decided to give Toronto a try. There were plenty of opportunities for incomers. My first job was working in elevators but then I got a job in insulation. Most people who arrive in a new country tend to gather with their own kind and we were no different. We lived with my brother-in-law and I began playing football with a team called St Andrews, where I met many expats. The Rangers supporters club was also a great meeting point for Scots. I went back to Glasgow in 1973 to give it another go but it didn't pan out so I returned to Canada a year later and joined the Toronto Number One. I became a committee member in 1975 and I have been there ever since.

The club was formed in 1967. It was the first Rangers supporters club in North America and we were around before the famous Toronto Blue Jays, the city's baseball team, which took another decade to come onto the scene.

Our website points out – and of course back then we never had anything like the internet, mobile phones or the television coverage that we have today – how and when we were formed.

On January 8th 1967 in the 'Sons and Daughters of Ulster' Hall, at Woodbine and Danforth, that a meeting was convened for the purpose of recruiting members who would commit to joining a supporters club.

The meeting was chaired by James 'Sugar' Henry and amongst the founding fathers were: Jimmy Lang, Jimmy McKinnon, John McKinnon, Duncan Cameron, Bobby Liddell, John Martin, Billy Black, Archie Wilson, Sammy Patterson, Jimmie Horne, George Tait, Billy Graham, Billy Clements, Alex Copeland, George Entwistle – and some others, about 30 in all.

At first ladies were not allowed to become members, although that has changed. Obviously it was more difficult to keep up with what was going on back home than it is now so we would listen to matches on shortwave radio and some people phoned back home for the results. It was more of a big deal to travel between Canada and Scotland in those days but the club would charter a plane once a year for trips back home and they were very popular.

When I joined the committee, we were a nomadic club with about fifty members, meeting in various pubs and halls around Toronto. But we continued to grow and decided that, rather than giving our money to other establishments, we would find our own premises. We have leased our present unit in Ellesmere Road, Scarborough for about fourteen years, and before that we had a permanent place in Kennedy Road, also in Scarborough. We open on Fridays and Saturdays unless there is a game on a Sunday or in midweek.

Unlike the early days, we have quite a few females in the club and, indeed, we have five women on our executive committee. The Bramalea

Rangers supporters club doesn't entertain female members, nor does the Cambridge branch. All I can say is that the women in this club are great; they put a lot of work in to keep it going. We have one social occasion every month and we have a Burns Night and St Andrews Night.

We don't charge children membership fees until they leave school. Out of all the youngsters who have come along over the years and grown up with the club, as far as I am aware, there are only two who stayed on to become adult members. Once they have to start paying they give it a body swerve. Recruiting kids to begin with is difficult. They have different interests and there are too many other sports for them to try over here, like ice hockey and baseball.

Typically, our members came from all over Toronto and beyond. We had a few who lived in the west end of the city, which is between thirty and forty-five minutes away, and because of the travelling – and, to be honest, the clamping down on drink driving – they decided to form their own club. There was no problem about that, we were all Rangers fans, but that is how the Bramalea RSC was started in the mid 1980s.

There used to be interaction between the various supporters clubs in the Toronto area. We would play dominoes against Bramalea and darts against Whitby RSC but it fell away. We should get it going again but the problem is that when you go to another RSC you are taking revenue away from your own club, and vice versa when they come here. It would be different if you didn't have to worry about the rent or electricity or things like that but those overheads are important and expensive.

We also have a good relationship with the Celtic supporters clubs in Toronto and if there is anyone in trouble we try and help each other out with benefit nights and the like. Of course there are times when they don't want to speak to us and we don't want to speak to them.

The biggest change in recent years is that we can now see Rangers games live on the television on a regular basis, most of which kick-off at 7.30 a.m. We buy the game from the broadcasters and split the cost among the clubs. But even the prospect of watching Rangers live on the telly is not as popular as it once was. Most people can access matches from their living rooms these days. It is mostly seniors in our club and if the match is during the week, in the winter and we are playing someone like St Mirren, then they will stay at home and watch it in the house.

But there is a great passion for Rangers among those who are still involved with the supporters clubs over here. Fans in Toronto had the same sense of excitement as those in Glasgow when Graeme Souness came to the club as player-manager in 1986. You have to give the guy his due. He turned it around. What he did at the end when he left for Liverpool was something else but when he was at Ibrox he did the business. We also felt the same sense of shock over here when Maurice Johnston signed a few years later. You got the odd bigot who said they wouldn't go back to Ibrox but they invariably did. If you are a Rangers supporter, it's not the individual you support but Rangers Football Club and that is the most important thing.

We have had some great nights in the club over the years. One of the best was when we invited former player Sammy Cox – who lives about an hour and a half away in Stratford – to become an honorary member. He brought down his Scottish Cup, League Cup and Glasgow Cup medals as well as his Scotland shirts and made a great speech. It was a night when the hairs on the back of your neck stood up.

We've got a fair bit of memorabilia on display in the club. Members and visitors bring stuff over from Scotland and among the better items we have in our collection – apart from what Sammy donated – is Ally McCoist's jersey from his testimonial game against Newcastle in 1993 and other mementoes from David Cooper's testimonial year in 1988/89.

Although there is no doubting the passion of the fans, even from afar, we have to accept that the numbers are dwindling. I still see guys like Rab Martin, Alex Copeland and Harry Mealyea – men who were there when I first joined the club and that's great – but new blood is needed. I would say that in the next five or ten years the club will not exist in its present format. There is a fear of the club losing its premises and having to go back to meeting in various halls and pubs again, which would be a shame.

But although individual supporters clubs are struggling, the North American Rangers Supporters Association – better known as NARSA – continues to thrive. That has been a big success since it was initiated seventeen years ago by the late Tommy Plunkett, a larger-than-life character, well-known to everyone in the Rangers community in North America. He had a vision of all the individual supporters clubs coming under one umbrella. He wrote to Rangers outlining his idea, they approved it and it has blossomed from there. NARSA began with seven member clubs and now we have fifty-four – every club in North America.

NARSA has a convention every year and that has grown into a huge event. There were a couple of hundred people present at the inaugural convention but nowadays a couple of thousand turn up, making their way from all over the world. At Niagara Falls in 2009, about 30 per cent were from overseas, mostly Scotland, and that figure has also grown over the years. The Toronto Number One is always well represented; we had about 180 members present at Niagara, about a tenth of all the people attending. The fundamental format hasn't changed. We have a 'meet and greet' on the Thursday, and, if we have a couple of players or former players over, we have a question-and-answer session. We try to invite a flute band over for the Friday night and on the Saturday night we have a grand banquet. It is always a huge success.

After the convention is over, we start preparing for the following year and there is always something to be done. I have been involved from day one and became a member of the NARSA committee after about six months. We have four committee meetings a year and depending where it is held, it can mean a four- or five-hour drive.

Before NARSA was established, the individual clubs didn't have much contact with Rangers but the club has been brilliant with us over the years. Sometimes I feel sorry for the punters back home. You could say we are the jam and they are the bread and butter but, at times, we seem to get looked after more. Some people will ask: 'What do Rangers do for us?' but they don't see the work that we, as a committee, do with the club and the benefits we can receive. If Rangers have broadcast rights to European games, for instance, they will sell them on to NARSA, which means that we save thousands of dollars.

The biggest problem we encounter – and it is the same for individual clubs – is getting current first-team players to visit. It is a sticking point with the fans and it always will be. Although we try our damndest to get players over, it's practically impossible. Some of our punters are continually moaning about it but they just can't get it in to their heads that players have lives of their own and they only have three or four weeks of a break. They can't see that the foreign players want to go home for the short period of time that they have off in the close season.

What we have to do is to invite former players and they always have a good time, especially at the convention. When Davie Wilson was over, he told me that in all his days at Rangers, he had never seen anything like it.

We would also like Rangers to visit North America more often. We would love to have them every year but unfortunately it just doesn't happen. Rangers toured Toronto a few times in the 1960s and the Toronto Number One had a big night for the players when they came over in 1976. They visited a few years later and then again in the early 1980s but the ties have been loosened since then. They did play Dinamo Zagreb in a friendly in the Sky Dome – now the Rogers Centre – in 2005 but we remain at the mercy of the club in terms of fixtures on this side of the Atlantic.

But are always lobbying and we will continue to support from afar, as we have done for four decades and more.

'I'm Reading About an Accies Player Who Broke His Leg at Ibrox'

Bobby Barr

I was one of thousands of Rangers fans who travelled up to Pittodrie on 2 May 1987 to see Graeme Souness's side bring the title back to Ibrox for the first time in nine years. I was up on the Kirkintilloch Rangers supporters-club bus. Some people might remember me – I was the guy hobbling around on crutches, recovering from a broken leg. There were Rangers fans everywhere that day, mostly in the beach end, but they managed to get tickets for every part of the ground and the atmosphere was electric.

But when Terry Butcher headed Rangers ahead just before half-time, scoring the goal that ultimately won the league, I probably felt different from every other Gers fans, not only inside Pittodrie, but also all over the world. It was Butcher who broke my leg in a league match at Ibrox around four months earlier, when I was a Hamilton Accies player: 17 January 1987, to be exact.

It was a day I'll never forget because the injury effectively ended my career. I never played another Premier League game. I had dreamt all my life about playing at Ibrox and when I eventually got to play there, it meant that I had played at every senior ground in Scotland, an achievement of which I am still proud. But my involvement lasted only seventeen minutes. I thought I had started well and certainly my mates who were at the game have since told me that. I was up against Ian Durrant and I was giving as good as I got. I got plenty of touches and was heavily involved.

Then teammate Kevin McKie got the ball in the right-back area and played a hospital pass between me and Butcher. My impression was that Terry came through me. Everyone in the stadium heard the crack. I didn't have shin pads on – and it might have made a difference – but as it was, I suffered a double leg break.

I was in shock. I kept trying to get up and look at my leg but I was told to lie back. Graham Roberts held my head but I couldn't see Butcher anywhere; I am quite sure he knew what he had done. It's funny the things that stick in your memory. Wee Davie Wilson, the former Rangers player, was a coach at Hamilton, and I noticed that, for some reason, he was at the side of the pitch wearing my sheepskin jacket. I don't know why, he must have liked the look of it hanging on the peg. My mum and dad were in the stand and there were some punters shouting, 'it should have been your neck you broke ya Fenian bastard'. My dad shook his head in disbelief at their attitude.

I heard through the grapevine that Butcher tried to get in to the changing room at half-time to see how I was but by then I had been whisked away to the Southern General. I got a morphine jag at Ibrox to kill the pain. Rangers offered a car and my mum and dad followed. My dad said that Campbell Ogilvie was great; he couldn't do enough for them. The game turned in to a kicking match. Rangers won 2–0 but they finished with nine men.

People often asked me how I felt about Terry's challenge. I would tell them that I am not one to hold grudges but that I was disappointed there was no apology at the time or even later when we met again. I haven't changed my view that it was a reckless tackle.

Accies had been relegated by the time Rangers went up to Pittodrie to win the title. As soon as the final whistle sounded, I left the ground as the Rangers fans invaded the pitch. I remember one of my mates coming back on to the bus with Ally McCoist's boot. I had always been a Rangers fan. Ironically enough, although I have spent all of my life in Kirkintilloch, I was born in 1962 at Lennox Castle maternity hospital, where Celtic's training ground is now. My dad and grandpa were Rangers fans and they would take me to games. The year Rangers won the European Cup Winners Cup – 1972 – I was at all the home games: Rennes, Sporting Lisbon, Torino and Bayern Munich. I was standing in the covered terracing across from the main stand, in line with Sandy Jardine, when he scored the first goal in the first minute of the 2–0 win over Bayern at in the semi-final.

My dad was quite strict with me in the way that I supported Rangers. I wasn't allowed to go up to the Rangers end of Ibrox; it was considered too rough and so I was either across from the main stand or in the Celtic end. And dad wouldn't allow me to wear colours. I didn't have a Rangers strip when I was a boy. I had other strips like Dundee United and Aberdeen, but never a Rangers strip. I attended Lenzie academy, which was a rugby-playing school. They didn't have a football team so I played for the rugby team. Again, there was some irony involved. Our physical-education teacher was Billy Williamson, a former Rangers player, who scored in successive Scottish Cup finals against Morton and Clyde. But he hated football and was only concerned with rugby. I was good at football and cross-country running so I struck a deal with the school: if I represented them at cross country, they would get me into the East Dunbartonshire football team. I kept my part of the bargain, winning a silver medal in the Scottish-schools-cross-country race. They kept their side of the bargain and so, although we never had a school football team, I was able to play for the East Dunbartonshire select.

I was into football in a big way, playing centre or right midfield where my running came in handy. I played for the Boys Brigade on a Saturday morning and as I got older I was asked to go to Campsie Blackwatch, one of the most famous amateur teams in Scotland. All the while, I was going to Rangers games. Although I was never a season-ticket holder, I went as often as I could but it was mostly midweek and European games. Like most young guys in Scotland I wanted to become a professional and I was chuffed when I was invited to a trial at Airdrie when I was sixteen. Bobby Watson, an ex-Rangers player, was the Airdrie manager then and the first thing he said to me was:

'Are you a bluenose son?'

'Yes, I support Rangers,' I replied.

'Okay, you are in my team for training.'

The training teams were picked on the basis of which Old Firm team you supported, so it was Rangers versus Celtic across the pitch, with my team including Bobby, Sandy Clark and Paul Jonquin. It was the first time I had encountered that mentality, but it wouldn't be the last. I played a couple of reserve games and nothing happened so I went back to Campsie and went through the age groups up to under-21. After that I then went to Queen's Park and chucked it after six months. I didn't like it there and so I went back to playing amateur, as you could after playing for the Spiders.

Rangers still played a big part in my life. One of my teammates at Campsie got me tickets for an Old Firm match at Parkhead. The only problem: it was for the Celtic end of the main stand. Jim Bett scored and I was up, cheering. I nearly got lynched. Celtic supporters were climbing over seats to get at me and a wee steward came and saved my life, taking me away to the Rangers end. It's not something you forget in a hurry.

At the end of the season I got a trial for Alloa. I played against Greenock Morton and even though we were beaten 5–0, I played well. I had another good game against Airdrie in my next run-out and manager Jimmy Thompson signed me after the game. I was twenty-two by then, quite old to be breaking into the senior game, but just two years later I found myself in the SPL. I had two good seasons at Alloa. In fact, in my first season, after twelve games or so, Alloa and Manchester United were the only two unbeaten teams in Britain. Then United were beaten, which left us as the only unbeaten team, at least for a while. We eventually finished second and won promotion to the second division.

Even when I was at Alloa, I tried to get to as many Rangers games as I could. I was at the Rangers–Celtic reserve game when Robert Fleck bared his arse, which was hilarious. I did well at Alloa and heard that Rangers were looking at me but nothing came of it. I was also told that Hibs were after me and that Alloa had knocked them back. Back then, that was the end of the story, there was no angling for a move. If your club didn't want you to go, you didn't go.

But when Falkirk, Hamilton and Motherwell all showed interest, I think Alloa realised they could not keep me forever. Hamilton were my last choice; I had it down to a straight fight between Motherwell and Falkirk. Motherwell manager Tommy McLean was on the phone to me every night, he was desperate to get me. In fact he was on the phone so often that he and my dad ended up talking about Rangers. It was all a bit messy though. I had no agent – few players did then – and there was a lot of politics going on. Eventually, however, it got sorted out and when John Lambie offered money plus a player to Alloa, I ended up going to Hamilton, who had just been promoted to the SPL. I stayed part-time; I was making more money that way, with two jobs.

Although I hadn't been keen to go to Hamilton, they had good players in their squad: the likes of Gerry McCabe, Ally Brazil, John Pelosi, John

Brogan, Gerry Collins, Graham Mitchell and Des Walker. Training at Accies was also Rangers versus Celtic, but again it was all good banter, good fun, nothing sinister. People would ask me if I tried harder against Celtic because I was a Rangers fan but nothing could be further from the truth. I would have loved to have scored against Rangers or been in a team that beat them.

I got my first chance in the first month of the new season when Rangers came to Douglas Park. Souness had taken over in the summer and Rangers were grabbing all the headlines with the players they were buying. New signings Colin West, Chris Woods and Terry Butcher were playing as were guys like Ally McCoist, Ian Durrant and Derek Ferguson. It was great, a real buzz. My dad and sister were in the stand with their Rangers scarves on. I remember shoulder-charging Butcher down at the corner flag and it was like hitting a brick wall. He was solid and I just bounced off him.

Lambie knew you would be chasing shadows against the Old Firm but he was a great man for his work ethic. If you did a job for him to the best of your ability then he would be okay with you. It was a great education playing against Celtic and Rangers. You don't knowingly try harder but you probably do. Davie Cooper was immense and I could never under-stand why people criticised Paul McStay; he was streets ahead of everyone. Peter Weir of Aberdeen was also fantastic and he had me turning round in circles when I faced him, as did Ted McMinn although maybe for dif-ferent reasons. But I was never in awe of anyone I played against. I had a strong mindset, and I never felt inferior. However, after the game against Rangers, Lambie said to me, 'you were like a rabbit in the headlights'. Obviously I didn't think that was the case but he told me not to make the same mistake again and that I was a better player than that.

It was well known in Kirkie that I was a Rangers supporter and just after that game, I played for the Kirkintilloch Rangers supporters club against a Rangers supporters club from Hamilton in a Sunday-morning challenge match. One of the opposition players asked:

'Did you not play for Hamilton against Rangers the other week?'

'Yes, but don't tell anyone, I'm just helping out the boys,' I replied.

Can you imagine that happening now? Can you imagine what Billy Reid and the media would do if they found out, for example, that James

McArthur had played for Castlemilk Rangers supporters club in a bounce game?

In the lead up to the game against Rangers at Ibrox, there was a lot of snow so we were training in a school gym. Lambie was going through set plays and I wasn't involved. So I remember saying to my mates and my parents that I wouldn't be playing but being Rangers fans they were still going to go to the game.

I was sitting in the dressing room, not really paying much attention, but when Lambie named the team I thought I heard my name. I can't remember who was sitting next to me but I whispered to him, 'Am I playing?' When it was confirmed I got stripped quickly and was first out on to the park. The Rangers groundsman tried to stop me, for some unknown reason, but I shoved him aside and ran on. I was looking all around the stadium, playing with the ball in a wee world of my own.

Due to the heavy snow in Scotland that day, the Rangers–Accies game was one of the few still on so a lot of people that I knew who might not have been at the game, amateur players and the like, were all there to see me suffer my worst nightmare, which continued when I was taken to hospital. The guy in the next bed was reading the *Evening Times*.

'I'm reading about an Accies player who broke his leg at Ibrox,' he said.

When I told him it was me, he barely believed me – as if I would make it up.

As I lay there feeling sorry for myself, two patients were brought in by the police. Both were handcuffed to their beds at either end of the ward. It turned out that one was a chip-shop owner and the other was a guy who had tried to rob him. Apparently the chip-shop guy put his hand in the chip fat and threw it over the guy's face. He had burnt hands and the robber had a burnt face. They spent the whole time shouting at each other across the ward.

I was in hospital for a week after some complications arose and I lost a lot of weight. The Saturday after I got out was the famous – or infamous – Scottish Cup game at Ibrox, which Hamilton won 1–0. There weren't as many games televised live in those days so I sat on the couch at home and listened on the radio. I couldn't believe it when Adrian Sprott scored. I kept turning the radio on and off as the second half went on. I kept it on nearer the end and I thought, 'we are going to beat Rangers here'. At the final whistle I was gutted because I realised the enormity of what had happened. I would have been playing in Accies' most famous game if I hadn't been injured by a Rangers player. The sports programme cut to Ibrox after the final whistle and showed our guys coming off the park after the game and there was wee Davie Wilson with my sheepskin coat on again.

My rehab was long and boring. Lambie used to come and take me to the hospital when I was going for examinations and not many managers would do that. I was sitting in my car outside Douglas Park one day, ready to go in for some physiotherapy, when a big Granada drew up beside me. The guy got out of the car and asked me, 'How are you doing?' I told him that I had broken my leg playing against Rangers and he replied, 'I used to manage them.'

It was Jock Wallace, who was in to get treatment for tennis elbow. He had lost a lot of weight and I didn't recognise him at first. He then asked:

'Who was it that broke your leg?'

'Terry Butcher.'

'Are you a poof son?'

'What?' I replied, somewhat taken aback.

'Letting a big English bastard break your leg.'

I got back to fitness but fourteen months after my initial leg break I broke it again. We were playing Airdrie and my studs got caught in the ground as a guy called Colin Lindsay tackled me. I got up and then collapsed. I went to hospital and they confirmed I had a double leg break. You could have put the new X-ray over the old one.

After breaking my leg the second time Gerry Collins and Danny McGrain organised a benefit night for me. Tommy Burns and Jock Wallace came along to offer support. I had got to know Jock fairly well after spending many weeks side by side on the treatment table. He invited me over to his villa in Seville. It was an offer I never took up but it was very generous of him and it showed the kind of man he was.

Alongside me at the top table at my benefit night were Andy Cameron, who was very funny, Tony Higgins, who gave us some good football stories mostly about George Best when they were teammates at Hibs, Chick Young, who was just starting his after-dinner speaking gigs and John Lambie. The night went well, a little too well for the gaffer, who grabbed the microphone at the end of the evening and started to sing 'The Sash'. Everybody took it in good spirit but that was John Lambie for you.

I was advised to chuck football but I got my fitness back and signed for Stranraer, where I lasted only two months, then played for Arthurlie, Stenhousemuir and Camelon Juniors. I went back to play amateur football until I was about forty-one then coached the youths at St Johnstone until they got relegated from the SPL.

After that I was invited by George Adams to do some youth coaching at Fir Park. George took me into his office at Fir Park one day to talk about the under-14 side I was coaching. Terry Butcher came in to the office.

'Terry, I don't know if you know Bobby Barr,' George said.

Butcher stuck his hand out and immediately froze. He didn't know that I was a coach at Motherwell. I stood up shook his hand and said, 'Yes George, we've come across each other before' and sat down. We blethered away and talked about this and that for fifteen minutes but we never spoke about what happened at Ibrox.

Like I said I am not one to hold grudges but I am still disappointed that he didn't offer any words of apology for what happened.

But that day at Ibrox and my time at Accies now seem like another life. You get older and wiser and move on. I'm doing media work most Saturdays but I still get along to Rangers games whenever possible. My son Robert was voted third-division player-of-the-year by his fellow players when he was with Albion Rovers but he now turns out for Livingston and I watch him when I can.

I was promised tickets for the UEFA Cup final in Manchester but they never materialised. My wife and father-in-law are season-ticket holders and they got tickets. My wife, Robert and I travelled down and I bumped into loads of people I hadn't seen for long and weary.

As for the game itself the chance was lost and who knows if we will see Rangers getting to a European final again.

I Can't Envisage a Time When I Won't Want to Go to See Rangers

Elaine Sommerville

For some reason, people can't match my personality with me being a Rangers fan. At work I am fairly quiet and my colleagues can't imagine me being at a game. I have a Brian Laudrup mouse map and there have been times when people have noticed it for the first time and they ask:

'Do you go to any of the games?'

'Yes, I've been a season-ticket holder for more than thirty years,' I usually reply.

There is a tendency for men to think, 'She's a female so she doesn't know anything about football' but I've always loved the game. Even now, if I meet somebody I used to work with, they will say, 'Are you still following the Rangers?'

There are more women and girls at games now, of course, but even though things have changed I am not aware of any other female in my office who goes to football.

I honestly don't know where the interest came from. I grew up in Coatbridge with mum Netta, dad Jim and older sister Christine and I recall playing football in the street with the boys. Christine liked football as well although I don't remember her playing. My dad had been a Rangers fan and Jock 'Tiger' Shaw, who lived nearby, occasionally got him tickets. My mum even went along with him for a couple of seasons around 1949/50 but by the sixties he had stopped going to games. I remember my dad and his brother Alex having an argument about who was the best player, George Young or Willie Woodburn.

I think my mum thought I would grow out of it. But if I had the choice of what I wanted to do I would play football. I went to my first game in February 1971, when we beat Hearts 1–0 at Ibrox and the famous Tiny Wharton was the referee. I have kept the programme, which has a picture of Colin Stein in a Scotland strip on the front, and it makes for interesting reading. Coincidentally, it was another female fan who had won the £50 from the last home game against Falkirk for having a lucky programme. The programme advertises a two-week holiday in Majorca costing £53 and Ronnie McKinnon speaking at the supporters rally in the Greens Playhouse cinema. It cost twelve shillings for a seat in the centre stand, ten shillings for the wings.

At that point in the season, Rangers were third in the table with 27 points from 22 games, Aberdeen on top on with 40 points from 23 games, and Celtic 38 from 22 games. Willie Johnston was top scorer with fifteen goals, of which seven were penalties. My dad took me and my sister to the main stand that day and I couldn't believe the size of the stadium. After that we would get taken to the occasional game, my dad didn't want to go every week and I was too young to go myself. But I was hooked.

By the time I was fourteen, I was going to matches with my friend, Karen Craig, and my sister. When girls at school had David Cassidy or Donny Osmond badges, I had a home-made badge with Derek Johnstone's picture on it. He was my first real hero. In fact, in a funny way, it was through DJ that I met Karen. It was the time when the song 'Nice One Cyril' was top of the charts. It was blaring out of someone's radio in the playground and I heard her singing 'Nice One Derek' along to it. I asked her: 'Which Derek are you talking about?' and that is how we got talking.

But even away back then it used to annoy me when people thought I was just going to the football because I fancied the players. There were a few other girls at games but not that many, nothing like the amount you see these days.

My mum was always keen that we would get into Ibrox early and wait behind afterwards until the crowd had dispersed. In fact, in all the time that I went to Ibrox before it was modernised, I never stood on the terracing. That was the deal with my mother. I was allowed to go as long as I went to the enclosure because it was slightly less rough. We would always get inside the ground early and be hanging over the tunnel to see the players coming out.

I started going regularly in 1974 when Christine started work full time and no longer had her Saturday job. We would get the 'blue train' (as it was called) from Blairhill station to Queen Street low level. Then we would get the underground from Buchanan Street to Copland Road. Of course that was the season we won the league to stop Celtic making it ten in a row. I remember being at Somerset Park for a game against Ayr United and the tune of that song by Pilot, 'It's Magic', was being used for our chant of 'It's magic, you know, never be ten in a row.'

It was mostly standing in those days – and it still is for the most part at Somerset Park – and you would get guys rubbing up against you a bit too close, but I can't really say I got hassled. Men would occasionally apologise for swearing but you kind of accepted that's what happened at the football.

After games at Ibrox, we would be hanging around outside the main door to get autographs and players like Tom Forsyth, Tommy McLean, Sandy Jardine and Alex MacDonald would talk away to you on a regular basis. Derek Johnstone used to kid us on when we asked for his signature, saying 'this is autograph 3,629' or some such ridiculous number. He actually came to open our school fete one day. We were asked by a teacher to invite him, which we did when we were yet again waiting to get his autograph and he told us to write to the club. Scotland were playing Wales at the same time as the fete was taking place and we thought he might be picked but fortunately for us, and unfortunately for him, he wasn't, so he was able to come along. Rather bizarrely, one of the teachers drove to Renfrew with Karen and me in his car to pick Derek up at his house! It's a different world now.

I used to buy a variety of newspapers and magazines and would cut out everything that mentioned Rangers. I had a vast number of scrapbooks that I've only got rid of in the last couple of years. I also had so many copies of *Rangers News* that I had to store some of them at mum's house and my sister's house. Eventually I got rid of the majority of them, keeping special ones like the early issues and ones following league and cup wins.

We would go through to Ibrox during the summer holidays and would meet some of the players, mostly reserves, on the underground, guys like Gordon Boyd and Johnny Hamilton. Karen's favourite was a reserve player called Isaac Farrell who had a twin, John Farrell, who was also at Ibrox.

Somehow I don't think you would bump into many players on the underground these days.

In 1974 Christine had won a season ticket in a *Rangers News* competition and then the following season her, Karen and I got season tickets for the main stand, section M, nearer the Celtic end. You didn't have a specific seat with your season book in those days so we would go early and go down to the front. It was crazy during Old Firm games because the enclosure in front of us would be full of Celtic fans.

As we got older, my dad would drive us to away games then go to the bookies while we were at the match. He started attending again after we signed Davie Cooper in 1977, but Karen had stopped going by the time she got married to a Celtic fan. Then she began to go to Parkhead with her husband and nowadays she is a season-ticket holder. She must be one of the few people who have been a season-ticket holder at Ibrox and Parkhead. I still see her occasionally and she admits that she feels like she has had two lives.

Even when I started going out with guys, I continued going to Rangers games. I remember one bloke chatting me up in a Glasgow disco and trying to impress me by saying he played for Rangers reserves. He soon realised his mistake when I started asking him questions about other reserve players. It never crossed my mind that I would not go to the football. Christine moved down south for a while so she stopped going, which left my dad and I going together.

I got to know Davie Cooper through Billy Coffield, a guy who used to drive him around. I remember when Davie played for Clydebank against Rangers at Ibrox and while I was getting his autograph after the game, I asked him about joining Rangers. He said he would wait and see but admitted that he would love to be at Ibrox and I was delighted when he signed.

We would occasionally go to Hamilton after games for a drink with Davie and he came to my twenty-first birthday party in the Georgian hotel in Coatbridge, which, even though I knew him by then, felt a bit strange. One of the presents I received, from an ex-boyfriend, David Mitchell, was a share in the club costing £15.90. I've still got the receipt. They had a share issue years later when my one share became one hundred shares and I gifted Christine some so that she could also be a shareholder.

I remember sitting beside Davie at Dens Park, during the John Greig era, when he had been dropped. Davie said to me a few times that he hoped that he would last longer than Greig because he didn't want to leave Rangers. I will never forgive John Greig for the way he treated Davie when he was the best player we had. My dad was never a Greig fan either. People go on about how loyal he was to the club when Celtic were dominating in the 1960s and early 1970s but my dad thinks he was responsible for those hard times.

You can't turn back the clock but you wish that Graeme Souness was there when Davie was a few years younger; he might have got the best out of him for longer. But even during Greig's time I would think nothing of going to the games myself, up to Dundee or wherever. It was second nature.

When Christine came back to Scotland, we teamed up together again, with her taking over my dad's season book when he died. We had moved over to section J in the main stand – the other side of the halfway line, row H, seats 122 and 123 – and I have been there ever since. You see people around you growing up and growing older. I remember the guy in front of me bringing his wee boy and all of a sudden he has turned in to a young man.

Christine got involved with the Rangers Supporters Trust when it was formed in 2003. I am also a member but, initially, I thought there was a little bit too much negativity. There was some debate over why the training ground was called Murray Park. I thought that was insignificant and a bit anti-David Murray. Don't get me wrong, there are things that David Murray has done that I disagree with but I am more concerned with the football than the politics. Christine, on the other hand, seems to like the politics and enjoys being involved.

For all the years that I have been following Rangers, my first trip overseas to see them was in 2007, when I went to the Champions League game against Barcelona in the Nou Camp. I had always been a bit reluctant to go abroad for a football game but I had been saying for years that I was going to do it one day. I had paid a tenner to join the Rangers Travel Club about four years earlier but it was only when Barcelona came out of the hat that I succumbed and booked the organised package through Thomas Cook.

Christine wasn't a member of the Travel Club so she travelled independently and we met up over there. I was in the back row of the stadium, which everyone who has been there knows is a long way from the pitch, but the occasion was just what I expected. What I didn't expect was for Rangers to get to the UEFA Cup final that season and for me to get my ticket for Manchester guaranteed like everyone else in the Travel Club.

The downside was that Christine obviously didn't have the same luck as me so I felt I couldn't enjoy having the ticket. She wasn't sure about going to the final but I persuaded her to come down with me and Bill Campbell, a work colleague of mine. We couldn't find a place in Manchester to stay so we booked a hotel I had used before in Huddersfield. I was still feeling guilty on the day of the game when we got the train in to Manchester. We met up with some friends: Ian Hardie, Graeme and his brother Scott. Christine and I walked up to the ground in the hope that touts would be selling tickets but there was nothing happening so we went back into town. I could see that she was becoming emotional with the thought of not getting a ticket. There were a couple of touts around but they were asking around £1,000, which was just too much.

Graeme's pal was also looking for a ticket and there were phone calls being made here, there and everywhere. At one point he disappeared and came back with two, one of which was for Christine. I don't know how much she paid for it but, as you can imagine, she was very happy and we could both enjoy it.

The result, of course, wasn't the best but there have been plenty of great nights over the years. My favourite was probably the night when we won nine in a row at Tannadice, just for the historic significance, but it was pretty surreal when we won the league at Hibs in 2005.

I am also a huge Neil Diamond fan and because I couldn't get a ticket for Easter Road, I went down to Hull to see him in concert. There was a crowd of us in our hotel and we had arranged to have an early dinner before we went to see the concert. When I left my hotel room Celtic were beating Motherwell 1–0 and Rangers were drawing 0–0 with Hibs. I had my radio with me and was listening to it in the restaurant but even when Nacho Novo scored I still wasn't thinking anything of it. Then Motherwell equalised and it was madness. I was banging my head on the table and when they scored the second, minutes later, I was jumping about. Looking at me with some bemusement were two Americans, two Dutch people, a couple from Shropshire and a Hearts fan, who at least understood. I still get slagged by those Neil Diamond fans for that when we meet up but who cares?

I don't know how I have kept my enthusiasm up over these past thirty-plus years. I have come away from games thinking, 'that was so bad' but I wouldn't think of not going.

I can't envisage a time when I won't want to go to see Rangers.

Rangers: a View from the East

Ian S. Wood

People know me for my historical work on Loyalism in Northern Ireland. I have also intervened in controversies over Orangeism in Scotland to call for a balanced approach to the Order's role in society. Nevertheless I am a proud Hibs fan of long standing.

We surely all remember the first time we saw Rangers play, even those of us from outside the Ibrox stockade. For me it was a Saturday in September 1951 at a packed Easter Road and Rangers were there to take on my heroes, Hibernian, the Scottish champions. I had been to Easter Road before but I was a small boy with no father to take me to such a big game and it was thanks to my mother that I got there at all. She was not in fact on her own for – as David Ross has pointed out in his book *The Roar of the Crowd* – women were following the game well ahead of family-friendly, all-seater grounds. He indeed uses photographs to prove the point.[1]

We were there early, right up beside the players' tunnel in the old west enclosure, so close that I could smell the teams before I saw them because of the pungent blend of Brylcreem and body embrocation that many players then used. Rangers came up the tunnel first and George Young and Willie Woodburn passed so close to me that they looked like giants. That was what they were, of course, in comparison to most of the Hibernian side – giants and titans, the very core of a defence known to sports writers of the time as the 'Iron Curtain'.

Apart from Young and Woodburn there was also Jock 'Tiger' Shaw, whose defensive technique, if that is the word for it, could best be described as uncompromising. His task was to mark, or try to, Gordon Smith, the greatest winger ever to wear a Hibs or any other Scottish jersey. He was part of a back five, along with Sammy Cox and Ian McColl, who with

Young and Woodburn, gave away goals with miserly reluctance whether playing either for club or for country.

I cannot have been alone in my premonitions about our Famous Five forward line's ability to get past such physically formidable opponents but with their extrovert and cavalier skills they did, many times, though the result of a pulsating but cleanly contested game was a one-all draw. The incomparable Gordon Smith was the tormentor-in-chief of Rangers on this occasion as he was of every other club we played in this golden era. Earlier that year, on 10 February, his mesmerising ball skills had played their part in eliminating Rangers from the Scottish Cup at Ibrox. Billy Simpson gave Rangers an early lead but Smith glided through the Iron Curtain to play a neat one-two with Willie Ormond before driving the ball beyond the reach of Bobby Brown. For a long time afterwards I kept a press photo of the 'Gay Gordon', as he was often called, seemingly smiling to the cameras as he completed a move of elegant yet lethal simplicity.

Rangers answered this equaliser with a second goal from Simpson but with fifteen minutes left Eddie Turnbull found the net with a fierce shot from the edge of the penalty area. Turnbull recalls in his memoirs how Rangers' Sammy Cox, whom he knew well, jogged up to him to say that it was looking as if they would be seeing each other on the following Wednesday.[2] Hibernian's Bobby Johnstone averted that possibility by connecting to a Turnbull free kick and lobbing the ball over his shoulder and into the net past a disbelieving Rangers defence.

Many parents in 1951 would rightly have flinched from taking a child to a game like this one, let alone allowing one to go on his own, for 106,000 people filled Ibrox for it. This can only be a chilling thought in the light of what was to happen twenty years later in a stadium where catastrophe was waiting to happen on the deadly Stairway 13.

The vast assembly who saw this February 1951 epic at Ibrox was not the biggest to watch the two clubs playing each other. Back in the spring of 1948 over 142,000 fans went to Hampden for a Scottish Cup semi-final, a figure never equalled since for a club or for any other game in these islands. On that occasion a Willie Thornton goal saw Rangers through but Hibernian ended the season as Scottish champions.

Playing Rangers, especially at Ibrox, was and is still an intimidating experience for any team but Hibernian in the post-war era had no reason to fear them. We were Scottish champions three times between 1948 and 1952 after all and the first club from Britain to play competitive football on the Continent after the Second World War. Also at an astonishing benefit match – or testimonial as it would later have been called – for Gordon Smith on the Monday evening of 15 September 1952 it rained goals at Easter Road. The visitors were Manchester United but seven of the goals were scored by Hibernian as they destroyed a great side managed by Matt Busby.

Beating Rangers was thus something we could take in our stride without getting carried away by it. This was still evident after the great team of the early 1950s had broken up and at no time more so than in Jock Stein's all-too-brief spell as manager, which he began in March of 1964. Inheriting from his predecessor Walter Galbraith players of the quality of Jimmy O'Rourke, Peter Cormack, Neil Martin and that wayward and self-destructive genius Willie Hamilton, Stein created an effective and elegant squad of players worthy of those who had gone before them.

He reinforced the team in central defence with the acquisition from Celtic of John MacNamee, a physically very strong and also creative player. Rangers appear however to have been a club for which he had a strong antipathy and he was not averse to making it known to their players. It has been said that the late Tom or 'Tiny' Wharton prior to taking charge of a game overheard MacNamee in the players tunnel telling Jim Forrest of Rangers just what would be in store for him when play started. Wharton, with the heavy formality that was his trademark, took the culprit aside to say: 'Mr. MacNamee, you are in grave danger of being the first man in football history to be sent off before the game has started.'3

Beating Rangers that season 1964/65 was something of an anti-climax after Hibernian had seen off the great Real Madrid in a memorable friendly at Easter Road. We were the first British club to do this but then again this triumph came not so long after we had knocked Barcelona out of the Inter Cities Fair Cup, later the UEFA Cup, netting seven goals against them in two tempestuous games in the 1960/61 season, surely a feat not equalled by many clubs and certainly not by Rangers or Celtic. The team that outplayed Real were all there a few days later to face Rangers at Ibrox and they ran them ragged in a 4–2 victory in which Cormack scored twice. Some of the Rangers faithful were not best pleased at the outcome and, not for the last time, Hibernian fans had a hazardous trip after the final whistle to their buses, which were attacked with bricks and bottles.[4]

Beating Rangers became a habit that season. On Saturday, 30 January 1965, the day of Churchill's funeral, Rangers came to Easter Road hoping to avenge their 4–2 home defeat at home but it was not to be. Heavy snow and no under-soil heating had required the Easter Road ground staff to work hard to clear the pitch. Prior to the kick-off many of us must have been watching the solemn pageantry of Churchill's funeral and both teams wore black armbands. The minute's silence before the game began was largely observed but home and travelling supporters were still not rigidly segregated and one Rangers fan could be heard calling out that Churchill would have 'given Ulster to the Fenians'. It must have been the 1912–14 Home Rule crisis he had in mind as the secret 1940 talks with de Valera were still a secret to nearly all historians.

A predictably tense encounter went ahead on what now would be deemed a dangerously hard surface and once more Rangers were out-played for long spells though only one goal was scored by Neil Martin to secure the points for Hibernian.

A few weeks later Rangers were back at Easter Road for a Scottish cup tie. The occasion was notable for the return of Jim Baxter after having his leg broken at a game in Vienna the previous year. He was clearly not fully fit and showed only a little of the nonchalant brilliance with which he would humiliate England's World Cup winning team at Wembley a couple of years later. Once again Hibernian left the pitch to rapturous acclaim from a huge home support after a diving header from Hamilton two minutes from the end delivered a 2–1 victory.

Moving forward in time, it is worth recalling that in the year of Rangers' European Cup Winners Cup triumph of 1972, Hibs eliminated the Gers to reach both a Scottish Cup and League Cup Final, and inflicted a 3–0 trouncing in the new pre-season Dryburgh Cup. Successes over Rangers became rare in the decades that followed, though when they arrived – as in the Skol Cup semi final of 1991 – they were sweet indeed.

Happy days returned to Easter Road with Tony Mowbray. In August 2005 a sparkling group of players managed by him ran rings round Rangers at Ibrox. Derek Riordan, Scott Brown, Gary O'Connor and not least Ivan Sproule excelled on this occasion. Brought up as a Rangers supporter in Castlederg in County Tyrone, Sproule became an overnight Hibernian hero with the stylish three goals he scored, leaving the home crowd close to speechless.

There was more to follow when Rangers came to Easter Road on Sunday, 25 November of the same season. On that date Alex McLeish suffered what was surely one of his darkest days as Rangers manager. The kick-off was preceded by a fervent tribute from all round the ground to George Best, who had died two days before, and the Hibernian perform-ance which followed would have received his imprimatur, not just because he had once worn the club strip but because of its sheer exuberant and effervescent quality.

Eighteen minutes into the game Riordan scored a dazzling opener and laid on a second goal for Gary O'Connor seven minutes later. Rangers pulled one back in the second half thanks to Barry Ferguson but never looked remotely like equalising. Indeed they hardly troubled Zibi Malkowski in the Hibernian goal, which was no doubt just as well given the eccentricities of which he was capable. The result left Rangers eleven points adrift of Hibernian and it was their eighth successive game with-out a win. Alan Pattulo in *The Scotsman* claimed that this had never happened to Rangers before and that not since 1891 had they been unable to record a single victory in the month of November.[5]

Alex McLeish – who had departed from the manager's job at Easter Road in 2001 – had the good grace to compliment the home side. He went further, declaring to the media that Hibernian's first-half performance was the best he had seen in a season that had included a game against Inter Milan.[6] Worse however was in store for him and his squad when in the New Year of 2006 they were drawn against none other than Hibernian in the third round of the Scottish Cup at Ibrox. The tie was played on Sunday, 5 February and there was more magic from Sproule in a second 3–0 victory which left Rangers playing out time as their fans streamed in droves to the exits. Sadly this virtuoso display yielded no silverware, only a disastrous semi-final against Hearts.

Worse still, an exceptional team soon broke up thanks to the chronic imbalance in financial power between an over-mighty Old Firm and Scotland's other Premier League clubs. The vultures were already hovering and before long five of the victors in that game would be wearing Celtic and Rangers strips or in Derek Riordan's case mostly a tracksuit in the Celtic dugout.

Thus far the casual reader might be forgiven for thinking that this chapter has simply been a catalogue of famous Hibernian victories over Rangers. Indeed it has been but it would be idle to deny that there have been defeats too. These, when they happen, are reverses which we must rise above, like any club's supporters. Is it though the case that for us there is a unique relish to be found in victory over Rangers? Were this so it would merely serve to bear out the familiar taunts from Rangers supporters that we are nothing more than Celtic fans without the cash for train or bus tickets to Parkhead.

Maybe some of them should slip incognito into the east terracing at Easter Road to hear the reception Celtic get when they play Hibernian. They might just begin to reconsider their view of our club. Some of us old enough could tell them that some of the worst violence at any Easter Road game was in 1968 after what seemed to me a reckless tackle from Celtic's John Hughes on Bobby Duncan.

I am referring here not just to the violence of a tackle that put Duncan on a stretcher in obvious agony and ended his career with Hibernian but to the fighting that broke out at once among still unsegregated supporters. It was a foul infinitely worse than Graeme Souness's late lunge that gashed George McCluskey's thigh in 1986. Then the resulting mayhem was confined to the field of play, in contrast to what happened in the 1968 Celtic game.

Yes, Hibernian is a club as Catholic and Irish as Celtic in its origins, in fact more so. It is also older than they are. Many of us at Easter Road with a sense of history still think of Celtic as late arrivals on the scene who, jealous of Hibernian's success, sought to lure away for cash some of our best players. As a result our club came as close to extinction as it did at the time of Mercer's takeover attempt.

If, as Alan Lugton claims in his book, *The Making of Hibernian*, it was some of our supporters who carried out the nocturnal removal of the symbolic square of Donegal turf laid in 1892 by Michael Davitt at the opening of the new Parkhead stadium then a kind of justice was done. It certainly was if the turf really did finish up at Easter Road after a sojourn at St Patrick's church in the Cowgate.[7]

We also think of Celtic as a club many of whose adherents, as well as the contributors to the *Celtic Minded* books, enjoy wallowing in the warm bath of victimhood long after the Irish community has achieved a high level of well-earned assimilation within Scottish society. Hibernian shed that baggage long ago and the religion of its managers and the players they signed never needed to be front-page news. Neither were war chants and songs in support of the Provisional IRA ever roared out at Easter Road the way they were at Parkhead. The day that started, had it done so, would have been the day many would have left Easter Road for good.

There is of course the James Connolly connection, which no doubt many Rangers fans suspect, while Celtic supporters deride us for not making more of it. Connolly does seem to have been an early well-wisher and possibly a kit boy with the club before he enlisted in the Royal Scots. It is an important link for the club and Connolly was a brave and tenacious man. He also hated sectarianism though whether he ever really understood the mind of Protestant Ulster remains very doubtful.

What he did not deserve was for even a few Hibernian supporters to dishonour the club by joining the Connolly Society's now abandoned marches in Edinburgh, supposedly to mark the anniversary of his birth in the city. These events – held for a number of years prior to and after the 1994 ceasefires in Northern Ireland – struck me as nothing other than hate-fuelled celebrations of the Provo-Fascist murder machine and about as welcome to the capital's population as the sight of a turd in a swimming pool.

The heavy predominance of Celtic strips on these occasions was a reminder to us at Easter Road of both what we are and what we have never wanted to be part of. The latter has to include what in my eyes are the paranoia and the suffocating, politically correct, self-righteousness of the *Celtic Minded* books compiled by Joseph Bradley.

So, when Rangers fans get off their buses to walk down Easter Road and feel aggrieved at not being offered afternoon tea, they should ponder the fact that we want to win not because we see Hibernian as some sort of Parkhead reserve force but because we are as proud of our club as Rangers supporters are of theirs. A prominent sign on the west stand looking out on Albion Road proclaims our ground as 'the home of the Hibernian family'. It is an extended family we are all happy to be part of and like every family it has its celebrations. Ours, if and when we beat Rangers, are no more or less fervent than when we beat Celtic or that other alien force from the nearer west, Heart of Midlothian.

Even the notorious Hibs casuals of the 1980s and early 1990s did not regard Rangers fans as their prime target. It might appear so from one or two episodes vividly recreated by Irvine Welsh in *Trainspotting* and elsewhere in his work. In reality some of the casuals' bloodiest encounters were with Aberdeen gangs. That wave appears to have passed. Some ageing ex-casuals have inevitably reinvented themselves as writers and others are no doubt studying for sociology degrees. At the moment Rangers fans traversing Easter Road on match days may not be admitted to many pubs but nothing more lethal will be thrown at them than pies and empty beer cans.

'Pride without prejudice' has been an admirable slogan that has featured in recent initiatives at Ibrox to try to deal with raw and aggressive sectarianism among a still vocal element of the club's support. It was tolerated and excused for too long just as Celtic have too often been portrayed by their numerous sympathisers among our intelligentsia as victims of sectarianism rather than as part of the problem.

This is why over in the east the Old Firm phenomenon is quite often seen as a relationship between two sectarian Siamese twins who have for too long lived lucratively off each other. Edinburgh of course is not Glasgow, even if John Cormack's Protestant Action party achieved some real electoral support here in the 1930s. Yet even then sectarianism in the capital did not infiltrate local football to the point where Hibernian versus Hearts games became a major public-order problem.[8]

This is why the UEFA report early in 2003, which identified the rivalry between the two clubs as sectarian, was such nonsense. It is true that Edinburgh's original football leagues were reluctant to accept a new club as overtly Irish and Catholic as Hibernian. The founders however had the wit to see that, with the city's Catholic population so much smaller than Glasgow's, the club had to broaden its appeal. The success with which it did this is history. None of the Famous Five were Catholics and nobody cared either.

UEFA in its report and on its website misrepresented the origin and evolution of the two Edinburgh clubs. Of Hearts it declared that support for them was 'a badge of honour for the capital's Protestant community'.

Two *Scotsman* contributors – one of them, Simon Pia, a noted Hibernian supporter – took apart this farrago of misinformation. Hearts, they stressed, have always been a non-denominational club, even if for a time in recent years a vocal element among its support have taken to a borrowed Ibrox song repertoire as well as displaying Union and Ulster Loyalist regalia.[9]

The Hearts owners somewhat belated response was to mount a campaign against them. Flags at what came to be called 'bigots corner' at the school end of the old enclosure were confiscated by stewards and some season-ticket holders were banned from Tynecastle.

Proof that there was still work to be done came on Sunday, 10 April 2005 when Hearts were to play Celtic in a Scottish Cup semi-final at Hampden. Pope John Paul II had died a few days before and the SFA decided that at all Scottish games there would be a pre-match minute of silence in tribute to him. At Hampden the referee curtailed this tribute because of the very audible jeers and whistles from a vocal element of the Hearts support. The club chief executive, Phil Anderton, was quick to condemn them and to apologise but what had happened was reported around the world.[10]

Whether the culprits acted as they did simply to provoke Celtic supporters, given that there had been one or two violent clashes between them at previous games or whether they were making a crude statement about Hearts' identity must remain problematic. Whatever some Gorgie knuckle-draggers may want to believe Edinburgh's great football divide has not historically been a sectarian one. Indeed it has to be very doubtful whether back in the early 1980s Bill Murray could have written a book on Edinburgh football reaching even half the length of his scholarly exploration of the Old Firm's long-running rivalry.

Possibly some huge, number-crunching survey of Edinburgh fans might illuminate the reasons for club loyalties distributing themselves the way they do. Personally, I would doubt the value of such an exercise. For me settling for Hibernian at a young age had nothing to do with being a Catholic but everything to do with the glorious football that seemed continuously on offer at Easter Road.

I actually lived nearer Tynecastle and I admit going to the odd game there but Easter Road was much more of an adventure and the raucous and raffish atmosphere there attracted me as it has continued to do. The douce men of Tynecastle with their pipes, belted raincoats and discreetly worn maroon scarves seemed to me an obviously lesser breed. I still recall a friend telling me that at one Edinburgh derby he was in the Tynecastle enclosure when Hearts scored and that an irate Hibs fan beside him had turned to the applauding Hearts fans in the stand above him to shout 'Awa hame to your bungalows.'

So, supporting Hibernian was a decision made long ago and one I have never regretted even if the club's relative underperformance in recent years and still, at the time of writing in the Scottish Cup, helps to define the element of unrequited love in the supporters' relationship with the club. For what other reason is the Proclaimers' lovely song 'Sunshine on Leith' now the club anthem?

That said, we have seen great days too, not least the victories over Rangers with which I began this chapter. I will spare a Rangers readership any repetition of these but there is one other game involving them at Easter Road so memorable that it demands a mention here to make this chapter complete. This was a midweek fixture on 12 October 1988 at which it was known that Mark Walters would be in the Rangers line-up.

As a black player he had already been, since Graeme Souness's bold decision to sign him, the target of sustained and vile racist abuse at Parkhead every time he got so much as a touch at the ball. Orchestrated jungle grunts and bunches of bananas dogged his footsteps every time he took a corner or a throw-in within reach of the Celtic support. To their enduring credit a group of Hibernian fans involved in producing the excellent *Proclaimer* fanzine decided to act in order to stop this gross conduct being imitated by fellow supporters.

The trouble was that elsewhere it already had. As a *Proclaimer* spokesman, Steve Tolmie, told the press: 'When we played Dundee United at Tannadice a few weeks ago some of our so-called supporters spent the ninety minutes abusing United's only black player, Raphael Meade.'[11]

Tolmie made clear what he had in mind: 'We're determined,' he told a reporter, 'to do what we can to stamp on the racists at Easter Road before things get out of hand.'[12]

Pathetically, the club gave no official backing to this initiative. On the day of the game David Duff – then effectively the owner of the club – had other priorities, namely putting his name to a fraudulent offer to supporters to buy into a share flotation. Many of us had smelt a rat when we saw one and Duff and one of his main financial backers in due course went to prison.

On the evening of the game thousands of leaflets were ready for distribution at all the home-supporters entrances to the ground and maybe some found their way into the hands of Rangers fans. The leaflet still merits quotation even twenty years on: 'Are you a real Hibernian supporter?' was the question on one side and on the other the point was put that 'Pele was one of the greatest players in the world. He was black. Would he have been booed and abused at Easter Road?' The club's history was invoked and the pledge given that 'We, the supporters, must make sure that it remains free of the racist stain.' A tough and uncompromising game went ahead but the result is still less important than the fact that there was no repetition of what had happened at Parkhead.

As it turned out Walters was not really a player we were ever going to love at Easter Road, any more than we did the constantly disputatious Neil Lennon. At least Hibernian with its Irish immigrant origins was not shamed by any rerun of what had happened at Parkhead and elsewhere. Perhaps there's a debt there owed us from Ibrox that we can call in one day. Meanwhile at our 'dear green place' at Easter Road we follow with keen interest all reports of Celtic and Rangers seeking to move into the English Premiership. We would of course wish them well in that can of worms. Some of us of course would support a more ambitious relocation plan, perhaps to the Falkland Islands or Patagonia, where they could form their very own two-club league. Failing these outcomes Rangers supporters will just have to be ready for more unpredictable encounters with Scottish football's sleeping giant.

Notes

1   D. Ross, *The Roar of the Crowd: Following Scottish Football Down the Years* (Argyll Publishing, 2005), pp. 58 and 82.

2   E. Turnbull, with Martin Hannan, *Having a Ball* (Mainstream, 2006), pp. 113–14.

3   T. Brack, *There is a Bonny Fitba Team: Fifty Years on the Hibee Highway* (Black and White Publishing, 2009), p. 40.

4   Ibid. p. 47.
5   *Scotsman*, 28 November 2005.
6   Ibid.
7   A. Lugton, *The Making of Hibernian* (John Donald, 1995), p. 195.
8   T. Gallagher, *Edinburgh Divided: John Cormack and No Popery in 1930s Edinburgh* (Polygon, 1987), pp. 116–17.
9   *Scotsman*, 23 April 2005.
10 Ibid. 11 April 2005.
11 Ibid. 12 October 1988.
12 Ibid.

LEGENDS AND FORGOTTEN HISTORY

It Was All About Standards

Campbell Ogilvie

My time working at Ibrox spanned three decades and during that time I worked with some of the biggest and most powerful characters, and over-saw some of the dramatic changes and developments in the club's history. Rangers played a huge part in my life. It was Mr Waddell who brought me to Ibrox from the Scottish Football League in 1978, although my links to the club go back much, much further.

I was steeped in the history of the club. I was brought up a Rangers fan from my early days when we lived in Jordanhill. My dad, Alasdair, was the reserve-team doctor for about forty years so in the 1960s I was always about Ibrox. George Brown was a midfielder who played for Rangers in the 1930s, and I knew him as uncle George. He gave me a cup winner's medal before he died. My boyhood heroes were John Greig, Ralph Brand, Billy Ritchie and Davie Wilson.

I went to lots of reserve games obviously, but the first first-team game I saw was against Dundee at Ibrox on 11 November 1961 and we lost 5–1. Years later a Dundee director gave me the programme from that game and I put it up on the wall at Ibrox. People would look at it and ask me why and I would make the point that it was easy to support Rangers when they were winning.

I spent my early years at Ibrox working under Willie Waddell, who had a reputation as being ferocious. Around May 1970, I had been working for only about two weeks as an assistant clerk for the Scottish Football League when I had my first experience of him. There was a dispute between Rangers and Celtic and there was nobody else in the office when Willie Waddell came on. He didn't know me from Adam but he was shouting down the phone at me. Ten minutes later Jock Stein was on doing the same thing. As time went on I got to know both men very well but it was Mr Waddell who took me to Ibrox in May 1978. I thought he was asking me over for SFL business. He had a light outside the manager's room, which showed red and green. He forgot that I was outside waiting to come in and so I sat there for about forty minutes looking at the red light. When I went in he offered me the job as assistant secretary to Frank King. I accepted there and then. I left the room and realised I hadn't even discussed the salary. I was getting married and I didn't even discuss it with my wife-to-be Kara, which was just as bad.

I became secretary in the summer of 1979 and my role grew and developed from there. Willie Waddell was a strong character. People would look up to him and I always had the greatest respect for him. Rae Simpson, a surgeon, was the chairman then and he was a gentleman. But Mr Waddell, the managing director, was the main voice at Rangers. I always say Mr Waddell; I would never call him Willie. It was the same with Rae Simpson. He would say, 'Just call me Rae' but I couldn't. It was all about standards.

I wouldn't say there was a fear of Mr Waddell because he was fair. However, if you made a mistake he came down on you like a ton of bricks. I was involved in the television deals during his time and there was one European game for which we had negotiated a fee of £60,000, a lot of money in those days. But twenty minutes before kick-off the signal went down and so we lost the money. It was due to a strike in London and we obviously had no influence over that. I was in the manager's room explaining this to him but I got it in the neck because, in his eyes, I had lost the club £60,000. Kara was in the Blue Room next door at the time and when we were coming downstairs afterwards she said:

'There was someone who was getting it in the manager's room a wee while ago.'

'Yes, that was me,' I replied.

But to be fair, if you did something wrong in the morning it would be forgotten about in the afternoon. I worked very closely with him and he was really good to me. He taught me a lot and started pushing a lot of the day-to-day stuff on to me. He would discuss things and you were allowed to have a point of view. Willie Thornton was assistant to Willie Waddell and he was quieter. Other former players, like Jock Shaw and Bob McPhail, were often around the place, which was great for me.

There weren't many backroom staff at the club in the 1970s. There was Frank King, myself, Laura the secretary, one telephonist, two ticket staff and four generations of one family, the Loves, who worked in the kitchen. In fact, it was very much like a family and certainly not run like you would see a football club run now. Some people say it is too businesslike these days but things happened over the years that meant that the game had to be run more professionally. I was at the Ibrox disaster as a fan and I count myself lucky. I used to leave by the Rangers end but for some reason that day we walked round and left by the Celtic end. I heard the sirens but we didn't know what had happened. That was a defining moment for the club.

After that, and by the time I was working at Ibrox, Willie Waddell took the decision to redevelop the ground. He and Tom Miller from Miller Partnership worked together on the project, with the refurbishment modelled on Borussia Dortmund's Westfalenstadion. It was a great learning curve for me. I certainly wasn't qualified at that time – nor now – but I was involved in the site meetings and you learn as you go along. We had this new 44,000-capacity stadium but of course we didn't do particularly well on the pitch at that time. Our average attendance was around 19,000 and we were getting all the jokes about building the new stands the wrong way.

The riot after the 1980 Old Firm Scottish Cup final at Hampden was another turning point for Scottish football. I remember sitting in the directors box at Hampden with a sinking feeling. I was watching it but not taking it in. It was horrific. There was legislation brought in banning alcohol from games and I was right behind it. People wouldn't even go to the toilet in those days, and relieved themselves as they stood on the terracing. There is a push from commercial departments to bring back alcohol to the concourses of stadium but not from me. I have reservations about that. There are hospitality suites now where you can get drink, but it is controlled. Fans accept the rules now and drunks are minimal, where before it was often the norm. Fans would smuggle drink in under their flared trousers. After one Old Firm game we got the police in after a package was left behind; it looked like a transistor radio with elastic bands on it. Given the times, we were obviously wary. But we noticed that there was a straw coming out if it – inside was a quarter-bottle.

I had been accustomed to facing the fans at the annual general meetings (AGMs), although I never enjoyed them because you never knew what was coming. Back in the 1960s they had them in the home dressing room because there was such a small number of shareholders and they would move very quickly up to the Blue Room and have a few drinks. An increasing amount of shareholders meant bigger premises were needed. My first AGM was the season after we had won the 1978 treble. It was around November and we had the three trophies at the front of the stage – and we got booed on! That highlighted the fickleness of some fans.

One year we had the AGM in the Broomloan Road stand and the wind was blowing papers away and then the speaker system broke down and I had to stand up at the front and start shouting to allow myself to be heard. People would complain about everything, from the birds messing the seats to the pies to major issues but to be fair it was the only opportunity the supporters had to air their grievances and some good things did come out of them. After one AGM in the McLellan galleries someone asked why we didn't have a club shop. Initially there was a wee shop inside the social club. Someone said they knew of an old property in Copland Road, a newsagent or greengrocer, and so on the afternoon of the AGM, Willie Waddell and I went down to have a look. It became the first Rangers shop.

But that ad-hoc way of working became a thing of the past in the mid-eighties when David Holmes arrived at Ibrox. We were taken aside and told that Holmes and Freddy Fletcher, from the John Lawrence organisation, were being brought in at the behest of Lawrence Marlborough, with David becoming chairman. Holmes started to shape the way the club would go in the future. Mr Waddell was a director when Holmes came in and he had handed over some of his day-to-day roles.

It wasn't a bloodless revolution. Some of the directors who had been there for a while lost their seats on the board. A totally new structure was put in place. It all changed, it moved to a different level. As a club we weren't moving forward but we quickly became more commercial in our outlook. Willie Waddell had brought in trackside advertising, kit sponsors and leasing offices but we didn't really have a proper commercial department. Hospitality was minimal; we had one suite, the Thornton suite, although that worked very well. David Holmes was very good to work with, he helped me; he had the business acumen. He and Freddy Fletcher were very proactive and they quickly increased the revenues from our commercial operation.

Marlborough had given Holmes the remit to sort out the club on and off the field. I knew about Graeme Souness becoming player-manager a good number of weeks before it was announced. Holmes said to me, 'There are going to be exciting times at this club – guess who the new manager is going to be?' I grew up in a doctor's house so there was no problem keeping a secret. That was invaluable during my time at Ibrox. There was a sense of excitement around Ibrox at that time. It had been flat and Graeme lifted it. Every player up until then had been on the same money and it was low. We had lost John McClelland to Watford because he wanted a basic wage of £240 per week and Rangers wouldn't break the pay structure.

The first thing Graeme did when he came in was abolish that wage structure. The Heysel disaster in 1985 had led to English clubs being banned from Europe and in consequence we were able to attract some of the top players from down south. Ian Redford had been a record signing for £220,000 but that was blown out of the water in pre-season when England captain Terry Butcher came in for £725,000, two months after England keeper Chris Woods had arrived for £600,000. It was a sign of things to come and the Butcher signing reverberated well beyond Scotland. David Holmes was invited to a small dinner party at Hopetoun House, at which Prince Charles was to be a guest. David couldn't make it and asked me to go in his place. I did the paperwork in a London airport for Terry's transfer and I had to fly back up for the dinner. When I was introduced to Prince Charles he said to me, 'I heard you signed Terry Butcher today.'

David Murray was quizzing me before he took over, asking me about this aspect of the club and that aspect of the club. I remember the night he bought the club, a Tuesday. I met the Murray lawyers, who took me aside and said that he was taking over tonight. It was as simple and as quick as that. When Murray came in it was a wee bit awkward because David Holmes was still there. It was difficult for me and I got caught up in it. I would get one instruction from David Murray and one from David Holmes and I am sure that David Holmes got upset with me at times. It was a difficult transition and I felt bad when Holmes left.

I had moved from Willie Waddell's time to David Murray's time. Murray came from a business background whereas Willie Waddell had come in from the football side of things but they were the key players in their own eras. Things evolve in football and over the years my role had changed. When Willie Waddell was there I would get involved more in the commercial side, then when David Holmes came in with Freddy Fletcher, I backed off from that. Then, in 1989, after David Murray had been in place a couple of years, I began my involvement with the SFA.

Discretion was still a key part of my responsibility. I knew that Maurice Johnston was signing for Rangers long before it happened. Celtic paraded him in May before the Old Firm Scottish Cup final and I later heard there was a possibility of him coming to Ibrox. The day that he signed, I became a director of the club. I remember looking out the window at Ibrox that day and there were a lot of people around and one guy was burning his scarf. I joked that he did that because I had been made a director!

That signing changed the club and took it forward although there was some bad feeling at the time. Some fans said they wouldn't be back and stayed away but there were a lot more who stayed and others who started to come to games. And as everyone remembers, Johnston scored a last-minute winner against Celtic at Ibrox. There was a photograph taken with the east enclosure in the background. That is where the diehard fans congregated in those days and every face was one of celebration.

I have a lot of friends who are Celtic fans. We just went our different ways on the day of the Old Firm game. So I was delighted that we changed the signing policy. Rangers had come out with a statement of intent in the 1970s (after the riot in a friendly at Aston Villa) but it hadn't changed until Maurice signed. That's the way it was. I suppose I should have questioned it but Rangers were, and still are, an institution.

I was directly involved in the signing of Johnston. We had to meet Maurice and his agent Bill McMurdo at the Royal Scot hotel in Glasgow Road, Edinburgh. It was all very cloak-and-dagger. We arranged for the two cars to park side by side and then they were to get into the back of our car. Maurice had a skip hat and glasses on in case he was spotted. Just before they switched over to our car, a British Rail lorry came into the car park and the workers got their sandwiches out. If they could only have seen what was happening that day, but we managed to get Bill and Maurice in to the car, then back in to their own car and off they went.

It took brave men to make that decision and Graeme Souness, Maurice and the chairman were brave men. I believed Graeme when he said he would sign anyone because he was such a strong character, as I would repeatedly discover during his tenure. He famously narrowed the Ibrox pitch before the second leg of a European Cup tie against Dynamo Kiev, when we were trailing 1-0 from the first game. Graeme never told anyone he was bringing the lines in, apart from the groundsman. I found out before the game but by that time it had been done. The night before Dynamo had trained at Ibrox and they kept pinging the ball to their wide players. Graeme obviously had someone watching this so he decided to reduce the width of the pitch. Halfway through the first half, as I'm sitting in the director's box, the Dynamo general manager, Oshemkov, waved his finger to me as if to say 'you are at it here'. Rangers won the game 2-0 and he demanded a pitch measurement. We went down to the pitch an hour after the game, when all the cameras had left. I tried to pick up the measuring tape but Oshemkov wouldn't let me near it. So he and the UEFA delegate measured it.

I was standing at the side of the pitch and I could hear some fans singing on their way home. I was worried, thinking: 'Is it the correct width?' and 'What if the groundsman's tape had a knot in it?' I feared that it could go from one of the best nights in the club's history to one of the worst. Thankfully, it was just the correct width and I went home and had a few drinks. We were at Falkirk a few weeks later and what did they do? They narrowed the pitch. They changed the laws after that and from then on you had to keep the dimensions of your pitch the same all season.

Graeme brought in a different approach to eating. In Jock Wallace's day it was all hamburgers and chips but Graeme introduced pastas and such like to the players' diet and there was a totally different outlook. But one day I was on the platform of Copland Road station, as it was called then, and a player came down the stairs eating a bag of chips – and asked me if I wanted one. Some took longer to adapt than others.

David Murray was keen to have representation on the SFA, which is why I got involved. David had business acumen and sitting on SFA committees wasn't high on his agenda. He had been used to making decisions for himself but it didn't work like that in football and he soon realised that you had to take people with you. I believed it was important for a club like Rangers to be represented at the SFA.

Some Hearts fans think the SFA are against them now but it became second nature to become involved in controversy when Graeme was at Ibrox. It started right from the first game, against Hibs at Easter Road, when there were twenty-one players booked (some retrospectively) after he got sent off for a challenge on George McCluskey. Hibs keeper Alan Rough was the only one not involved. There were a few dust-ups and I was up and down to Park Gardens – where the SFA had their headquarters before moving to Hampden – all the time.

I did my best to keep Graeme on a tight rein and was forever telling him, 'You can't do this or you can't do that.' I'm sure he saw the governing body as a nuisance. I felt in the latter part of Graeme's time that he had become exasperated and fed-up. I don't think the infamous bust-up with Aggie at St Johnstone helped and it may have affected his decision to leave.

After David Murray's takeover, board meetings became a lot less frequent. You had the statutory number but it wasn't even as regular as once a month. When I started at Ibrox, board meetings were every Tuesday at 3 p.m. and the ones that were the worst were the ones that didn't have a set agenda. They became talking shops and it could be nine o'clock before I got out of Ibrox. But David made all the decisions and it was easy for me to work that way. He would let me get on with my job and other people, like the financial director, would report to him. We wouldn't see David apart from on a match day or if you went through to Edinburgh to see him.

David Murray would get on to me and say 'you're not hard enough' but I am what I am. I'm not aggressive; I'm a great believer in working with people. I have always tried to work through things, I have not gone head-on and maybe he thought I should have been more of a hard-nosed businessman. But you can't change yourself, you are what you are. I wasn't a known face; only once did someone have a swing at me in a pub. I was more in the background.

There was a seamless transition when Graeme left and Walter took over. There was great team spirit in Walter's side, with a lot of Scottish players. The nine-in-a-row years were great, with characters like McCoist and Durrant and then of course Gazza came in. He was probably the biggest character at Ibrox in my time there. He was another signing that we had known about for weeks beforehand. Gazza was involved in a lot of things. I was in the boardroom at Celtic Park that day when he came in for a swift half before the game with his strip on. I had been warned but I didn't believe he would do it; more fool me, of course. But Bob McPhail told me later that players in his time would do the same.

If we had a home game on the Saturday, I would go into Ibrox about nine and Walter and I would have a run round the track. Gazza would be there, walking about with a leather bag full of tricks, false eyes and all that stuff. He was great with children. Gazza took dollars with him to Bucharest and after the game he kept the bus waiting because he was upstairs giving the money away to kids.

The transition from Walter to Dick was also smooth and my regret from my time there was not qualifying for Europe after Christmas regularly. We would be training on Jordanhill cricket ground. We built a new stadium and spent a lot of money on players, and it was embarrassing telling them that we didn't have a training centre like clubs in England and on the Continent. But to be fair, clubs on the Continent didn't own their own grounds; we did and money went into that. Where the argument fell down was in England, where they owned both. When Graeme looked at sites and companies realised it was Rangers that were interested, prices rocketed. So Murray Park was one of the best things to happen to the club.

Working for Rangers, at one time, had been all-encompassing. One day my wife had arrived home and discovered that our flat had been burgled but she wouldn't phone me because I was in a board meeting. I was mad at her. It was the same when my oldest daughter was born. We were playing a Glasgow Cup final against Celtic and she went in to labour but wouldn't phone until afterwards. I got married the day after we played Chesterfield on the Monday and I had to miss the rehearsal. I missed five games in twenty-seven years home and away, and that was only because I was away on Rangers business.

But latterly the structure changed. I was aware that bits and pieces had been taken off me. I was more involved with the SFA, SPL and UEFA. I was doing less and less on a day-to-day basis and I wasn't enjoying it. It was obvious that there wasn't a future for me. My time had come and it was time to move on. I could have continued in a lesser role but the last thing I would do is hang on to someone's coat tails just to be there. We came to an agreement that I would stay on as a consultant for a fixed period but that lasted about a week. After years of coming in at nine on the day of the game, here I was in the boardroom at quarter to two. I said to myself: 'What are you doing here?' I couldn't go down to the police-control room or anything. These things weren't in my remit so I decided to call it a day.

I left in 2005, a year after my dad died. I don't know how he would have felt. He worked there for forty years and didn't get paid. My girls, Kayleigh and Faith, had grown up at Ibrox so it was hard but there is no point in hanging on. I would never say a bad word against Rangers. As I said, I have no axe to grind and my only regret is that in all the years I was there, we only got past Christmas, two or three times, in Europe.

I'm heavily involved with the SFA and Hearts but you can't work in a place for twenty-seven years and it not have an effect on your life. I found it difficult going back to Ibrox with Hearts the first time. But it is like a player or a manager going back, you have to give it your all and I want Hearts to beat Rangers. People don't believe me but you've got to be like that.

My wife and I still keep in touch with a lot of people at Ibrox, and I still go out with them. I didn't socialise with David Murray when I was there but we get on fine. I've been at Hearts for four years, it's a good club and has a lot of good people associated with it.

I worked with seven managers at Rangers, and I worked with Scot Symon when he was at Thistle and I was at the SFL. I know Davie White from way back so I've known nine Rangers managers and not many people can say that.

'Jock Wallace Here Son. How Would You Like to Come to Rangers as My Assistant?'

Alex Totten

Big Jock Wallace would say to me, 'Alex, if you cut me I would bleed blue blood.' He was a big Rangers man. There was only one team for him.

When we travelled to away games – irrespective of whether it was Rugby Park, Dens Park or Pittodrie – when we were half a mile from the stadium, he would say to Stan the bus driver, 'Right Stan, put the tape on,' and 'Follow Follow' would come through the speakers. Big Jock would shout 'up louder Stan,' and all the boys would be singing away.

He was larger than life but he was also open to everybody and treated everyone the same, the young guys and the first-team players. People often get the wrong impression of Jock. He was a hard man, a fitness fanatic and as we all know we would go to Gullane for pre-season training. The players would shit themselves if they met Jock in the corridor. He would punch them in the stomach and ask: 'How are those stomach muscles coming on?'

But he loved to play good football, loved the good things about the game and he was good with tactics. He didn't get credit for his football knowledge. People thought he was just a big, hard man, but he won ten trophies and you need more than fitness for that. Like me, he loved wingers and we always played with wide men but you don't get that any more.

He treated me like a son and you couldn't help but like him. He told me why he left Ibrox to go to Leicester but I have never divulged it and I never will. But he was a Rangers man through and through and he went back in a minute when he was given the opportunity.

When he asked me to join him as assistant, it was unexpected. I was about thirty-seven at the time and had no connections with Rangers. As a wee boy I used to go and see Falkirk but occasionally my dad would take me to see Rangers; he was a Rangers man. I can remember teams like Niven, Shearer, Caldow, Greig, McKinnon, Baxter, Henderson, McMillan, Miller, Brand and Wilson.

But I barely knew Jock Wallace. When I was manager of Falkirk the first time, Jock was boss of Motherwell and I was looking to buy a player called Bruce Clelland from them. I called big Jock and he told me to come through to Fir Park to see him. I was only ten minutes in his company and the transfer didn't materialise. So I thought that was that.

But on 11 November 1983, at eight in the morning, the phone rang. My wife answered it and said 'it's for you'.

'Jock Wallace here son. How would you like to come to Rangers as my assistant? I'm going to Aberdeen tomorrow for my first game. Keep it quiet and I will phone you on Monday.'

On the Saturday I went to the Dutch Inn with the Falkirk players before our game against Clyde and who comes up on the big screen, on the *Saint and Greavsie* show, but big Jock. I was thinking to myself, 'I'll be with him next week and nobody knows it.'

But after our game I was told that the Motherwell chairman wanted to speak to me. So I met him at a hotel, where he made me a great offer.

'Alex, we've had so many managers, between Jock Wallace, Davie Hay, Roger Hynd and Ally MacLeod. We want continuity so we will offer you a five-year contract if you take the job.'

It was a brilliant contract but I told him I would have to call him on the Wednesday. I did, but only to thank him sincerely and to turn it down.

I had been manager at Alloa and Falkirk and could have been my own man at Motherwell but I couldn't turn Rangers down. Falkirk obviously got compensation for me and when I travelled through to Ibrox on my first day, Stan, the commissioner, told me Mr Wallace was waiting for me upstairs. I went up the famous marble staircase with a combination of joy, pride and trepidation. I walked past the portrait of Alan Morton, the wee Blue Devil, and went in to the office. Big Jock said, 'Great to see you son, come in and meet the directors.' Willie Waddell, Rae Simpson and John Paton were there. It was a fabulous moment.

A lot of people didn't like Deedle (Willie Waddell) but I got on well with him. I always take people as I find them and he gave me respect. He was still a big character at the club, although he wasn't the chairman. I met the players – guys like Davie McPherson, Davie Cooper and Ally McCoist – before the home game against Dundee United on the Saturday. Jock wanted me to go out on the pitch with him before kick-off to take the acclaim of the crowd and they were going daft. We drew 0–0 but then we went about twenty games or more with just one defeat and we beat Celtic in the League Cup final with McCoist getting a hat-trick. So it wasn't a bad start.

We then went on a tour of America, New Zealand and Canada at the end of the season. It was great, everyone wanted to meet you. There were so many expats who would come and see us, people who had not been home for twenty or thirty years. Every night there was a function on. I would even run into people who I played with before I had gone in to coaching.

But Jock believed strongly in getting out to meet the Rangers fans. We went to a lot of supporters' functions, especially at the end of the season. Once we were in this tough area of Glasgow and when we arrived the fans were noisy and Jock bellowed, 'quiet!' and it went quiet. After a few seconds of silence, with people wondering what he was going to say next, Jock started singing, 'Though the straits be broad or narrow, it's follow we will.' The punters were up on the tables singing along, it was absolutely brilliant. The fans loved him. Everybody took to him. He was good company.

I had to find out why he wanted me to join him. We were in Switzerland for pre-season and we had had a really good drink so I asked him, 'come on gaffer, why did you come in for me?' He replied: 'That ten-minute chat was enough.' Obviously he made enquiries but he said, 'I could have gone for other people but I went for you,' which of course gave me a fantastic boost.

He had a lot of faith in me and after working with him for a while he told me he was tutoring me for his job. He said that he was stepping up to general manager and I would take over as team manager. John Paton became chairman and about six months later he said the very same thing in a newspaper article.

It was a difficult time for Rangers. There were a great bunch of boys and there was a good team spirit but Jock was frustrated by the lack of cash. The boys that were there were good players but he wanted to improve, as all clubs have to do. He always treated the boys to the best and his attitude was, 'if we can afford it we will do it'. But he was curtailed by the money.

We didn't have the money to improve but money was no object when Graeme Souness came in. Good luck to him. Obviously he changed Scottish football but it should have been the same for us. We should have had the best. Aberdeen were *the* team then and they were offering more than us. How could an Aberdeen player get a bigger basic than a Rangers player? When I went to Ibrox there were four internationals on the playing staff: John McClelland, Jimmy Nicholl, Robert Prytz and Davie Cooper. When I left there was only one: Cooper. The rest had left because of money. Everyone was on the same wage, a basic of £300 per week.

When Souness came it changed completely. Big Jock spent about £600,000 in three years and Souness spent £16 million. I went looking for players that I knew from the first division, like Kevin McAllister, Alan McInally, Bobby Connor and Bobby Williamson. He sent Willie Thornton to see Bobby and we paid £100,000 to Clydebank for him. When I was at Alloa I had signed Stuart Munro so I told Jock that he could do a job for us. He took me along to see Alloa at Douglas Park and Munro was the best man on the park. Jock said, 'go and offer your former chairman £15,000'. He was at Rangers for six years – and all for £15,000.

Craig Levein, John Brown and Gordon Durie were on our radar but we were turned down for one reason or another. When we were in Australia, big Jock got word that John Brown had signed for Dundee and he was raging. Both Brown and Durie turned up at Ibrox later and did a great job for Rangers.

It seemed to me that John McClelland was always looking for money. We went to Canada and were invited to a Rangers supporters club and he stood up and he was moaning and groaning about money. Big Jock was raging. He wanted to keep it in-house, not tell all the supporters in Canada about our problems. We played Inter Milan in the UEFA Cup and Graham Taylor came up from Watford for the return game at Ibrox and signed him after the game. My God, the thought of a Rangers captain leaving to go to Watford, but he was getting more money so he was away.

Of course, good players stayed with us, players who would go on to become legends at the club although I wouldn't have bet on a certain Ally McCoist achieving that status the day we were beaten 1–0 by Dundee at Ibrox in the Scottish Cup. All the chances fell to Ally but it was one of those days when he just couldn't score. The fans started singing 'Ally, Ally get to fuck'. He came off the park with tears streaming down his face. I will never forget that although obviously he won them over in the end. He was so upset but I knew he would recover. He had a tremendous personality and was full of confidence and of course the rest was history.

We played Chelsea at Stamford Bridge in a benefit game for the Bradford disaster. After twenty minutes their manager, John Hollins, shouted over to our dugout:

'Who is your number seven?'

'Ian Durrant,' I replied.

He's brilliant,' Hollins said and Durrant was brilliant in his prime.

Big Jock often predicted that someone would get the benefit of our work and that is exactly what happened. Robert Fleck, Derek Ferguson and Durrant all went on to play for Souness. Those three stood out. I loved Durrant. He wanted to start moves and also to finish them. It was a shame what happened to him.

I don't know if there were boardroom influences with regards the issue of religion. Colin Stein took the under-14s and Jock and I were sitting in his office when he came to the door. He said to Jock:

'I've got a player for you but there is a wee problem. The mother is a Catholic and his dad is a Protestant – or vice versa. I can't remember and I wasn't interested.'

Jock asked, 'Is he good enough?' and Colin replied 'yes', so we signed him. It was John Spencer.

Jock had no problems with it; he had no hesitation and John Spencer was a good player for Rangers. And as far as I'm concerned, as long as they can play football, irrespective of what religion they are, or what colour they are, I would sign them. Money was more of a problem than religion.

When David Holmes took over that was the end for Jock and me. Jock said to me, 'I don't think he likes me' and, of course, soon afterwards Souness came in. I was in the boot room when I got a phone call from David to go and meet Souness. When we shook hands he looked away from me, which I thought was really ignorant. I introduced him to the players. He said a few words and went back to Italy.

I looked after the team for a week. Then John Haggerty, Stan Anderson and I were called up to David Holmes's office, where our contracts were terminated. I had no problems with that, I had done the same thing myself when I had taken over as boss but, David, whom I knew from Falkirk, said, 'I'm sorry Alex.'

It is galling to think that we spent so little on players and Souness paid out so much. It wasn't as if David Murray was there at the time. So how did the club find the money? Terry Butcher told me he had no intentions of going to Rangers, he was going to Tottenham. But he met Souness and told him: 'If I'm going to come to Scotland I want this, that and this' and Souness said, 'okay.' Big Peter McCloy was the goalkeeping coach and he once told me, 'Alex, if you want it, you get it – if you don't want it, you still get it!' It was incredible, the money that was available.

I have no regrets. I enjoyed my time at Ibrox. Being the Rangers manager would have been fantastic and I would have liked to have managed in England at some stage in my career. But I am involved with Falkirk as business-development manager and that's great.

I went to see Jock after he moved to Fuengirola; he thought the heat would help him with his illness. He seemed in good form then. Later, when I was manager at Kilmarnock, he said to me: 'You know, I think the sun shines out of your arse, don't you?'

I've never forgotten that. That was the last time I spoke to him.

The Ultimate High:
Captaining Rangers to a Cup-Final Win at Hampden

Craig Paterson

It wasn't really a case of me wanting to leave Hibs in the summer of 1982 to join Rangers. I didn't have a choice. In those days the club owned you. You were just a piece of meat to be traded. There were no agents and it was a matter of waiting for clubs to decide what your future was and that was the way it worked with my transfer to Ibrox.

The first time I got wind of a possible move was when John MacDonald asked me at a Scotland under-21 gathering if I would fancy playing for Rangers. John was such a piss taker that I didn't know whether to believe him or not. He later admitted that he had been sounding me out but I just wasn't sure at the time.

Speculation had been building and during pre-season I got a call from Hibs saying that they had done a deal with Rangers and their manager at the time, John Greig, would be in touch. I spoke to Greig on the phone and he was an impressive character. There were no wage negotiations. I was told, 'this is what Rangers pay' and to be fair it was double what I was on at Hibs. I moved from £120 a week to £240, a big difference, and I also got £5,000 as a signing-on fee for each year of my three-year contract. I flew out to Lille to meet my new teammates a couple of days after signing at Ibrox.

I don't know what would have happened if I had said I didn't want to go to Rangers. The thought never crossed my mind. Rangers had offered around £225,000 for me and Hibs could not afford to turn it down. It was as simple as that. I certainly wasn't looking to move. I had a year left on my contract at Hibs and was playing every week. Although I was a Scotland under-21 player, I was still a novice. On top of that I was steeped in Hibs. Rangers were just a big team from Glasgow that Hibs found hard to beat.

My dad, John, was part of the Hibs Famous Five side of the 1950s; he was one of the not-so-famous six. He had also been a centre half like me and is still in the top ten when it comes to appearances for the club. My dad played in two championship-winning teams and I think he was the only ever-present in those two seasons. But as a youngster that meant nothing to me. I didn't realise how famous that side was but, as it transpired, I was known as the son of Hibs legend John Paterson for my entire spell at Easter Road.

I would go along to games with my dad and with Famous Five players like Lawrie Reilly and people would be asking them for autographs. I was puzzled. I knew my dad's pals were nice lads but I didn't know why people were asking for their autographs. I eventually found out of course but when I started watching Hibs regularly it was the teams from the 1970s of Herriot, Brownlie, Schaedler, Blackley, Black, Stanton, Edwards, O'Rourke, Cropley, Gordon and Duncan.

I wanted to become an Easter Road player like them, rather than emulating Reilly, Smith, Johnstone, Ormond or Turnbull, although ironically, Ned – as I would never call him to his face – was the manager when I signed for Hibs.

I had a chance to go to Rangers when I was fifteen but my dad didn't want me to get buses and trains from our home in Penicuik to Ibrox. I didn't really want to do that either but I wanted to tell my mates in school so I went in the huff and didn't speak to him for a fortnight. The weirdest thing about it was that someone from Rangers asked my dad about his background. He had played football for Dalkeith St David's, a Catholic school, because they didn't have enough players and his school, Penicuik High, didn't have a team. I'm not sure if that was a thorough background check but at that point I didn't know what it was all about.

I played a trial for Jim McLean at Dundee United and he wanted me to go to back to Tannadice for a week so they could have a better look at me but I had just started work and couldn't get time off. Then I got a phone call from Easter Road. I played two reserve games for Hibs, signed a professional contract then broke my ankle playing against Ayr United on the following Saturday. Such is football.

My dad was really proud when I signed for Hibs. He could see that Jim McLean had something but he knew that Eddie Turnbull, a friend of his, was also a good coach. But he was also pleased when I moved to Rangers. He knew that I was moving to a big club and that it was a good career move.

Strangely enough, I don't know who my dad followed as a boy but my granddad was a Rangers fan and so were some of my uncles. He had often played against Willie Waddell and Willie Thornton and would ask me: 'How's Deedle and Bustle getting on?' Waddell – a former Rangers manager – and Thornton were both Rangers greats, and they were always around the club. They sat at the front of the Rangers team bus going to games and they, in return, would ask me how my dad was keeping. Another legendary Ibrox figure, Willie Woodburn, would occasionally meet my dad for coffee in Edinburgh.

It took ten minutes to settle in at Ibrox. Players are players all over the world and I knew John MacDonald and Jim Bett from the Scotland under-21s. There was always talk of Greig struggling with the move from the dressing room up the marble staircase but when I got to Ibrox, Alex Miller and Peter McCloy were really the only ones who had played alongside him.

I had been signed to replace big Tam Forsyth, who had retired, and Colin Jackson, who had moved on. John McClelland had had a great World Cup in Spain with Northern Ireland that summer and the idea was for me to play with him in the centre of defence. As fate would have it, my first competitive game for Rangers was at Easter Road. I got merciless stick, as I knew I would, with the Hibs fans singing 'What's it like to be a Hun?' throughout the 1–1 draw.

I don't suppose Ibrox was a happy place at that time. Aside from the traditional battle for honours with Celtic, Aberdeen and Dundee United both had the best teams and best managers in their history. Aberdeen, under Alex Ferguson, had already won the league to break the Old Firm's monopoly, and, in addition to winning their fair share of domestic trophies, they would go on to win the European Cup Winners Cup. Jim McLean's United would soon win their first SPL title and would feature in a European Cup semi-final, so it was a purple patch for both those clubs.

That was hard for Rangers fans to take because they wanted and demanded success.

There was pressure on you at Ibrox. Whether it was a European tie or a domestic game, you were expected to win. But to be honest the expectancy didn't bother me at first. It was later on in my Rangers career, as I battled with a frustrating ankle injury, that I felt under pressure. I once read that I had been sold to Rangers with the injury but that is bullshit. I hadn't missed a game for Hibs the previous season and the one before that the only game I missed was when I was away with the Scotland under-21 team. You are not talking about a third-division club. Rangers gave me a proper medical before I signed so that rumour is nonsense.

I picked up the ankle injury after about six games, against Cologne at Ibrox in October 1982, and I feel shattered when I look back on it because you think about what might have been if I had got it sorted properly and quickly rather than trying to patch it up. The injury came in innocuous circumstances. I knocked the ball back to Jim Stewart and one of their players came down on my ankle. They brought a stretcher on but I thought, 'I'm not getting on that, it will make me look weak in front of the Rangers support.' So I hobbled off. It was a stupid thing to do.

Nothing showed up on the X-ray, which was strange because the pain was still there although it would come and go. The League Cup final against Celtic came along soon afterwards and I took a jag before the game and another one at half-time and on the Saturday night. I felt pain that I had never felt in my life because of the damage I had done. But my thought process was: 'I have to get out there and play,' because I was a big-money signing. Jim Bett cost more but my transfer fee was a record between two Scottish clubs and you want to justify that to yourself and to your new club. So I felt under pressure from myself.

What I didn't realise, but what I was about to learn, was that if you pull a jersey on you declare yourself fit and you will be judged as a fully fit player. Don't ask for sympathy or leeway when you are getting stick because you are not doing well enough.

Cortisone was the cure-all in those days and I don't know how many injections I took. Players or clubs would not do that now. I can't blame anyone, that was what you did but even then I only played twenty league games that season. When you look someone in the eye, and they want you to take a jag and play, my question is: 'What would he do in my situation?' And when you looked John Greig in the eye you knew he would be out there with his sleeves rolled up doing what he could for the team. With some other managers or coaches you would think: 'In this situation, you would be up in the stand' but you couldn't point the finger at Greig. That is why I would volunteer to take the jags but neither he nor I realised I was doing more damage.

Don't get me wrong, bonus money was also important, it could double your wages. In my entire career, I never played for a club where the basic wage was enough. You had to be playing and winning to make a living. I could earn around £500 a week if Rangers won, so it made a difference.

But the good start I had made at Ibrox – scoring in pre-season friendlies and then against Airdrie – had gone down the toilet because I was playing with an injury. It was so frustrating. I could train all week without a problem and then on the Friday it would go again. You wouldn't want to tell anyone in case they thought you were at it so you would take more jags. I imagine Greig was beginning to wonder: 'What is going on with this lad? He was flying in training on Thursday, and I come in on Friday and he's hobbling in the warm up.' The problem wasn't just physical, it became destructive mentally.

This went on for a couple of years until I eventually got an operation in my third season. The specialist told me that they knew something was wrong but they didn't know what. The last resort was to open up the joint and when they did that, they discovered that a loose piece of bone was rubbing inside the ankle joint, which was causing the pain. Sometimes it would move and I would feel okay but then it would move again and I would be in agony. That's why I was starting to lose the plot. They put the bit of bone in a jar to take away with me.

From my point of view, the end of John Greig's tenure and that of his successor, Jock Wallace, were similar. I was sitting there doing fuck-all to help, which was soul-destroying because they were men who I would have loved to have seen go on for years and years.

When the going got tough, you wanted to be out there doing your bit to help but in reality I wasn't pulling my weight. I was sitting in the main stand in a plaster cast or whatever. I felt I was on the outside looking in.

I hadn't met Jock Wallace before he took over from Greigy but one of the first things he did was to tell me to get my injury sorted, which I duly did. There was more to Wallace than the battle. He liked his footballers and we had a fair few good players in that side. I tend to put Davie

Cooper and Bobby Russell together in that respect. I have never seen two guys who were so in tune with each other. It was telepathic at times and a treat to watch. Most people know about Coops but Russell was also an excellent player. He would take the ball from you with his back to goal and he had some sort of radar because he would know what was going on behind and around him without being able to see. John McClelland was a fine defender, very hard to beat, and we had other good players like Derek Johnstone, John MacDonald and Jim Bett.

There seemed to be more of a bond between fans and players then. Players earned more than most fans but maybe only double, whereas nowadays the differential is colossal. Modern-day players have country estates whereas in the 1980s you would live next door to supporters.

There was a rota drawn up for players to go to supporters' functions and no club was overlooked. From the oldest to the newest, the biggest to the smallest, both Greig and Wallace made sure the fans got two or three hours of your time. It was a small price to pay, you were always well treated and it was good fun. I remember one night my wife sold raffle tickets to help with club funds – I'm not sure you would get that nowadays.

When I went to Rangers I knew by then that they didn't play Catholics. You sang the songs at the supporters' clubs – there were no camera phones in those days! If the songs that they were singing at the club meant something to them then so be it, it was doing nobody any harm. But from the players' point of view, it made no difference and I wasn't interested in the Protestant/Catholic thing. I can honestly say I never played in an Old Firm game when I was called an Orange bastard and I would never have called Celtic players the other stuff.

I had a few good patches of form in between injury but, frustratingly, those spells did not last long enough. However, it was during one good spell in 1984 that Jock Wallace made me captain. He didn't ask me to be captain; he summoned me up the stairs and told me I was to be his captain. That was Jock. If he had asked me to wash his car when I went in to his office I would have done it.

I thought immediately of the captains who had gone before me. I was joining a list that included players like Greig, Bobby Shearer and George Young. It was a huge honour but if Jock Wallace thought I was up to the job then that was good enough for me.

My elevation to captain had come as a result of a dispute between the club and John McClelland, who was looking for a signing-on fee to sign a new contract. John was still in the team but because the row had spilled over in to the papers, there was to be a change of skipper. I don't know how much John was asking for to re-sign but that wasn't Rangers' policy and they probably didn't want to set a precedent. Nowadays it's every man for himself but if the club had succumbed to John's demands, it would have led to other players asking for the same.

The clear mistake that big John made, as far as I was concerned, was after I had captained the side to the League Cup-final win over Dundee United at Hampden. John passed the cup on without lifting it up to the fans. I thought: 'No, your gripe is with the club, not the fans, you don't do that to them' and one or two people picked up on that.

John was good about losing the armband to me and there was no problem between us. He never changed in the dressing room, he was a bubbly character and his form never altered. He was just standing up for what he thought was right. It was unfortunate because we did well at the beginning of the 1984/85 season. I had taken over as captain and we had won the League Cup against Dundee United in October. When John was sold, we sustained a couple of injuries and suspensions and it went flat very quickly. We finished fourth in the table that season, behind Aberdeen, Celtic and Dundee United.

It came to an end for me at Ibrox the following season when Graeme Souness arrived and brought in England skipper Terry Butcher. I just kept my head down in the reserves and helped the younger boys, the way older players had helped me. Big Slim McPherson was injured one week and I got in beside Butcher and enjoyed it. He was terrific, a super player, and we beat Hearts 3–0 at Ibrox. At Easter Road the following week I played again in a goalless draw and I felt good but the following week Rangers signed Graham Roberts. The writing was on the wall for me but I have to say that I had no problems with Souness.

He also had no problems with me staying. He knew my attitude was good but that I wanted to play first-team football. Once you've played regular first-team football, turning out for the reserves is soul-destroying. Motherwell came in for me and to be fair to Graeme, he made sure Rangers took less from them than they might have just to make sure I got a signing-on fee to make up the difference in wages at Fir Park, which were being halved.

Even though I hadn't been brought up in the Rangers tradition, the club does something to you. I've always thought of football as a job, with highs and lows. To me, there's never been any more to it than that. But I remember walking out of Ibrox for the last time carrying my boots and there was a sinking feeling in the pit of my stomach. I knew I would be back there playing, but that was the last time I would be Craig Paterson of Rangers.

I went on to win the Scottish Cup with Motherwell, which was great, and then moved to Kilmarnock where I helped bring them back to the Premier League, where they have been ever since. I had followed in my father's footsteps at Hibs and I couldn't have been prouder.

But as a one-off event, captaining Rangers to a cup-final win at Hampden eclipses all that. I had been up the Hampden steps the season before as a loser and when we had beaten our biggest rivals in a final, but being the first person up there after beating Dundee United was something else.

There is the wonderful couple of seconds after they hand you the cup when you can decide how you lift it. I don't know if it is a power thing but you know that there is nothing that can go wrong. You know that when you lift that trophy above your head, the thousands upon thousands of fans who are in the stadium will go bonkers. They did and it remains a great memory. I wish I could do it again. If anybody is ever thinking about taking drugs, then I would say to them to go and achieve something, whether it's at your work or hobby or pastime because there is nothing like it. It is the ultimate high.

The downside was that I then proceeded to give one of the craziest interviews of my career on the pitch to Dougie Donnelly, who roasts me about it any time I see him. I don't even remember what Dougie asked me but I blurted out, 'If the bears want trophies then the bears had better get trophies.' The point I was trying to make was that if they didn't then I wouldn't be doing the job for long but I didn't get to say that. I've had nothing but stick for it ever since. Even now, when I go in to the pub in Penicuik somebody will repeat those words to me.

However, something so inconsequential could never devalue those great Hampden memories. I had never known a buzz like it. I still feel affection for Rangers and I still like them to beat Celtic to the title.

But I would also like Hibs to win the Scottish Cup again one day – 1902 and waiting.

'Daddy, Did You Kill a Man?'

Terence Murray

'Daddy, did you kill a man?'

That question was a dagger in Sam English's heart. It was asked by his daughter Eleanor, then just five years old. The little girl had been approached by a stranger in the park, where she had been playing with her two older sisters. It was now 1937, six years since the death of John Thomson in that fateful Old Firm encounter, but still English's tormentors would not leave him in peace. They were remorseless, unforgiving, heartless. He heard them only too clearly on the field of play. 'Watch the killer, watch the keeper,' the crowd would bellow when his team had a corner kick. When he clashed with a player an opponent would run alongside him and drip poison into his ear: 'That will be another man you have killed.' Now they had targeted his little girl.

How could anyone stoop so low?

In his own little community of Dalmuir he found nothing but kindness after Thomson's demise. They saw him as one of their own and held him close; his neighbours, Protestant and Catholic, rallied round. The wider world was different. The poison-pen letters flooded in, forcing him constantly to relive that afternoon at Ibrox. When he was in Glasgow he pulled his cap tight over his face, afraid to look anyone in the eye in case they stared back and didn't stop staring. On holiday in Fife, Thomson's home county, he overheard men saying, 'That's the laddie that killed Johnny Tamson.'

For the rest of his life Sam English asked himself one question. Why me? He was not one of the game's hard men, relying instead on guile, skill and speed. Nor was he a football fanatic, as some players were. Despite his undoubted feelings for Rangers football was a way of making money, of providing for a young family. There was no question of a grudge against

Celtic in general or John Thomson in particular. That game at Ibrox was his first Old Firm experience and he had never met or spoken to Thomson.

While some Celtic fans offered him only sympathy he was pilloried when he played at Celtic Park. The first game Rangers played there after the tragedy might have ended in a riot had it not been for the prompt action of his captain Davie Meiklejohn, who asked the referee to intervene. Abuse from crowds Sam English could take but what he found harder to accept was the attitude of Celtic manager Willie Maley. Maley, an unprincipled man, cast vile slurs on his character, inflaming an already volatile situation.

His father, steeped in the tribal loyalties of Ulster and the Glasgow shipyards, had seen it coming. 'Get out of football, go to America. You will never be allowed to forget it,' he told his son. He was right but Sam English played on, and played to a standard that does him great credit, until he could take no more.

So much has been said and written about John Thomson, and rightly so. He was a great player and a true gentleman. But there were two victims that day and Sam English was also a great player and a true gentleman, something that has often been overlooked. After 5 September 1931 he found what it was like to live 'less as a person than one half of an accident'.

It is time to remember the person.

*

The facts of Sam English's career in football can be found in any number of sources. But they do not tell us how he felt about the hand he was dealt, the agonies he suffered, the persecution he endured. So we are fortunate that eventually he did choose to bare his soul, more than three decades after the event that changed his life. It was not an easy decision to make but at the age of fifty-four he felt compelled to put the record straight. He had been silent for too long and in consequence, as he puts it, 'the Sam English story has been twisted into a kind of hideous folk tale. One generation has warped it and passed it onto the next.' So, in early 1963, English poured his heart out in the pages of the *Scottish Daily Express*, then the most influential newspaper in the land. The *Express* knew there would be huge interest in his story and gave it a considerable amount of space, spreading the serialisation over five days ('The Sam English Story', *Scottish Daily Express*, 27 February–5 March 1963). It is an invaluable supplement to what others have written about him and a significant part of this essay is based on those remarkable interviews.

*

Sam English was an Ulsterman, born in 1908, in a farm cottage in the hamlet of Crevolea (sometimes Crivolea) on the outskirts of the village of Aghadowey, itself close to the large town of Coleraine in County Londonderry. He was one of eleven children, of whom six were boys and five were girls. No doubt finding it hard to make a living on the land his father uprooted the family and headed to Glasgow, then one of the greatest industrial cities in the world. English senior found work as a storeman in John Brown's, one of the many shipyards on the banks of the river Clyde and the family settled in Dalmuir, in the town of Clydebank. Like most of their neighbours the Englishes struggled to make ends meet. As Sam recalls there wasn't enough money to buy him and his brothers a proper football or 'bladder'. They made do with tin cans, stones or, when their finances could stretch to it, a 'tanner ba'. Undaunted he and his brother Dick played football constantly, no matter the weather.

> Even on the rainiest days we were off with it up to the Somerville Park. Often just the two of us. On cold, damp grass we chased and trapped and punted through endless wet afternoons. And in the evenings our mother often had to call us up from the dirt yard beside the house, still practising.

It was perhaps just as well the young Sam was so dedicated to football, for he was no scholar. His teacher, a Miss Mitchell, used to tell him that all his brains were in his feet. There were other promising players at school, particularly Neil Dewar, whom his classmates nicknamed Silver-sleeves because he never had a handkerchief or, alternatively, Cleeks, because of his hen toes. He and Sam, united by their exceptional talent, became firm friends. Despite being an occasional figure of fun Cleeks Dewar, a wonderfully skilful player, would like his classmate make it in the professional game. After school, as is often the way, the two friends lost touch. But a decade later Cleeks would come back into Sam's life just when he needed him most.

After he left school Sam English's life was to an even greater extent ruled by football. His first job was as a grocer's boy but he gave that up because it interfered with Saturday-afternoon football. He went to work at Beardmore's shipyard as a plater's boy, a yard he chose for the very simple reason that it had, as he explains, 'a great team at the time, Dalmuir Albion'. Beardmore's was a soccer hothouse and every lunchtime there would be three games going in the yard, helping the young apprentice to hone his skills. English was signed by Junior side Old Kilpatrick, and received the princely sum of one shilling per game, before moving onto a new club, Port Glasgow, where, surprisingly in view of what was to follow, he was given a free transfer after just one season.

Disillusioned he thought about giving up football and concentrating on his new job as a sheet-metal worker at his father's yard, John Brown's. He also loved the bright lights, and by his own admission was more 'interested in going dancing every night' than in the hard slog of training. All that changed when officials from Yoker Athletic appeared at his door one Sunday afternoon. They were keen to sign him and were not put off by an admonition from his father, who informed his visitors that his son enjoyed a rather hectic social life: 'This boy will be no good to you. He's never home any night before midnight.' Sam signed a contract, was paid a £3 signing-on fee and £2 a game, of which there were sometimes three in a week. It was good money. The average weekly wage for a journeyman at the time was less than £3.

Three great years followed. The Junior game was thriving, with big crowds and a high standard of player. Yoker's main rivals were Clydebank Juniors and games between the two clubs often attracted gates in excess of ten thousand. In the estimation of Sam English the standard of play in the Juniors was 'the highest ever reached in Scotland and better even than Continental teams today' [that is, in 1963]. He may have been looking at the past through rose-tinted spectacles but there is no doubt that he was a sensation in this grade of football. In three seasons with Yoker he averaged around one hundred goals per season and not surprisingly became one of the most sought-after players in Scotland.

Scouts from senior teams flocked to watch this goal machine and one would have signed him but for a dispute between the SFA and the Junior game, which meant among other things that transfers between the two jurisdictions were banned. Despite this the big clubs courted English assiduously. They reasoned that one day the ban on transfers would be lifted and they would be able to get their hands on the young Ulsterman with dynamite in his boots. The managers did more than just keep a weather eye on Sam English. They filled his pockets with gold. Long before the terms 'tapping up' and 'bung' were coined the leading British managers were well practised in both.

Willie McCartney, manager of Hearts, was a regular visitor to Yoker, slipping Sam a few pounds with a request that the Ulsterman should 'remember me when the time comes'. Other managers did the same: Paddy Travers of Aberdeen, Jack Tinn of Portsmouth ('spats and all'), Willie Orr of Leicester City; all of them and more besides came to court the young striker nicknamed Blondie due to his unruly thatch of flaxen hair. But there was one manager who did more than the rest to keep Sam English sweet.

His name was Bill Struth.

The legendary Struth, who brought unparalleled success to Rangers in the inter-war years, wasn't about to let another club steal a march on him when the player he was after not only supported Rangers but also plied his trade just a couple of miles from Ibrox. No doubt worried about Rangers being implicated in making under-the-counter payments Struth was careful to cover his tracks. For two seasons Sam English received four pound notes in an envelope at his place of work. The money might have been handed over at John Brown's shipyard but the real paymaster was Rangers Football Club.

Sam English felt not a shred of guilt in accepting this money. As he writes in the *Express* articles.

> Their tips plus my shipyard wages meant a lot of money coming into a house where nearly all the others were unemployed. I always played football for money. For I know what it means to be short of money. I know what it meant for my mother to be short of it.

By the summer of 1931 the rift between the two jurisdictions in Scotland had been healed. Sam English was now free to join a senior club. Rangers were strong favourites for his signature but the move was almost hijacked at the last minute by the biggest team in the land. Herbert Chapman was the most successful manager England had ever known. He had won three league titles in a row with lowly Huddersfield Town in the early 1920s before being tempted to Highbury where he would enjoy huge success, turning Arsenal into the establishment club, a team so aristocratic that the Royal Family is said to support it.

So it was that after Yoker's last game of the season Sam English had two invitations. One to meet Chapman. The other to go to Ibrox for signing talks with Bill Struth.

Yoker stood to make a lot more money from the transfer if their star centre forward chose to move to England. So when the ninety minutes had come and gone, and the crowd had dispersed, Sam English was smuggled out of the little ground and sent in a taxi to St Enoch's hotel in Glasgow city centre, before Rangers could get their hands on him. Herbert Chapman was recovering from a cartilage operation and received his young visitor in his bedroom, got up as English recalls 'in his dressing gown'.

'I have never seen you play. But everyone else seems to want you. So I might as well join the queue,' the great man informed him.

The Arsenal supremo was nothing if not persuasive. He told English that he would do better for himself in London than anywhere else, that opportunities there were unequalled. He boasted about the many audacious transfers Arsenal had been involved in, including the 1928 purchase of David Jack from Bolton Wanderers for £10,340, which not only broke the world record but also doubled the previous highest fee. Chapman promised to better any offers Rangers made and, when the man from Yoker was still not convinced, 'virtually offered me,' as English vividly remembers, 'a blank cheque to go to Highbury'. For this young man the streets of London were indeed paved with gold, a tempting prospect for someone who had just got married. But he left the St Enoch hotel that night without signing for Arsenal, despite the riches on offer. His heart lay elsewhere.

At Ibrox Park.

It was after midnight when Sam English climbed that famous marble staircase and walked into Bill Struth's office. English recalls that Struth was brisk and businesslike during their meeting. The Rangers boss told him that he was good enough to go straight into the top team at Rangers, the first Junior in history to do so. The money was not to be sneezed at either, even if it was less than Arsenal were offering. His basic wage would be £12 per week – about six times what a tradesman earned – with bonuses on top. There was another incentive: a massive signing-on payment of £600, which Struth handed to him in crisp new banknotes. At long last he was a Ranger.

It was a huge step up from Yoker to Rangers, notwithstanding his incredible haul of goals in the Junior game. English remembers that, 'He reported nervously to Ibrox, where the championship flag was still flying.' This was hardly surprising. Rangers had dominated Scottish football since the end of the First World War, winning ten of the last twelve championships, which included a run of five-in-a-row from 1926/27 to 1930/31. The dressing room was full of genuinely great players: Alan Morton, the Wee Blue Devil himself, a Wembley Wizard, and someone, according to English, 'who could put the ball in your hip pocket'; Davie Meiklejohn, one of the most redoubtable captains in the history of the Scottish game, and a rock in the centre of defence; Bob McPhail, the record goalscorer at Rangers for fifty years; George Brown, a cultured left half, who, like his teammate Morton, would later become a director of the club. And then there was Struth, who was, according to English and almost every observer, 'an autocratic man. He was the boss. His word was law.'

If the boy from the Ulster back country was apprehensive it didn't affect him on the field. He was a sensation from day one, slotting easily into a side that had no discernible weaknesses.

His first league match was against Dundee at Ibrox on 8 August 1931. It was an unforgettable debut. He carved the Dens Parkers' defence open time and again with his lighting pace and scored two goals, both with his head. Skilful with the ball at his feet, pacey and direct, outstanding in the air, despite not being the tallest; Rangers had unearthed a gem. That debut performance was no flash in the pan. He continued to score freely in the league, notching an astonishing five goals at home to Morton and a double away to Ayr United. The goals came from both feet and from his head. The practice sessions with his brother Dick all those years ago in Somerville park were now paying dividends. After eight league games he had twelve goals to his credit.

He felt he had earned a jersey for what would be the biggest game of his life. Against Celtic at Ibrox on Saturday, 5 September 1931. It was an experience he almost missed. In a midweek game before the Old Firm clash he had been kicked on the ankle, leading some newspapers to speculate that Jimmy Smith would take his place in the side. Although he recovered in time it was a nagging worry in the build up. He was desperate to face Celtic, desperate to play in the biggest derby in the world.

Be careful what you wish for.

As he got changed Sam English was nervous. As nervous as he had ever been in his life. But he wasn't the only one. Even veterans like Davie Meiklejohn and Bob McPhail seemed on edge, while experienced right back Dougie Gray, English recalls, was as 'jumpy as a cat'. That is what the biggest club game on the planet does to players. The young Ulsterman sneaked out of the dressing room to have a look at the crowd, which he remembers 'looked like a vast tidal wave moving down the terracing'.

Kick-off approached. It was time to walk into the crucible that was Ibrox stadium. Perhaps surprisingly, there were no stirring words from Bill Struth; no great oratory. He sent his team onto the pitch that day with a single sentence, which in its simplicity said it all:

'Well, you know what this means to you.'

The teams:

Rangers: Dawson, Gray, McAulay; Meiklejohn (c), Simpson, Brown; Fleming, Marshall, English, McPhail, Morton.

Celtic: Thomson, Cook, McGonagle; Wilson, McStay (c), Geatons; R. Thomson, A. Thomson, McGrory, Scarff, Napier.

Referee: W. Graham Holburn (or Holborn)

The first half was a disappointment, a scrappy affair, distinguished only by the number of fouls conceded by both sides. Sam English, keen to make his mark, did not have a single shot at goal. He had only one chance, when a cross was floated into the box. He jumped but the Celtic keeper, an inch or so taller, took it off his head.

'Hard lines, young fellow.'

The only words ever spoken by John Thomson to Sam English.

Half-time came, something of a relief after a forgettable first period. Then five minutes after the restart came the moment that changed the lives of two fine young men. Sam English's own words are more eloquent than anything I could write.

Jimmy Fleming had the ball making ground right out on the wing. His cross came over low towards me just outside the 18-yard line.

Both Celtic backs are lying wide. Billy Cook is left of me and behind. I can see McGonagle to my right. He is maybe six yards away, I don't know. Anyway, it's too far away for it to matter. There is only the keeper to beat.

The ball comes to me from the side. I can see John Thomson moving out of his goal. He hesitates about the six-yard line to balance himself.

He's got the goalmouth completely blocked. There is no bounce on the ball. I can't lift it over his head.

But if John Thomson comes out further I have a chance to go round him. I can run forward faster than he can run back.

He does come out. I have a view of two feet to a yard of the goal.

By now I have pulled the ball round in line with my body, using my right foot. I kick it, again with my right, cutting across the front of the ball, to try to swerve it in.

John Thomson is on me in a rugby tackle. His head thumps into the inside of my left knee. I feel nothing.

I fall over him. The ball trickles over the byline, barely rolling.

I bend over John Thomson. Billy Cook pulls me back. 'It wasn't your fault,' he says.

Cheering swells out from the terracing of Rangers supporters behind the goal. Davie Meiklejohn runs forward, waving it down. A sudden heavy silence fills Ibrox.

The game continued with Chic Geatons taking over in goal for the stricken Thomson. No goals are scored. The players' hearts were just not in it.

Leaving the pitch the young Ulsterman learns that John Thomson has been taken to the Victoria infirmary with a fractured skull. Even a layman knows how serious such an injury could be. Sam was desperate to get home to his family and was given a lift to Dalmuir by Tommy Hamilton, the Rangers reserve goalkeeper. As he walks out of the dressing room Davie Meiklejohn makes a vain attempt to keep his spirits up. 'You'll be all right, Blondie,' the respected skipper assures him.

But Sam English would never be all right again.

Later that night, suddenly restless, he had to get out of the house. He went to a billiard hall owned by Tommy Hamilton, which was very close to where he lived. He was deep in conversation with his teammate when a customer came in. It was a quarter to eleven. 'John Thomson is dead,' the man said. 'Special papers have been printed.'

The two Rangers players had to confirm it for themselves and they ran to the nearest phone box. Hamilton rang the hospital, with English squeezed into the box next to him. From what Hamilton was saying he knew that the unthinkable had happened. On the walk back home he still could not believe what had happened. Then he heard the cries of the street-corner newspaper sellers.

'JOHN THOMSON DEAD. JOHN THOMSON DEAD.'

*

No blame can be attached to Sam English for what happened to Thomson. Billy Cook was the closest player to the incident and his immediate comment to English that it wasn't his fault is telling. Others who took part in the game took the same view. Jimmy McGrory – the Celtic centre forward and universally recognised as an honourable man – writes in his autobiography (*A Lifetime in Paradise*): 'I can state here and now that not one Celtic player blamed Sam English for what happened. It was an accident.' Chic Geatons was the Celtic left half and took over in goals when Thomson was stretchered off. Years later he expressed his admiration for the Ranger, as well as his sympathy: 'Sam English was a gentleman footballer as well as a great one. I can assure Sam that from that moment the sympathy of every Celtic player was with him.'

Newspaper reports lead to the same conclusion. 'Clutha', covering the game for the *Evening Times*, is unequivocal: 'Everyone I am sure completely exonerated English of the smallest semblance of blame.' There are photographs of the moment when English and Thomson collided, most notably one taken by Jack Gibson of the *Scottish Daily Express*. It is clear from this image that the collision was the result of two highly committed players going for the ball. But the most compelling record of all is on a remarkable piece of newsreel, shot by British Movietone (it can be viewed on YouTube). The film shows English running in on goal at speed and Thomson advancing towards him. No one who watches it can come to any other conclusion about the accidental nature of the incident. The footage is equally telling about the aftermath: when English gets up his instinctive reaction is to check on Thomson's injury. Seconds later he gestures to the bench for assistance. These are the actions of a man whose first concern was for the welfare of a fellow professional.

Further affirmation of English's blamelessness came from the most unlikely of sources – the *Glasgow Observer*, which, with its strong sales in the city and its thirty-four local editions was the most widely read and influential newspaper among Scottish Catholics in the 1920s and 1930s. The paper was however highly partisan in those days, with an editorial line that rendered it little more than a mouthpiece for the Catholic Church in Scotland (and, frequently, for Celtic Football Club). Its disdain for Rangers and Rangers supporters was striking. In one fairly typical piece from 1924 the *Observer* describes followers of the Light Blues as.

> The dregs and scourings of filthy slumdom, unwashed yahoos, jailbirds, nighthawks, won't works, burroo barnacles and pavement pirates . . . This ragged army of insanitary pests was lavishly provided with orange and blue remnants and these were flaunted as . . . the football tide flowed this way and that.

The *Observer's* editor/founder Charlie Diamond went much further than simply insulting Rangers fans. He was a fervent advocate of, and apologist for, violent Irish Republicanism and in 1920 was jailed for openly advocating terrorism. For much of the inter-war period the *Observer's* broader political opinions were equally reprehensible. It admired two of the leading fascist dictators of the time, Franco and Mussolini, and both were the recipients of lavish praise in its columns. Nor should its attitude to the situation in Hitler's Germany be overlooked. In his groundbreaking book on sectarian strife in the west of Scotland (*Glasgow: the Uneasy Peace*, 1987) Tom Gallagher comments that the *Observer* under Diamond was not averse to 'crude Jew-baiting', and argues that the following statement is a typical example: 'The Jew is an odious and unscrupulous exploiter . . . the most intolerant on earth and the least amenable to social discipline.'

So for the *Glasgow Observer* to absolve English of any blame in the tragedy is instructive indeed. And it did so in unequivocal terms, even praising the Rangers player for his concern for the prostrate custodian.

> The said occurrence was, of course, a sheer accident and no blame attaches to the Rangers player, Sam English, who was in possession of the

ball when Thomson took his fatal dive. English instantly saw the dreadful nature of the accident and shouted a frenzied appeal for players, officials, trainers and doctors to come to the assistance of the injured goalkeeper.

If Sam English's conduct was impeccable so too was that of Rangers Football Club. Bill Struth insisted on sending a car to Thomson's home town of Cardenden, Fife to collect his parents and bring them to Glasgow. Meiklejohn, Struth's on-field lieutenant, as we have seen, silenced those Rangers fans who began to cheer when Thomson collapsed. How should we judge those fans? On the face of it for anyone to cheer in such circumstances is unsavoury. It has also been seized on by the Celtic-minded, desperate to blame Rangers for something. 'Man in the Know', the *Glasgow Observer*'s football reporter, is typical of that group: 'Even in the presence of death some cheering fanatics [in the Rangers end] gave vent to their insane hatred of all things Celtic.'

The truth is a little more complicated.

There was of course no way the Rangers fans could have known the seriousness of Thomson's injury. It was customary in the 1930s for fans to barrack injured opponents, just like today. It is also clear that when Meiklejohn gestured at them to desist a respectful hush descended over the Rangers end of Ibrox. Despite this many of a light-blue persuasion were uneasy, perhaps even a little ashamed, at the attitude of a small minority of their fellow supporters. On Monday, 7 September 1931, two days after the game, both the *Evening Times* and the *Evening Citizen* noted that they had received several letters from Rangers fans protesting about the unsporting conduct. This letter, from 'True Blue', Secretary, Loyal Orange Lodge, is typical.

> As a supporter of Glasgow Rangers of not a few years standing, I would like to express my feelings of disgust at the behaviour of a certain section of the crowd at Ibrox Park on Saturday when Thomson, the popular Celtic goalkeeper, was injured. The cheering of a few nincompoops at the rear of the Celtic goal was surely the very personification of ignorance . . . and I trust those who took part had the grace to be thoroughly ashamed of themselves when David Meiklejohn had of necessity to ask them to desist.

Rangers and their players, as shocked as anyone in Glasgow about the tragedy, were to the fore as obsequies were observed. On the Tuesday after the game a memorial service for Thomson was held in the Trinity Congregational church, near Charing Cross. The idea for the service came from the church's minister, Revd H. S. McClelland; a keen football man, he had been at the game and had witnessed what happened. Glasgow, as warm-hearted as ever, came out to pay its respects to the courageous young man from Fife. Accounts vary but it is estimated that upwards of three thousand crowded into West Claremont Street, hoping to gain entry to the service. Many were disappointed; so many that another service was put on immediately after the first one. Every Rangers player who had taken part in the match was present, while Meiklejohn read one of the lessons. For his part Sam English got a foretaste of the life that was to come. As he squeezed through the huge crowd every eye was upon him.

'But he's only a boy,' one woman exclaimed. English would later say that she sounded almost disappointed, somehow wanting him to be older.

The service was an ordeal for the young man from Crevolea. When the first organ note of 'Nearer My God to Thee' was played Sam began to weep and did not stop weeping until he left the church. It was the same at John Thomson's funeral, held on Wednesday, 9 September in Bowhill cemetery, near to Cardenden. If the service in Glasgow had been well attended it was as nothing compared to the turnout in Fife. They came from all over Scotland to pay their last respects. Three special trains carrying two thousand mourners left Glasgow Central station for the east. Many men, impoverished due to the dire economic circumstances of the early 1930s, were unable to afford the bus or train fare. So they walked to Fife, camping out in the hills of Auchenderran at night before attending the funeral. The next day they trooped home, completing a journey that for some was a hundred miles or more. It is said thirty thousand were in and around the cemetery, including the great and good of Scottish football. Those who could not be there sent wreaths, so many that a lorry was needed to carry them.

In that mighty throng were twenty-one men who had played at Ibrox on the Saturday, among them Sam English. He could have stayed away. He had ready-made excuses, as his presence might well have detracted from the solemnity of the occasion or even worse led to an outbreak of violence. But it never crossed his mind not to attend. He had to be there. It was his duty. English remembers walking alone in the cemetery, before teammate Alan Morton pushed his way through the crowds to be at his side. Just to be on the safe side the police crowded around the two Rangers, forming a thick cordon.

Five weeks after John Thomson was laid to rest official Scotland gave its verdict. A fatal accident enquiry was convened in Glasgow on 15 October 1931. Although the police investigations into what had happened at Ibrox pointed strongly to accidental death the inquiry was nevertheless a legal requirement. Witnesses were summoned, including the referee, the two club managers, Dr Kivlichan, the Celtic club doctor, a press photographer and Sam English himself, although he was not called to give evidence. The referee and Dr Kivlichan both testified that the incident was accidental, as did others summoned to the stand. Sheriff Wilton, presiding, was in no doubt; nor was the jury, among whom there were no dissenting voices. The finding was that the cause of death was 'fracture of skull sustained by accidental injury while playing football'.

That is a fact.

But there was one verdict that meant more to Sam English than any other. That of the Thomson family, and, in particular, John's mother. Many have commented on the similarities between Sam and John. Both were young men who had escaped the drudgery of a life in Scotland's traditional heavy industries; both were from a Northern Irish background (Thomson on his mother's side); both were Protestants; both were from large families, English being one of eleven siblings, Thomson one of five; both had distinguished themselves on the field of play at an early age, Thomson being capped for Scotland at the age of twenty-one, very young for a goalkeeper. But most of all both men were very close to their mothers, using their earnings from football to make life easier for the most important women in their lives. Under different circumstances the two families would have been friends or neighbours.

So it must have been a great comfort to Sam when he learnt that the Thomson family had asked local newspapers in Fife to carry a special article. Headed 'A Message from Bowhill' it was printed in several papers and reads.

> The parents of John Thomson have made a request to us to publicly announce that they entirely exonerate the Rangers centre forward, Sam English, of any responsibility for the accident which resulted in their son's death. They realise that it was an accident, pure and simple. The

family also wish to express their gratitude for the uniform sympathy that has been extended to them from people all over the land.

English was invited to the Thomson home a week after the funeral. He remembered shaking hands with the family and then visiting the grave with John's father. Even in the midst of a terrible bereavement the Thomsons were anxious to reach out to a man they knew must be suffering. It was a truly Christian gesture.

Sam English always treasured the letter he got from John's mother on the third anniversary of his death.

Dear Mr and Mrs English,

Received the beautiful floral tribute that you sent in memory of our beloved son John. His resting place was lovely with all the wreaths.

The Celtic company was here with their tributes also.

Our hearts are sad at this time. But nothing can bring our dear one back again.

I hope you are well as this leaves us. With kind regards.

Yours sincerely,

Mrs Thomson

In 1963, the *Express*, as part of its serialisation, arranged for John Thomson's brother, Jim, to meet Sam and during their meeting Jim confirmed how the Thomsons felt: 'I never blamed you for what happened, Sam. Neither did my mother. Even when she was at her lowest she spared a thought for you. I'm sorry you have been so troubled.'

Jim Thomson's sentiments were typical of how decent, fair-minded people felt. In fact everyone with a close connection to what happened was satisfied that it was an accident. Except that is for Celtic manager Willie Maley.

*

Willie Maley's leading role in the development of Celtic, and more broadly of Scottish football, is undeniable. He was a distinguished player and administrator with the Parkhead club and he won sixteen league titles and fourteen Scottish Cups in four decades as Celtic manager. For these achievements he deserves to be bracketed with Struth, Stein, Smith and Ferguson.

But after the death of his star goalkeeper, Maley did more than anyone else to keep the bitterness going. Quite simply his conduct was disgraceful. At the fatal accident inquiry he was asked if he thought Thomson's death was an accident.

'I hope it was an accident. I cannot form any opinion as to what happened as I did not actually see the accident,' he replied.

This was not a man blurting out something he did not mean in the rarefied and unfamiliar atmosphere of the courtroom. He clearly suspected Sam English of foul play and had no compunction about making life difficult for the Ranger. In the immediate aftermath of the tragedy, and even before he left Ibrox stadium, Maley began his smear campaign. In *A Lifetime in Paradise* Jimmy McGrory recalls the following conversation between the Celtic manager and a representative of the press:

'Was it an accident?' asked the journalist.

'I hope so,' Maley replied.

Some will be surprised by his attitude. But not those who knew the man behind the facade. Willie Maley was deceitful, disloyal, corrupt, money-grubbing and cruel. (His brother Tom was even more venal. In 1905, while manager of Manchester City, he was thrown out of English football by the Football Association for his part in a bribery scandal.) Even the Maley name was a fraud; the family name was O'Malley but his father, a soldier in the British Army, anglicised it. No doubt he reasoned that the new name would be more acceptable to his superiors. It is telling that even Celtic-minded historians, never knowingly objective when it comes to their club, find it hard to defend the man who was manager at Parkhead for forty-three years.

Willie Maley's first brush with notoriety occurred in 1894 when, as secretary-administrator, he rigged the election for the committee that ran Celtic, forcing the club to order a rerun. It is also clear that he used Celtic to enrich his other businesses, notably the Bank restaurant in Glasgow city centre, a favoured haunt of bookies, barflies and other ne'er do wells. Maley always insisted that official club functions were held at the Bank and encouraged Celtic players to eat and drink there, knowing that the pull of the Old Firm would draw in the punters. After games at Celtic Park, and without the knowledge of his employers, he used the appropriately named Bank to count the takings, slicing off a percentage to top up his slush fund, which was used to bung promising young players he wished to sign. Then there were the bets on matches placed by his Celtic players, an illegal practice then as now, but one that was an everyday occurrence in the Bank.

As for his attitude to players it often verged on the vindictive. In a book on Celtic managers (*The Head Bhoys* by Graham McColl) many examples are cited: when one of his young players, Alex Millar, bought a car he told him that he was not the sort of person who should own a motor vehicle and forced him to sell it; on another occasion Maley accused teetotaller Johnnie Wilson of frequenting pubs despite compelling evidence to the contrary. Wilson, a true Celtic fan, left the club shortly after the incident, a thoroughly disillusioned man.

But it was how Maley dealt with Jimmy McGrory – the club's record goalscorer and a Celtic man to his fingertips – that shows the depths of his vindictiveness. This was on the face of it all the more surprising given that McGrory looked up to Maley as a son looks up to his father. In the summer of 1928 Maley and McGrory went on holiday together to the Catholic shrine of Lourdes, in southern France. But Maley had an ulterior motive. En route to Lourdes they got off the train in London, where they were met by Arsenal manager Herbert Chapman. Without informing McGrory, Maley had arranged a meeting with the Arsenal supremo for just one reason: to finalise his star centre forward's move to the Gunners. Arsenal had offered the incredible sum of £10,000 for McGrory's services, a transfer fee that would have equalled the world record.

There was just one problem. McGrory had no intention of leaving Celtic for Arsenal or for anyone else. Although the talks went on all night, with Chapman trying everything he could to persuade the Celt to sign, McGrory would not budge. 'Celtic was the only team I wanted to play for,' he writes in *A Lifetime in Paradise* (and unlike Mo Johnston six decades later he meant every word). Many managers would have accepted their player's decision with good grace and moved on, especially if they had been as close as the Celtic manager and the young man who so admired him.

But not Willie Maley.

In an act of spite Maley kept McGrory on £8-per-week basic wages for the rest of his career at the Parkhead club even though most other first-team men, much less talented, were on £9. McGrory only found out what

Maley had done years later but such was his respect for his mentor that he refused to criticise him or to let it affect their friendship.

Wille Maley was inducted into the Scotland hall of fame in 2009 as one of the sixth batch of inductees. We can only assume that integrity was not one of the criteria for admission.

Sam English always felt that what Maley had said at the fatal accident inquiry was not only deeply unfair but was also responsible for many of the on- and off-field problems he would endure. Thirty years on from the accident he was still baffled and hurt by Maley's actions, as he points out in his articles for the *Express*.

'I still cannot imagine why Mr William Maley, the Celtic manager, said what he said that day.'

Even years later Maley's views on what had happened were ambiguous. In his book on the history of Celtic (*The Story of the Celtic, 1888–1938*, published in 1939) he refers to Thomson's death as a '*regrettable* accident' (my italics), a strange choice of word given that he could have used 'complete' or 'unavoidable' or 'total' or any number of synonyms. Never one who failed to capitalise on a crisis Maley also blamed Celtic's lack of success in the 1930s on Thomson's death, arguing in the same book that, 'The shock had a tremendous effect on our players, one which we firmly believe was responsible for many failures during the next few years.' So for Willie Maley at least this particular cloud had a silver lining.

*

It is often asserted by modern-day journalists that after the accident Sam English was never the same player again. They are correct.

He was even better than before.

It might also be assumed that having been through such a trauma he would be sidelined by Rangers for weeks, perhaps even months, before being allowed to set foot on a football pitch. In fact Sam English played the *day after* Thomson's funeral, on Thursday, 10 September 1931. And scored a wonder goal.

There was a home game against Third Lanark scheduled for that night in the Glasgow Charities Cup, a competition that clubs at the time took very seriously. English did not expect to be selected. His family also thought he would be given leave of absence, with his mother making the heartfelt comment 'Surely they'll not ask you to turn out today.' The newspapers too were blindsided, among them the *Daily Record*, which informed its readers that the Rangers team would be minus English, noting that 'Jamie Smith leads the attack'.

So when the young Ulsterman arrived at Ibrox he fully expected to be sitting in the stand. His manager had other ideas: 'I remember the dull shock of getting to the stadium to find that Mr Struth had listed me to play,' he later recalled. The manager's explanation was that Smith had a heavy cold – but was this a ruse on Struth's part to ease English back into the side without giving him time to brood? It is doubtful if English was in the right frame of mind, in fact he even thought of refusing to play, but with a disciplinarian like Bill Struth that was a Rubicon he dared not cross.

'Keep your eye on the ball and remember you are playing football,' the manager advised him, in a gruff yet somehow kindly tone.

And play football he did, scoring what the *Record* describes as 'a beautiful goal – a bit of quick thinking and coolness' in the 4–1 victory. He was helped by a chance reunion with someone from his schoolboy days: the Third Lanark centre forward was none other than Neil 'Cleeks' Dewar and his presence was crucial.

> I ran out to him in the centre circle. We shook hands. We said just the usual things about how long it had been since we met. But the relief of having an old friend on the field helped me through that first game.

From that day on English's form was exceptional. While he failed to score in the next league game against Partick Thistle several papers noted that his overall performance was excellent. Normal service was soon resumed. He notched a brace in a 6–1 rout of Cowdenbeath on 3 October, and a hat trick against Dundee United on the last day of that month. By the season's end he had added another four hat-tricks, including four goals in a match against Queen's Park in February 1932. He finished up with forty-four league goals for the season, a Rangers record and one that endures to this day. English was no less prolific in the Scottish Cup, scoring a further two hat tricks and a double. Rangers advanced to the final where they met Kilmarnock and after a first match that was drawn the teams returned to Hampden for the replay. In front of a record crowd for a midweek game of 105,000 Rangers ran out easy winners by three goals to nil with Sam English, despite sustaining a bad head knock, scoring the third. Fifty-six goals in all competitions and a Scottish Cup medal; surely no other Ranger in history has achieved so much in his first season.

If his second season in light blue was not quite so glorious it was nothing to be sneezed at. He got ten league goals in twenty-five games (twenty-two in all competitions) as Rangers powered to a sixth title in seven years. After another productive season and with a championship medal in his pocket Sam English left for his summer holidays in Girvan in fine fettle. So it must have been a shock when he was summoned back to Ibrox in the middle of his vacation to meet Bill Struth. The manager bluntly informed him that his time at Ibrox was up and that he was being moved on, as English recalls in the *Express* articles.

> [Struth told him] Liverpool had made an offer and I would be transferred. Some of the edge had gone off my game. Goals came less readily. The heart had gone out of me.

English did not want to leave Ibrox. He loved it there. Indeed, when Struth told him that Rangers had accepted Liverpool's offer his first thought was that he 'might as well give up the game'. But he decided to go to Anfield, persuaded by Liverpool's manager, George Paterson, that he 'would find it different there'.

Many Rangers fans take the view that it was a shabby way to treat someone who had endured so much, as well as being a poor decision in purely football terms. They also believe that the powers-that-be at Ibrox gave in to what amounted to an unprincipled campaign to chase him out of Scottish football. Let us examine each of these assertions in turn.

There is no doubt his scoring record was remarkable. He racked up seventy-eight goals in eighty-seven first-team games at Ibrox, despite the dip in 1932/33. But Struth may have been concerned about his record against the top teams. Rangers' main rivals at the time English was at Ibrox were Celtic and Motherwell but in ten games in all competitions against these two sides he scored only once – against Motherwell in the league. Struth could also call on the services of Bob McPhail and Jimmy Smith, two of the best strikers ever to pull on the famous light-blue jersey. Results vindicated Struth's decision; the team won the league-and-cup double in 1933/34 and again in1934/35 and both McPhail and Smith were prolific scorers in these campaigns.

In addition the transfer fee paid by Liverpool was substantial, £5,000 some papers said, a record fee for the Merseyside club, and one of the highest ever between Scottish and English clubs. The decision to let him go could therefore be justified on financial grounds. Or could it? Some informed pundits were more than a little sceptical. 'Waverley', writing in the *Daily Record* on 31 July 1933, observes that the fee was reported to be 'a cool five thou', but added 'I hae ma doots'. A possible interpretation of Waverley's remark is that the size of the fee was being exaggerated, perhaps to appease Rangers fans aggrieved that one of their favourites, someone who had suffered grievously for the cause, was being shown the door.

Despite his misgivings about the reported size of the fee, 'Waverley' shared Struth's analysis from a football perspective. He argued that Rangers were well off for centre forwards and therefore 'Sam's going does not surprise me'. Another *Record* journalist, 'Rufus', also thought Struth had called it correctly because Rangers had 'an embarrassment of riches in English and Smith so better to let one go elsewhere so that both may take their rightful place in first-class football'.

Whether the fee was £5,000 or a lesser amount it was no doubt substantial and would have enabled Rangers to strengthen other areas of the team. So the transfer would have made perfect sense to Struth, a man who dedicated his life to making Rangers successful.

But did the reaction to English from opposition fans play any part in Struth's decision? Did he, as is sometimes suggested, cravenly give in to a campaign, organised or ad hoc, against Sam English? The evidence is unclear.

The first real test would come when Rangers played in the cauldron of Celtic Park. It was the semi-final of the Glasgow Cup and the game took place just twenty-three days after Thomson's death, on 28 September 1931, in front of a crowd of 55,000. While the *Glasgow Observer* did its best to gloss over what happened that day by claiming that 'perfect decorum was observed at both ends' (3 October 1931) more objective observers refused to excuse the disgraceful conduct of the Celtic fans. There was sustained barracking of English right from the kick-off by those in green and white, which the *Daily Record* calls 'bad sportsmanship'. The same paper also notes that Davie Meiklejohn, concerned by the abuse of his teammate, made a formal protest to the referee. This is confirmed by the *Evening Citizen*: 'Meiklejohn had protested to the referee against the conduct of some spectators, who, he alleged, were barracking one of the Rangers players. The referee informed a Celtic official and there was no further complaint.' English himself was only too aware of what was happening: 'The crowd in one corner surged forward, threatening to break in,' he recalled. Not that he was intimidated, with most papers pointing out that he had an excellent game.

Sam English played in two more Old Firm games at Celtic Park. The first was the traditional Ne'erday league fixture on 1 January 1932. If the Celtic fans were going to persist with their barracking this was a good opportunity, especially when Rangers left the east end of the city with a comfortable 2–1 win. But trouble there was none. The *Glasgow Herald* reported that 'The game was played in a sporting spirit and passed off without a single unseemly incident' while there are no reports of anything untoward in the *Evening Times*, *Evening Citizen* or *Daily Record*. English had a great game, with the *Daily Record* naming him 'the best player on the Rangers team'.

This does not mean that the Celtic fans had either forgiven or forgotten the Ulsterman. In the Old Firm match at Celtic Park on 10 September 1932, English went down injured after a collision, 'a fact that was heralded by a mighty roar from partisans behind the goal,' according to the *Evening Times*.

We shall never know for sure what Struth's reasons were for transferring English. On face value it was done for football reasons, but the continuing vitriol from Celtic fans, the despicable comments of Maley and the abuse the young striker had to face in his daily life may well have played a part in his decision. There is also the possibility that Struth thought he was doing English a favour, allowing him to make a fresh start away from the bitter enmities of Glasgow.

At Anfield his performances were highly creditable. He scored twenty-six goals in fifty goals for the Reds, including one in the derby against Everton. But when his form shaded in his second season on Merseyside he was sold to Queen of the South for £1,700, a huge sum for a club that is small even by provincial standards. The English signing was one of the biggest things ever to happen to Queens, with local paper *The Dumfries and Galloway Standard* (24 July 1935) describing the new man as 'a real big name in British football'. Such was the excitement generated by his capture that 11,000 rolled up to Palmerston Park for the season opener against Hibs.

In the early part of his time at the Doonhamers Sam English performed admirably and one game in particular must have given him great satisfaction. In mid September 1935 he faced Celtic at Palmerston and scored an excellent goal, although it didn't prevent Queen's going down by three goals to one. Then in November 1935, came the fixture he must have been anticipating most of all – at home to Rangers. If English had mixed feelings about facing his old club it was not evident on the field. The *Standard* of 13 November 1935 describes his play as 'delightful' and notes that 'English continues to improve and his bustling methods had Simpson and his backs in a quandary and glad to pass back to Dawson for relief'.

It was not to last. His performances, whether through injury or loss of form, began to deteriorate. The *Standard* was quick to criticise, using words like 'feeble' and 'failed' to sum up his displays. He was moved from centre forward to the right wing and when that did not improve matters he was left out of the team altogether. He neither played in the return league fixture at Celtic Park in January 1936 nor in the away game with Rangers in April of the same year. On 22 April 1936 the *Standard* reported that Sam English was on the transfer list and available for a fee of £1,000.

In May 1936, with Queens unable to find a buyer, English was given a free transfer and joined Hartlepool United, a 'lowly' team in his view. Once again his early performances were of a very high standard. In his first season he scored eighteen league goals in thirty-four starts. His second campaign was not so successful, with a return of nine goals in thirty-five league matches. By this time he had become disillusioned with football. He was tired of the snide remarks from opponents, the taunts from sections of opposition supporters and the stream of poison-pen letters. In the end the never-ending abuse simply wore him out. So, aged twenty-eight, he retired after, as he describes it, 'seven years of joyless sport'.

Today, thanks largely to the efforts of Rangers fans, a process is underway to restore Sam English to his rightful place in the pantheon of Ibrox greats. He has always been a fans' favourite, as a song written in his honour, 'The Ballad of Sam English', clearly illustrates. It notes English's Protestant and Ulster roots and encourages Rangers fans to sing 'Derry's Walls' when he scores a goal. It is also, incidentally, very complimentary about John Thomson.

But it was the centenary of Sam English's birth, on 18 August 2008, that became the focal point. Rangers Supporters Trust – thanks to a considerable fundraising effort by its members – commissioned silversmith Cara Murphy to make the Sam English Bowl, a piece of solid silver containing forty-four silver balls, which is presented each year to the top scorer at Ibrox. Then in February 2009 members of the English family were invited to a civic reception by Coleraine Borough Council at which two plaques in his memory were unveiled at the family home in Crevolea. Rangers Football Club belatedly recognised their former player when Sam English was inducted into the hall of fame at Ibrox.

Elsewhere in this book Gregory Campbell MP, of the Democratic Unionist Party, tells of how in March 2008 he tabled a parliamentary motion entitled 'Centenary of the Birth of Sam English' in the House of Commons asking the House to mark the centenary of his birth. He might also have questioned why there is no place for his countryman in the Scottish football hall of fame. After all in 2008 a place was found for John Thomson, following a campaign by Tom Greig, who wrote a highly authoritative book on the Celtic keeper.

Thomson is in the hall of fame not for his prowess as a goalkeeper, which was admittedly considerable, but because he was killed in an accident on the field of play. He won only four Scotland caps and a solitary Scottish Cup medal. Sam English was also a victim of that terrible day and if playing records are taken into account his is superior to Thomson's: he has a league-championship medal and was also a Scottish Cup winner, as well as being capped for Northern Ireland, and there is no way of knowing how much he was handicapped by the trauma of the accident. In addition he retained his dignity under the fiercest provocation and was able successfully to return to the game despite the terrible events of 5 September 1931. These things are surely worth commemorating.

*

After his playing career had drawn to a close English had spells as a coach with Duntocher Hibernians and Yoker Athletic before he again found work as a sheet-metal worker in John Brown's shipyard. In those years he and his wife, Sadie, lived in a four-room house in Dalmuir, where, to keep out of her hair, he became a keen gardener. It took a long time but in the late 1950s he started to venture out to football again, initially at Firhill and then, as he explains, 'thanks to director George Brown and manager Scot Symon' at the place he loved above all others, Ibrox. He relished his trips to watch Rangers, despite still 'being some kind of grisly peepshow'.

Sam English gave his interviews to the *Express* in 1963 and some time thereafter he contracted the deadly motor-neurone disease. He died in the Vale of Leven hospital in 1967 at the age of fifty-eight. It was no doubt some kind of release from the whispered asides and furtive glances that followed him wherever he went. But no matter what fate threw at him he never retreated into bitterness or self-pity. Most of all he kept a place in his heart for the young man whose death he would have done anything to avoid. People, trying to be kind, would often say to him.

'You are the unluckiest player in Scotland.'

'Not the unluckiest,' Sam would reply, 'the second unluckiest.'

David White: a Manager's Record Reassessed

David Mason

It was back in 2000 that former Rangers boss David White granted me the privilege of an interview for my book *Rangers: The Managers*, published later that year. It was a rare honour. Such was the trauma of leaving Ibrox that White had never before talked publicly of his time at Rangers. Although four decades had elapsed since he walked sadly from Ibrox back in 1969, his dreams in tatters, the pain of his departure still cut deep. It took some time before he could even bring himself to return to the stadium, particularly since his nemesis and successor, Willie Waddell, had assumed a prominent role in the Ibrox boardroom. If my book brought some balance to the events through White's own recollections, the rehabilitation of a man who was cut so cruelly from office was incomplete. He still appeared haunted any time I saw him walk through the great oak doors to the inner sanctums of a club he once ruled.

We became good friends over the next few years, sharing a passion for both football and golf. However, I was reluctant to compromise that relationship when the producers of Rangers TV called me early in 2009 to seek a screen interview with David. White owed neither Rangers nor me a thing, but I was sure that if we could get him in front of the cameras, the interview would prove illuminating. To my surprise, David agreed, but insisted I conduct the interview, an honour I proudly accepted. So chastened had he been with the press that little trust remained. He knew that he could trust me, as club historian, to stick to the facts and not to speculate. A date was set and the interview would be conducted in the Blue Room at Ibrox.

It was a very nervous David White who appeared in the great hallway at Ibrox and slowly climbed the marble staircase to where I waited with the camera crew.

'I almost didn't come,' he admitted. 'I sat in the car for a time and wondered whether I should go through with it, but I'm here.'

With his wife now departed, I could imagine how he had wrestled with his conscience and the wisdom of going through with the interview. She would have been pleased, however, that we referred to him as David and not Davie and I know he prefers that too.

With the microphone adjusted and the lighting positioned, we started some general chat about golf and Rangers, as I tried to ease him into the interview with no cameras running. He wasn't the only one who was nervous. I had done all my research, but I had no idea where this interview would go. Perhaps it would even end up on the cutting-room floor. In fact, it was one of my most memorable moments in over twenty-three years' service to the club. When the former Gers boss settled, his frankness proved quite disarming to even the sternest of his critics. The interview was far reaching and as White dipped deeper and deeper into the events of the past, there was a real sense that he was unburdening himself of feelings that had lain dormant for so long. He looked refreshed, relieved even, at the end, then headed home with a smile.

When the show went out in two parts a few weeks later, the response from the fans was incredible. 'Lovely man' was a recurring comment, but, more importantly for the historical context, there was a general consensus that White had been wronged by Rangers.

The next time he was at Ibrox on a match day, I met him at the top of the staircase.

'Did you watch the programme?' I enquired.

He hadn't and still hasn't to this day. He can't bring himself to watch.

However, as we stood there chatting, a fan came over to shake his hand. 'I really enjoyed your interview, Mr White,' he said as David stood in a kind of stunned silence. Then another approached with similar sentiments, then another. I watched him that afternoon as he sat in the director's box, glowing with contentment.

Since then, his whole demeanour has changed markedly as he enters Ibrox for a game. Gone is the haunted figure that, for many years, slipped up the staircase almost unnoticed to stand alone in the corner of the Blue Room. Today the rehabilitation of David White is complete and a balanced perspective of his time at Ibrox can be considered.

It hardly seems more than forty years since he was handed the biggest job in football and the unenviable task of succeeding where predecessor Scot Symon had failed. One of Bill Struth's boys, Symon provided an almost seamless transition in management style from his mentor when he was appointed in 1956. However, the late Sixties brought winds of change which favoured the tracksuit boss – a style that characterised Jock Stein's stewardship at Celtic Park. Symon seemed dated in comparison, almost yesterday's man, as Stein drove Celtic on to European Cup success, attaining heights that they had never before reached, or are ever destined to again.

Ironically, it was Scot Symon who brought David White to Ibrox in June 1967. According to White he was told that when he was appointed he was being groomed for the position of manager, but he could scarcely have imagined that the opportunity would come along so quickly or in such circumstances. Symon was dismissed just five months after White moved to Ibrox to take up the role of assistant manager. Naturally disappointed at the loss of Symon, White was nevertheless excited about his new role as Rangers manager. Such was his enthusiasm that he turned down the offer of a contract. He didn't see the need for one and was looking forward to success. He later admitted it was one of the biggest mistakes of his life.

Although the job came sooner than anyone expected, David White had supreme confidence in his ability to turn the club around. Although he had never attained great heights as a player or managed at a higher level than Clyde, he was a keen student of the game. His enthusiasm was such that he moved in the highest circles in Scottish football and took every opportunity to watch the top bosses in action. He was also invited to attend Rangers' European Cup Winners Cup-final clash in Nuremberg, before which he had travelled to Lisbon to watch Celtic win the European Cup. He had already impressed as part-time manager of Clyde, taking them to third place behind the Old Firm one season. Despite this success, he continued to ply his trade as a draughtsman and even considered emigrating to Canada before the opportunity to join Rangers arose.

White's move to Ibrox as assistant to Symon was not without its difficulties. He found Bobby Seith in the role of first-team coach, leaving White to look after the reserves. Perhaps Seith saw White's arrival as an obstacle to his own ambitions. Their relationship was fractious, but

White's dedication to the reserves bore fruit. He became a popular figure with the second string and provided a more varied training routine than the first team experienced. In his autobiography, John Greig talks of the 'dressing-room grapevine' that carried good reports from the reserves of White's work with the side. His tactical ability was also beginning to shine through as he played with formations and adjusted player movements to capitalise on the pace of the likes of the explosive Willie Johnston. The young fringe players that White coached would not only carve their place in his team, but would also feature prominently in the major success the club achieved in the Seventies.

Bobby Seith resigned within twenty-four hours of Symon's dismissal, a move possibly motivated by White's appointment as manager. White was alone at a club in crisis, but he rallied the players quickly despite the fact that many observers voiced doubts about his ability to succeed, something that he must have been all too aware of. It was argued that he didn't have the credentials or the experience to manage Rangers and its big stars. Ironically, he was to find that the strongest bonds came from the senior players and John Greig, in particular, eased the new boss into a good relationship with the dressing room. The squad had respected Scot Symon and was solidly behind him right up until the end of his stewardship, but White also commanded the respect of the players from an early stage. In reality, the players depended on White perhaps more than he needed their commitment. They had failed to halt the march of Celtic and Ibrox is no hiding place for players who don't succeed.

It was the players who ultimately cost Symon his job. He had dismantled the ageing, but tremendously successful, side that won the domestic treble in 1963/64, with Billy Ritchie, Eric Caldow, Ian McMillan, Jimmy Millar and Davy Wilson all having effectively gone. Symon had also lost the main creative force with the departure of Jim Baxter in 1965. The reconstruction of a side is not instantaneous, but time is a gift rarely available to any manager of Rangers. White would be expected to mould a team capable of wresting the championship from Celtic. He worked at building his relationship with the players, who were generally receptive. They found the new manager to be quite different from the reserved and stoical Symon. After a good result one Saturday the team travelled to their Largs base in preparation for a midweek European tie. White astounded the players as they sat in the hotel bar by coming in to buy them a few beers. They had never known the like before.

The players were encouraged to mix freely with him and he would join them for practice games but, although he courted their affections, he also instilled discipline. He was approachable, but they knew that they daren't step out of line. In many respects, he was ahead of his time – his approach being of a modernist, not a traditionalist. Ironically it would be his undoing; making him an easy target for dissenters should things go wrong. It was former club secretary Campbell Ogilvie who once voiced the opinion that the club should always be prepared to dispense with the bad traditions while retaining the good ones. However, long hair and moustaches were not seen by many as typical of the Rangers player.

While White worked hard to create a good atmosphere, he knew that he would be judged solely on results. The manager was bursting with ideas on how to shape the side, but he was reluctant to make too many changes in the early stages – Rangers were top of the league, after all! Chairman John Lawrence had cited the lack of goals as a key reason for Symon's dismissal, despite the board's shameful influence in the removal of the precocious Jim Forrest and George McLean following the Scottish Cup defeat to Berwick Rangers earlier that year. It was a decision that probably cost Rangers the European Cup Winners Cup a few months later. Centre forward Alex Ferguson had scored just six goals in sixteen games, but the goals weren't exactly flowing freely from other parts of the team.

In his first match as boss, against St Johnstone, White reorganised his front line to sharpen the penetration that had been lacking in previous games. He reintroduced Willie Henderson to the wing and shifted Willie Johnston to inside forward. The switch paid off with Johnston scoring the opener. With that sound start in his first few weeks in charge, he steered the side through a perilous Fair Cities Cup tie with Cologne and then saw it string nine successive league wins together, which maintained Rangers' position at the top of the table.

He also safely negotiated his first Old Firm match, the Ne'erday fixture at Celtic Park. A stirring fight back by the Ibrox side produced an equaliser from Kai Johansen with just two minutes left after Celtic's Bobby Murdoch had shot Stein's side into a 2–1 lead. When the manager returned to Ibrox, relieved and elated, he stepped into his office to take his place behind the desk, which he had refused to use until, in his own words, he 'had earned the right'.

However, White was under no illusions that a favourable result at Parkhead would earn acceptance at Ibrox. 'You have got to win one of the major honours for this club before the fans and the people in football think of you as successful,' he admitted. He was only partly correct. The fans expected the side to deliver a cup, but it was the championship flag that they coveted.

Unable to extend the lead over Celtic despite the continuation of their 100 per cent record, Rangers realised that the title might ultimately be decided on goal average. White instructed his players to go out and score as many goals as they could. By the end of March they had extended the run to eighteen league victories, interrupted only by that Ne'er Day draw with Celtic. They had scored a remarkable ten goals against Raith Rovers, six against St Johnstone, five over Partick Thistle and Stirling Albion, and four in many other fixtures. But they still remained behind Celtic's three-per-game strike rate. White's prediction that goals would be crucial in determining the destination of the flag was correct.

In the closing stages of the season, Rangers dropped valuable points in draws at Tannadice and Cappielow leaving Celtic top on goal average with two games remaining. A last-minute goal by Aberdeen at Ibrox saw Rangers lose their final match 3–2, sending the 1967/68 league flag to the east of the city. Remarkably they were only a minute away from completing the league campaign without defeat, although even that would have been scant consolation with the honours going elsewhere.

White had avoided widespread change as he tried to guide the club to the championship using men that Symon had signed. They had failed so now was the time for the manager to enforce change, introducing the sweeping ideas he felt could bring success back to Ibrox. Essentially, he had to restart the reconstruction process that Symon had initiated. He entered season 1968/69, his first full term in charge, with no new personnel although he had tried unsuccessfully to add to his squad. He did, however, introduce youngsters Colin Jackson and Sandy Jardine to the side.

The season opened with League Cup sectional ties and White would ideally have liked to ease the team into the campaign with a comfortable draw. Fate dealt him a cruel hand, however, when Rangers were drawn in the same section as Celtic, along with Partick Thistle and Morton. It was almost a boom-or-bust scenario at the earliest stage in what would be a long season. Victory could launch the side into a good league challenge. Poor results on top of the disappointments of the previous season would be too much to bear for many. White's worst fears were realised. Defeats at both Ibrox and Parkhead at the hands of Celtic got the side off to a dismal start as it crashed out of the cup.

Some pride was regained with victory in the first league clash with Celtic, at Parkhead (4–2), but the fans were unimpressed by a start that provided little of the consistency of the previous season. By the end of October 1968 the side had slid to fifth place in the table, although they remained only two points behind leaders Celtic. The Light Blue legions called for the board to pull out the chequebook. It was painfully apparent that the squad could not sustain a challenge to Celtic without new blood. White responded by bringing a striker to Ibrox in the first six-figure transfer in Scottish football. The loyal Rangers support had a new hero – Colin Stein, who burst on to the scene in a manner that exceeded his wildest dreams. He scored a hat trick on his debut at Arbroath's Gayfield Park then followed it up in the next match, his Ibrox debut, with another three goals in a 6–1 win over former club Hibernian. Two more followed in his next game, a European Fairs Cities Cup tie against Dundalk.

Less than three weeks after Stein's arrival, Alex MacDonald was signed from St Johnstone for a fee of around £50,000. The new men boosted the team, but they could not shake off the inconsistency that had marred their early-season performances. By the turn of the year they had slipped five points behind Celtic, closed the gap to three with victory in the Ne'er Day fixture, but surrendered another point at Rugby Park a week later. White knew it would be a hard struggle to overcome Celtic but, as he battled to close the gap, he was dealt a major blow to his title ambitions as the closing stages approached. Colin Stein was called before the SFA beaks and punished with a five-week suspension following two ordering-off offences within ten weeks, compounding previous incidents during his spell at Easter Road. He would be out for the remainder of the campaign, missing seven league matches. Disabled by the loss of their star striker, the side won only three of these matches and dropped six points in the remaining four games. Celtic ran out winners of the championship, with Rangers languishing five points behind.

The torment for White had not ended. The side surged impressively into the Scottish Cup final – where they would meet Celtic – after a crushing 6–1 win over Aberdeen. With the suspended Colin Stein sitting disconsolately in the stand, Alex Ferguson took the number-nine jersey. Players were assigned their responsibilities at set pieces. White maintains that Ferguson was given the task of marking Celtic's Billy McNeill, but later learned that the striker had apparently asked Ronnie McKinnon to deal with the aerial strength of the big Celt. The circumstances are unclear, but there was definite confusion in the Rangers box as McNeill was left unmarked. When the ball was floated into the box from a corner kick in the first minute, the Celtic captain rose unchallenged and scored with a header.

This early goal set the pattern and a series of defensive blunders handed Jock Stein's men a 4–0 victory; one of their most convincing cup-final wins over Rangers. In fact, it was Rangers' first defeat in a Scottish Cup final in forty years. The victory gave Celtic the domestic treble, while Rangers' trophy famine was extended to three years. White had spent around £400,000 on players and despite the bad luck that marked his tenure in the Ibrox hot seat the growing discontent on the terracing and in the Ibrox boardroom placed a question mark over his future.

With all hope of domestic success in season 1968/69 gone White turned his attention to the Fairs Cities Cup, a tournament that provided Rangers with some respite from the ever-present shadow of Celtic. They had gamely fought their way through to the semi-final where Newcastle United awaited. White's plans were savaged by the loss of two key defenders, Mathieson and McKinnon, on the eve of the game, compounding the selection problems already presented by the suspension of the incisive Willie Johnston. If ever White had a feeling that all luck had drained from his office at Ibrox, it was manifestly evident in a sorry first half against the St James' Park outfit when keeper Ian McFaul dived full stretch to his right to save an Andy Penman penalty. The young Belfast-born keeper – who had supported the Ibrox side as a boy – piled on the agony for Penman with a wonderful save from a thirty-yard shot that streaked through the Newcastle goal area. In the second half Rangers continued to dominate, but try as they might they could not breach the resolute Tyneside defence. When the final whistle sounded most of the 75,000 crowd agreed that

Newcastle were fortunate to leave Ibrox with a 0–0 scoreline. However, the result provided the platform for the Geordies to progress, and they won the second leg by two goals to nil. Rangers had looked a shadow of their normal selves. It was now evident that the manager's spending had brought no tangible rewards in terms of trophies.

White had already lost the confidence of many in the boardroom before the Newcastle tie, and the discontent among the Rangers support had now reached epidemic proportions. He knew that he needed to inject some inspiration into the ailing club, although it was unlikely that the board would sanction further transfer activity on the scale of the Stein acquisition. Then just a few days after the heartbreak of Newcastle, White seemed to have his first stroke of luck. The prodigal son, Jim Baxter, became available, with Nottingham Forest placing a £15,000 valuation on his head.

The manager moved quickly and on 28 May 1969 the club's loyal followers got the news that would help dispel the disappointments of the season past – Jim Baxter, 'The King', would return to Ibrox Park. White pledged that Baxter would have to play for his place like everyone else on the staff, but no one was under any illusion that this was a final throw of the dice for the manager. Quite simply, he would rely on Baxter to resurrect the ailing fortunes of the club – and to save his own job. The two men had built up a good relationship during their playing days and Baxter respected the tenacity of the Clyde midfielder.

However, it was clear they would both need tenacity to turn the tide. In an interview after his signing had been completed, Baxter said, 'I know that I have got to be a success here. There is no room for failure at Ibrox . . . there never has been.' It was a reality that White was all too familiar with. The problem was that Baxter had lost shape and was no longer the 'Slim Jim' who had left four years earlier. Before he even kicked a ball, many influential characters had proffered an opinion on the move. For some it characterised the malaise at Ibrox.

After just twenty-one months in the hot seat, White entered a critical phase with the opening of the 1969/70 season. He had failed to capture any of the six domestic competitions the team had played for, while Celtic had won five of them. There was little doubt that luck had deserted him, but that cut little ice with either the fans or, importantly, with the board.

The first competition of the season provided little respite. Incredibly, Rangers and Celtic were drawn together in the same League Cup section for the third successive season. Victory in the Old Firm clashes went with the venue – Rangers winning the opening fixture at Ibrox and Celtic edging the return at Parkhead. However, the Ibrox side's aspirations of a run in the tournament ended when they failed to beat Raith Rovers at Ibrox. The despair continued in the league and a haemorrhaging of points through the autumn saw the side slip to sixth place by November, although just two points behind the leaders. However, when Celtic won their first league match at Ibrox in twelve years, the rumblings on the terracing became incessant.

The old guard in whom he had placed so much faith began to fail him. Comparisons were drawn with the Celtic conveyor belt of talent, which came from their successful youth policy. Stung by the criticism, a frustrated White introduced the young Brian Heron in defiance at those who questioned his willingness to blood youth. Heron was thrown into a Cup Winners Cup tie with Gornik Zabrze, in Poland, a tie Rangers were expected to win. He had a nightmare of a match as the Poles romped to a 3–1 win. Heron was again pitched in for the second leg and for thirty minutes it looked as if the Ibrox side would recover the tie. Jim Baxter, who otherwise had failed to reach the heights he previously enjoyed, scored the opener early in the first half. However, any thoughts of a great Rangers recovery were dashed when, first, Gornik scored with thirty minutes to go and then added a second twelve minutes later. By the time they scored the third near the end, many fans had left the stadium.

While most left quietly, a vociferous few headed for the front entrance chanting 'White must go'. The next day, the manager was summoned to meet the board. The end was inevitable, beginning a long period of turmoil for David White. There is little doubt that the press were unkind to him, led by former Rangers star Willie Waddell, then a journalist with the *Scottish Daily Express*. Waddell, disappointed by the decline in the club's fortunes, had waged what seemed a personal campaign to oust the manager. One headline, referring to 'the boy David', cut deep and is remembered by many today. White is still embittered by the role Waddell had in his departure and talked of seeing the journalist's car outside the ground as he departed.

The players were genuinely shocked and disappointed by his departure, although some thought that standards had slipped. One player confided that he felt there had been a lack of professionalism among some of his teammates. Sandy Jardine felt there was much to admire in David White's tactical ability, but believed that the job came at a bad time for him. 'He was unfortunate that he was pitched in at the start of Celtic's nine-in-a-row run, with our rivals having their best-ever team. The problem was compounded when you consider he inherited the team at a time when the fans were used to success.'

The fortunes of Rangers are always judged against their rivals from across the city. White came into the role as Celtic enjoyed the most successful period in their history, led by one of the greatest managers the country has ever produced. If he was a failure, the responsibility lay as much with the players upon whom he relied. Managers need time to rebuild sides and the twenty-one-month period that David White held the reins at Ibrox was clearly not enough. Ironically, he took great satisfaction as Rangers won the European Cup Winner Cup in Barcelona, just thirty months later, in 1972. In the side were many of the players he had groomed in the reserves, assisted by his two big-money signings Alex MacDonald and Colin Stein.

Who knows how things would have evolved for Rangers and White if he had been allowed to complete the job. What cannot be gainsaid is that he had a hand in the success the club would later enjoy. His contribution is now widely recognised, even if his tenure in the Ibrox hot seat brought him a degree of personal sadness. I asked him if he looked back on his days as manager with satisfaction. Without hesitation, he replied, 'Absolutely, I am very proud to have been manager of Rangers.'

The rehabilitation of David White was complete.

THE CONTRIBUTORS

Graham Walker

Is an academic who has written widely in the fields of Scottish and Irish political history. He is author of *A History of the Ulster Unionist Party* (2004), and co-editor with Ronnie Esplin of *It's Rangers For Me?* (2007).

Ronnie Esplin

Is a sports reporter, football writer and author. His last book was *Totally Frank*, the story of former Celtic and St Mirren striker Frank McGarvey and prior to that he wrote *Down the Copland Road*, co-authored *Barcelona Here We Come* and *The Advocaat Years* with Alex Anderson. He also edited *Ten Days That Shook Rangers* and co-edited *It's Rangers For Me?* with Graham Walker.

Scott Dougal

Has been a sports journalist for ten years and a Rangers fan for a lot longer. Born in Berwick and now living in Yorkshire, he is currently deputy sports editor at the Press Association.

Peter Millward

Is a lecturer in Sport Policy and Sport Sociology at Leeds Metropolitan University and has written widely on football culture. He is a Wigan supporter.

Andy Kerr

Was born in Biggar, Lanarkshire in 1957 and spent over thirty years in the town before moving south to Lancashire then to Yorkshire where he currently resides. A lifelong Rangers fan he has been secretary of his local Rangers supporters club for over ten years. He is currently president of the Rangers Supporters Assembly, the body that represents Rangers fans worldwide.

David Edgar

Is media spokesman for the Rangers Supporters Trust and has been a board member since 2004. Born in Kilwinning, Ayrshire, he now lives in Glasgow and has been attending Rangers games since 1983.

Roddy Forsyth

Is the Scottish-football correspondent for BBC Radio Sport, London, and held the same position for *The Times* before moving to the *Daily Telegraph* in 1993. He writes a weekly column for the Irish *Mail on Sunday* and reports on Scottish football for RTE Radio, Ireland. He has written three books – *The Only Game* (*The Scots and World Football*), *Blue and True – Unforgettable Rangers Days* and *Fields of Green – Unforgettable Celtic Days*.

Daniel Taylor

Is a graduate of the University of Edinburgh and currently works in the museum and stadium tours department of Chelsea Football Club.

Steve Bruce

Is professor of sociology at the University of Aberdeen and a distinguished author. He has published extensively on the subject of religion and society. Among his recent publications is the co-authored work, *Sectarianism in Scotland* (2004).

Alan Truman

Has supported Rangers since the early 1960s. He is a board member of the Rangers Supporters Trust.

Gregory Campbell

Is Democratic Unionist Party (DUP) MP for East Londonderry, and a member of the Northern Ireland legislative assembly.

Stevie Clark

Is a lifelong Rangers fan who lived in Forfar and Montrose before moving to the Republic of Ireland in 1999. Now living in Drogheda, County Louth, he co-founded the Dublin Loyal RSC in 2001 and the club is now forty-strong. He is looking forward to celebrating its tenth anniversary in 2011.

Bobby Smith

Was born in Tradeston, Glasgow in 1944 and emigrated to Toronto, Canada in 1965. He became involved in the GRSC Toronto #1 in 1974 and has been an active member ever since. He was also a founding member of the North American Rangers Supporters Association (NARSA), which was established in 1993 and has been on the executive committee since.

Bobby Barr

Has played for Queens Park, Alloa Athletic, Hamilton Accies, Stranraer and Stenhousemuir in a career spanning over ten years. During that time he played at every senior ground in Scotland. He also coached at youth level for St Johnstone and Motherwell. Currently he is part of the Football Live project for the Press Association.

Elaine Sommerville

Was born and brought up in Coatbridge. She has been a Rangers fan since she was ten. Her parents bought her first season ticket in 1975 and she has been a season-ticket holder since. Her all-time favourite player is Davie Cooper, closely followed by Brian Laudrup. Highlights include the trebles in 1976 and 1978, Pittodrie 1987, nine-in-a-row at Tannadice in 1997, Helicopter Sunday in 2005, Manchester 2008 and regaining the title at Tannadice in 2009.

Ian S. Wood

Is one of Scotland's most distinguished historians and has written extensively on the Protestant paramilitary groups of Northern Ireland. One of his best-known works is the book, *God, Guns and Ulster: a History of the Loyalist Paramilitaries* (2003). He is a former associate lecturer with the Open University in Scotland and his latest book is *Crimes of Loyalty: a History of the UDA* (2006). Nevertheless he is a proud Hibs fan and his memories of Easter Road stretch back to the 1950s.

Campbell Ogilvie

Is managing director of Hearts and vice-president of the Scottish Football Association. His links to Rangers go back to his childhood where his father was the club's reserve-team doctor. In 1978 Ogilvie was recruited from the Scottish Football League as general secretary at Ibrox by Willie Waddell. He later became a director at Ibrox but relinquished his executive duties in September 2005, following a boardroom reshuffle.

Alex Totten

Began his football career with Liverpool and played for Dundee, Dunfermline, Falkirk, Queen of the South and Alloa. He managed Alloa and Falkirk before moving to Rangers in 1983 to become assistant to Jock Wallace, where he remained until Graeme Souness took over in 1986. Totten then had spells managing Dumbarton, St Johnstone, East Fife and Kilmarnock before returning to boss the Bairns where he guided them to the 1997 Scottish Cup final. He now works in the commercial department at Falkirk.

Craig Paterson

Joined Rangers from Hibs in 1982 and stayed for four years, captaining the Ibrox side to a League Cup-final triumph over Dundee United. He later played for Motherwell, Kilmarnock and Hamilton before ending his career at Junior side Glenafton. He is now enjoying a successful career as a pundit with the BBC.

Terence Murray

Who lives in Ayrshire, is a writer in the field of Scottish football history. He is currently assisting Rangers legend Tom Forsyth with his autobiography.

David Mason

Is the official historian of Rangers Football Club and has written *Rangers: the Managers* (2000).

Acknowledgements

Thanks to Iain Patterson for the photo of the Sam English mural (page 8 of the plate section) and for the research he did on English's life. Thanks also to Peter Drury, Nina Warhurst, Alexey Morozov, Pavel Astafiev, Alex Anderson, John MacDonald, Falkirk fan Denise Laird, Tom Greig, publisher James McCarroll and of course all the contributors.

Photo credits
Pages 1 and 2 of plate section: courtesy of Mirrorpix
Page 3: courtesy Eric McCowat
Pages 4–5: Getty Images
Page 6: Dublin Loyal Rangers Supporters Club
Page 7: North American Rangers Supporters Association (NARSA) and the Toronto number 1 Rangers Supporters Club